W9-AVE-797

The Economics of Household Behaviour

Peter Kooreman
Professor of Economics
Groningen University
The Netherlands

and

Sophia Wunderink
Lecturer in Economics
Erasmus University
Rotterdam, The Netherlands

St. Martin's Press
New York

THE ECONOMICS OF HOUSEHOLD BEHAVIOUR
Copyright © 1997 by Peter Kooreman and Sophia Wunderink
All rights reserved. No part of this book may be used or reproduced
in any manner whatsoever without written permission except in the
case of brief quotations embodied in critical articles or reviews.
For information, address:

St. Martin's Press, Scholarly and Reference Division,
175 Fifth Avenue, New York, N.Y. 10010

First published in the United States of America in 1997

This book is printed on paper suitable for recycling and
made from fully managed and sustained forest sources.

Printed in Great Britain

ISBN 0–312–17305–9

Library of Congress Cataloging-in-Publication Data
Kooreman, Peter, 1955–
The economics of household behavior / Peter Kooreman, Sophia
Wunderink.
p.   cm.
Includes bibliographical references and index.
ISBN 0–312–17305–9
1. Households—Economic aspects—Mathematical models.
2. Consumption (Economics)—Mathematical models.   I. Wunderink,
Sophia.   II. Title.
HB820.K66 1997
339.4'7—dc21   96-48551
                                                              CIP

To the memory of Aldi J. M. Hagenaars (1954–93)

Contents

List of Tables, Figures and Exercises

Tables

Figures

Exercises

Acknowledgements

The authors and publishers wish to thank the following for permission to use copyright material: American Economic Association for Table 6.7 from F. T. Juster and F. P. Stafford (1991) 'The Allocation of Time Empirical Findings, Behavioural Models and Problems of Measurement', *Journal of Economic Literature*, 29, table 1, p. 175, and Table 7.1 from R. A. Pollak and T. J. Wales (1978) 'Estimation of Complete Demand Systems from Household Budget Data: The Linear and Quadratic Expenditure Systems', *American Economic Review*, 68, table 2, p. 365; Amsterdam University Press for Tables 5.2, 5.3, 5.4, 5.5 from H. A. Pott-Buter (1993) *Facts and Fairy Tales about Female Labor, Family and Fertility*, tables 2.5, 2.6, 4.12, 4.13; Blackwell Publishers for table 5.6 from R. Blundell and I. Walker (1982) 'Modelling the Joint Determination of Household Labour Supplies and Community Demands', *Economic Journal*, 92, table 3, p. 362; and Table 4.2 from R. Alessie and A. Kapteyn (1991) 'Habit Formation, Independent Preferences and Demographic Effects in the Almost Ideal Demand System', *Economic Journal*, 101, table 1, p. 413; Bohn Stafleu Van Loghum bv for Table 6.3 from M. Bruyn-Hundt (1985) *Housekeeping=Unpaid work*, table 4, p. 86; Chapman and Hall for Table 6.4 from E. Quah (1987) 'Valuing Family Household Production: A Contigent Evaluation Approach', *Applied Economic*, 19, table 1, p. 220; Columbia University Press for material from S. B. Linder (1970) *The Harried Leisure Class*. Copyright © 1970 by Columbia University Press; The Econometric Society for Figure 4.3 from R. Moffit (1989) 'Estimating the Value of an In-kind Transfer: The Case of Food Stamps', *Econometrica*, 57 figure 1, p. 387; Elsevier Science S A for Table 6.6 from P. L. Menchik and B. A. Weisbrod (1987) 'Volunteer Labor Supply', *Journal of Public Economics*, 32, table 3, p. 175; Elsevier Science NL for Table 7.6 from B. M. S. van Praag (1985) 'Linking Economics with Psychology: An Economist's View', *Journal of Economic Psychology*, 6, table 1, p. 296; Figure 5.6 from A. Kapteyn, P. Kooreman and A. van Soest (1990) 'Quantity Rationing and Concavity in a Flexible Household Labor Supply Model', *Review of Economics and Statistics*, 57, figure 1, p. 62; and Table 5.7 from M. P. Pradhan and A. H. van Soest (1995) 'Formal and Informal Sector Employment in Urban Areas of Bolivia', *Labour Economics*; International Association for Review of Income and Wealth for Table 6.5 from J. Fitzgerald and J. Wicks (1990) 'Measuring the Value of Household Output: A Comparison of Direct and Indirect Approaches', *Review of Income and Wealth*, 36; and Table 12.2 from P. Saunders, H. Stott and G. A. Hobbes (1991) 'Income Inequality in Australia and New Zealand: International Comparisons and Recent Trends', *Review of Income and Wealth*, 37; JAI Press Inc. for Table 2.1 from H. Theil, C. F. Chung and J. L. Seale (1989) *Advances in Econometrics*, table 5.5, p. 106 and 5.6. p. 112; National Bureau of Economic Research, Inc. for Figure 11.3 from J. Mincer (1974) *Schooling, Experience and Earnings, New York*, chart 4.1; OECD for Table 11.4 from (1992) *Education at a Glance*, OECD Indicators, table P. 1, p. 41. Copyright © 1992 OECD; Timothy M. Smeeding for Table 4.1 from M. O'Higgins, G. Schmaus and G. Stephenson (1990) 'Income Distribution and Redistribution' in T. M. Smeeding, M. O'Higgins and L. Rainwater (eds), *Poverty, Inequality and Comparative Income Distribution in Perspective*, Harvester/Wheatsheaf, table 2.1, pp. 30–1; Springer-Verlag GmbH & Co KG for Table 8.1 from W. Groot and H. Pott-Buter (1992) 'The Timing of Maternity in the Netherlands', *Journal of Population Economics*, 5, table 6; SWOKA Institute for Consumer Research for Table 9.2 from H. J. Ritzema and M. E. Homan (1991) *Debts and Assets in the Netherlands*, 13; and Tables 6.1, 6.2, 7.2, 7.3 from Y. K. Grift, J. J. Siegers and G. N. C. Suy (1989) *Time Use in the Netherlands*, SWOKA Report 65, tables 1, 2; SWPH for Figure 8.1 from A. N. Baanders (1991) 'Leaving the Parental Home; Changes Since the Fifties', *Huishoudstudies*, vol. 1, pp. 14–21; The University of Chicago Press for Table 11.5 from M. R. Rosenzweig and T. P. Schultz (1983) 'Estimating a Household Production Function', *Journal of Political Economy*, 91, table 2, pp. 736–7; Table 7.5 from E. P. Lazear and R. T. Michael (1988) *Allocation of Income within the Household*, table 5.11, panel A; and extract from G. J. Stigler (1960) 'The Economics of Information', *Journal of Political Economy* pp. 213–25; The University of Wisconsin Press for Table 12.3 from A. Hagenaars and Klaas de Vos (1988) 'The Definition and Measurements of Poverty', *Journal of Human Resources*, 23, 2, Spring, table 1, pp. 211–21; Figure 11.5 from J. P. Strauss, O. Rahman and K. Fox (1993) 'Gender and Life-Cycle Differentials in the Patterns and Determinants of Adult Health', *The Journal of Human Resources*, 28, 4, figure 4, pp. 791–837; Table 7.4 from C. Michalopoulos, P. K. Robins and I. Garfinkel (1992) 'A Structural Model of Labour Supply and Child Care Demand', *The Journal of Human Resources*, 27, 1, Winter, table 3, pp. 166–203; Table 11.3 from J. Mincer and H. Ofek (1982) 'Interrupted Work Careers: Depreciation and Restoration of Human Capital', *Journal of Human Resources*, 17, 1, Winter, table 1, pp. 3–24; and Table 11.1 from P. T. Schultz (1993) 'Investments in the Schooling and Health of Women and Men: Quantities and Returns', *The Journal of Human Resources*, 28, 4, table 1, pp. 694–734.

Every effort has been made to trace the copyright-holders, but if any have been inadvertently overlooked the publishers will be pleased to make the necessary arrangement at the first opportunity.

Preface

This book deals with the economic behaviour of members of private households. It does so by using the familiar utility theory, but unlike most books on household behaviour it emphasizes the interaction between household members. The choices of household members with respect to consumption, labour market participation, fertility and so on are interrelated. The book integrates theoretical views with empirical evidence, integrates economic theory with social science views of behaviour, and deals with both static and dynamic models. Economic psychologists and economic sociologists used to criticize economic theories based on the idea of the existence of a rational consumer because, according to them, rationality is often not very obvious. We listened to their criticism and to their ideas about economic behaviour, and we have tried to incorporate these into the book. In our opinion, several ideas originating from psychologists and sociologists can certainly improve the quality of models of economic behaviour.

We have chosen to touch upon quite a large number of topics. Given space constraints, this rules out comprehensive, in-depth treatment of all subjects. Rather, we aim to provide introductions, focus on essentials and offer guidance to further reading. Our readers should have some knowledge of elementary microeconomics and calculus, including partial differentiation and integration. Although the book is primarily written for students at the graduate level, economists and policy-makers who wish to bring their knowledge of household behaviour up to date without reading all articles in the relevant economic journals, will find it interesting and useful.

The book has a history that started around 1987, when Aldi Hagenaars became a professor of Economics of the Household Sector at Erasmus University Rotterdam. With her econometric and sociological background she started writing a book in Dutch, with Sophia Wunderink, on the subjects mentioned above. The book was published in The Netherlands in 1990. Reaching a more international audience seemed quite logical, but unfortunately by that time Aldi knew she had an incurable disease. She was glad to know that Peter Kooreman was willing to work with her and Sophia on the book, but she herself had to give up very soon. We missed her clever, cheerful and inspirational participation. She passed away in 1993.

Although Aldi Hagenaars gave us the inspiration for this book, we also wish to make explicit acknowledgement to those who advised and commented on the book in its earlier stages. In this respect we would like to thank Arianne Baanders, Tim Barmby, Michiel Bliemer, Jan van Daal, Simone Dobbelsteen and Menno Pradhan. A part of the first author's work on the book was done while he was at the Department of Household and Consumer Studies of Wageningen Agricultural University.

PETER KOOREMAN
SOPHIA WUNDERINK

CHAPTER 1

Introduction

1.1 Why this book?

There is one thing all people of the world have in common: they all belong to a household. Therefore they all belong to the household sector of the economy. This sector comprises many activities. Incomes are earned and spent, taxes and social security premiums are paid, money is saved and borrowed, time and money are invested in health and education, houses are cleaned and maintained, meals are prepared, and household members enjoy leisure activities, decide whether or not to move, or to change jobs, and so on.

One of the main features of this book is that it considers the consumer, the taxpayer, the saver and borrower, the supplier of labour and the student all explicitly as members of a household. The (economic) behaviour of members of the same household is interrelated. The earnings of two partners living together form the household's income, which will at least partly be used for joint household expenditures, such as the rent, durable goods, and food. If a wife has a higher wage rate than a husband, the partners may decide that she should work more hours in the labour market, while he should do more in the household. This theme runs through the book like a continuous thread. For singles, who form a household by themselves, these interactions are, of course, absent.

A second characteristic, which distinguishes this book from others, is that it shows how the theories on household behaviour have been applied in empirical work and what the results look like. In these studies, data on individual behaviour are used to test hypotheses that are based on the theories. In many cases we shall also show data on the 'state of the world'. These data show averages of characteristics of groups of households, or household members.

Households are not static; they change continuously. The dynamics of the nature and existence of the household form the third theme of this book. Households are formed, and the number of people belonging to the household changes, as do their ages. Finally, the household dissolves, either because its members die, or because of a divorce. Along with the different (life-cycle) stages of the household, it is involved in different activities. In the second half of the book we shall focus on these dynamic aspects.

The activities taking place in the household sector are not only important for the households themselves; they will certainly also be of interest for the other sectors of the economy: the private and public sectors. The household and the private and public sectors of the economy are connected by many ties. We shall give two examples:

1. When a household earns income it pays taxes. If income decreases it will pay less taxes and consequently government income decreases. The household may also consume less, or borrow more money, which affects the private sector.
2. Activities that take place in the household sector often have a market substitute. For example, household members can either clean their own house or hire somebody to do the job for them; they can look after their young children themselves, or take them to a day-care center. If the price or quality of the market substitute changes, the household may revise its choice between the two alternatives. It may even have consequences for the labour market behaviour of the household members. Although nobody pays for activities in the household one cannot say that they are free. Instead of doing work in the home, a person could spend his or her time working and earning money. If the amount one can earn increases, this might also lead to a different choice. So changes in the private and public sectors affect household decisions and vice versa.

Although these aspects of household behaviour have received much attention in the economic journals, they have not been central in economic textbooks. We hope this book will fill the gap between existing traditional textbooks and modern research on household behaviour.

1.2   The consumer and producer roles of households

The household is the consumer of the goods and services produced in the private and public sectors. Some of these goods can be consumed immediately, while others are essential as inputs of household activities. These activities can be directed to satisfy various kinds of need of household members. We will call this *household or home production*. Market goods and services are not the only inputs; others are time, physical or mental energy, knowhow and skills. Through these activities value is added to the market goods. Some of these activities are clearly productive, others may have a leisure characteristic. When food is bought in the supermarket, someone has to prepare the meal before the household members can enjoy their dinner. Preparing the meal is a productive activity. When a football is bought, one has to play soccer to enjoy the football. This activity is more in the recreational sphere, but one could still say that value is added to the football by playing with it. So the household is not only a consumption unit, it is a production unit as well.

In general, there is no market price for the products of the household. Still there is a form of competition between 'home-produced goods' and 'market goods'. Such a competition exists, for example, with respect to child care. The price that the day-care center charges is an ordinary price, but it is less obvious what the value (or price) of the private care is. Still, the household has to decide either to consume the market product or the home-produced product.

Individuals also have to decide to which sector they will supply their labour: to the private or public sector and earn money, or to the household sector for home production. Since time is limited, individuals who form a household with others can look for an optimal allocation of tasks among household members. In particular, we shall analyse to what extent the allocation of time of household members is interrelated.

To a certain extent, the economic organization of the household is determined by the structure of the society. The function of the household and the allocation of tasks among household members is influenced by a combination of economic, social, cultural and legal factors. Within this framework there still exists freedom of choice. For a better understanding of household behaviour we shall make use of models that contain the essential determinants of this behaviour.

1.3   A general model of household behaviour

What should such a model look like in theory? Given the existence of a household, it should consist of:

(a) functions describing the household members' objectives and preferences;
(b) the restrictions and uncertainties that the household members are facing; and
(c) functions that indicate how the objectives, preferences and restrictions of different household members are interrelated.

It should be made clear in such a model which variables are choice variables and which are out of control of the household or determined in the past (exogenous variables).

Objectives and preferences
In the economic theory on household behaviour it is assumed that the preferences of individuals are more or less structured. If so, they can be represented by a utility function. This function should contain information on those items that affect the individual's utility in both current and future periods. Preferences may be affected by what an individual experienced in the past, so the utility function may have dynamic components. Preferences may

also be affected by what other members of the society choose, so the utility functions of different households may be interdependent. We shall assume that individuals try to maximize utility; that is, make an optimal choice, given the constraints they are facing.

Restrictions and uncertainties
The restrictions the individual faces concern current and future periods. For example, one may think of general restrictions concerning the laws of the country, its climate and the opening hours of shops and schools, but also of particular restrictions with respect to the individual's own limitations, such as the limited amount of knowledge, skills, wealth and time that the individual and his or her fellow household members can use in each period. Past, present and future are interrelated in several ways. For example, durable goods that were bought in the past can still be used in both current and future periods. Loans from the past have to be paid back, and savings can be used in the future. Knowledge gained from education in the past can be important for an individual's current and future income.

Interrelationship of objectives, preferences and restrictions
Household members not only have to share household income, they also have to make decisions about the way they are going to spend their time. If one member spends more money, the others can spend less, but many of the goods that are bought are shared by the household members. For example, members share kitchen equipment, furniture and the food that is bought. Sharing is a typical characteristic of households. More or less the same kind of relationships exist for the use of time. Each member has 168 hours per week to spend. These hours can be spent on paid labour, household production, education, leisure and so on. If one partner decides to do the cooking, the other can spend his/her time on other activities. However, household members may also like to do things together, such as going to a theatre, or going on vacation. Therefore, if one household member decides to do something this will usually affect the way the other members will spend their time.

One of the items that may affect the utility level of an individual is the utility the other household members experience. If it is assumed that one person, say the head of the family, decides about consumption and time spending of all other members, it is quite possible that this person's utility level increases not only when his or her own consumption increases, but also when the other household members can consume more. This is a form of altruism. But also when each individual household member can decide for him or herself, the utility levels the others can reach may affect the individual's utility level. Even if household members have independent utility functions, the fact that they share at least part of the income and household production makes, for example, their labour supply interdependent. They also share at least some consumption goods, the so-called public goods, that every household member can enjoy, without decreasing the utility for the others. Examples are the paintings or posters on the wall, kitchen equipment and so on.

Joint decision-making may be common practice. However, there could be a difference of opinion between partners about the way income and time should be spent. In that case, who decides about who gets what? With a game theoretic approach to household behaviour, this interaction can be modeled. As long as partners stay together it is assumed that they can reach a higher utility level within the household than outside it. However, the division of the utility gain depends on the partners' characteristics and their positions in the relationship.

Traditionally, microeconomic models of consumer behaviour took into account only a one-consumer utility function. This consumer was supposed to represent a whole household, but the models did not analyse the effects of the different interests of household members on the outcome. In this book we shall emphasize the fact that a household is a collection of different individuals. One model that would take all these factors into account would become very complicated; in fact, it would become unworkably complicated from an analytical and computational point of view. Therefore, we shall formulate models in which only a few of those aspects of household behaviour are analysed at a time. In each chapter of the book we shall focus on a different set of issues.

1.4 Data collection

In order to put the models into practice and to test hypotheses that are based on these models, one needs data on many variables, such as individual incomes, wage rates and time use, and the prices of goods and services.

Since it is impossible to question the whole population, information is gathered from a subgroup of the population. This subgroup should be representative for the population that is to be studied. It is beyond the scope of this book to go into details about sampling techniques. The statistical procedures can be found in books on sampling theory; for instance, in Levy and Lemeshow (1991).

The concepts that are used in the models should be well *defined* before one can start *measuring*. Sometimes it is not so obvious which practical concept corresponds with a theoretical variable. Take, for example, income. Which income value do we need to know? Is it gross or net income? Do we need to know only total household income, or the income of all household members separately? Do we include or exclude income in kind? After deciding which concept should be used, one can start measuring.

Income

It may seem simple to measure net income, but are respondents capable and willing to provide that information? Problems arise when part of the income is in kind or when part of it is earned in the informal sector or the black market. The very rich and the very poor are often not willing to answer questions about their income. Self-employed individuals quite often do not exactly know what their income is over a given period. These measurement problems may cause inaccuracy in the data. Part of the problem can be solved by confronting the respondent with a detailed list of income components. If not, respondents are apt to underestimate their income systematically (Kapteyn *et al.*, 1988).

Prices

Models often distinguish many goods and services, but for practical purposes these are aggregated into broader categories. The price index numbers for these categories must be determined. There are several ways to do this. For example, Laspeyres, Paasche, Fisher and Tornquist price index numbers are widely used. For most static models they are not relevant because at one given point in time all individuals are supposed to pay the same price for the goods they buy. By choosing the quantity units suitably, the price index numbers of all categories are equal to 1. However, as soon as regional price differences exist, one should take these price differences into account.

In reality, not everybody pays the same price for the same good, not even people living in the same region. Consumers spend time on searching for a bargain. It is impossible to determine *the* price of a good. In many countries the government subsidizes basic needs for the poorer households, and they pay less for food (food stamps), housing (rent subsidy), education (school fee reduction) and so on. These prices become income-dependent. This complicates the calculation of price index numbers. Even if individual prices and quantities bought are observed, the quality of the goods is usually not observed. It means that a higher price may reflect a higher quality, but not necessarily.

Wages

When wage rates or wages are used in models one should also be aware of the different wage concepts that could be used. Should gross or net wage, average or marginal wage be used? What is the wage rate of individuals who do not participate in the labour market? In some models no distinction is made between average and marginal wage rate, as though they are equal, but usually they are not equal. When estimating the parameters of such models one should have data about the correct wage concept of individuals.

Time use

Time use of individuals is also not easy to measure. Most common is to ask households to keep *a diary* and write down their activities. Sometimes people are asked to note their main activity every 15 minutes of the day. However, people are often doing many things at the same time: for example, cooking, listening to the radio and keeping an eye on the children. These joint activities will not be noted if not asked for. Very short-lasting activities will also not be observed: for example, a one-minute telephone call. The respondent will only write down 15 minutes 'cooking'.

A second possibility is to let *an outsider* observe the activities of a person during a certain period. The observer should live with the household for some time. This form of participating observation is, of course, very costly; moreover, the observed person may change his or her behaviour because of the presence of the observer.

A third possibility is to interview an individual, personally or by means of a computer questionnaire and ask about his or her allocation of time the previous day (and the day before). This retrospective way of questioning will be inaccurate, because the respondent may not remember exactly what s/he was doing and how long it took him/her.

A fourth method that is applied is the 'buzzer' method. The respondent receives a 'buzzer' during some days in the observation period. The buzzer emits a signal at random time intervals. When a signal is heard the respondent makes a note of his/her activity at that time. But even this rather advanced method is not perfect. For example, it could change behaviour because the respondent is disturbed during his/her activities, and may not continue in the same way as if no disturbance had occurred.

Three types of data set

Research in the field of economics of household behaviour is performed with three types of data: (i) cross-sections; (ii) time series; and (iii) panel data. In a cross-section, observations of individual households are gathered at a certain moment in time, or during a short period. Times series usually contain aggregate data: for example, national data on households, prices and time use during several periods (years or quarters of years). Panel data contain time series on an individual or household level. The same households are questioned during several periods (years, months) so that their individual reactions on changing circumstances can be observed. Panel data seem to be ideal for testing the models that are mentioned in this book, but there are some drawbacks. Quite often households withdraw from a panel and then they must be replaced by other households, which complicates the estimation procedures. However, the dropouts may form a selective subsample of the panel; there may be a reason for their withdrawal, such as a divorce or a house move. If the panel is supplemented with randomly selected households, the new sample is no longer random. Information on panel data analysis can be found in Hsiao (1989), for example.

Interest in international comparison has grown and resulted in the settlement of institutions such as Eurostat and LIS (Luxembourg Income Studies). These institutions, alongside organizations such as the World Bank and the UN (United Nations), collect data from several countries in a consistent way, so that international comparison becomes possible and is not disturbed by differences in definition and measurement.

1.5   The structure of the book

The first seven chapters of the book consider only static models; that is, models without a time dimension. In each chapter we shall focus on a different aspect of the economic behaviour of the household. In the later chapters of the book dynamic models, in which past and future are explicitly taken into account, are presented.

In Chapter 2 we start with a short survey of the theory of the neo-classical model of consumer demand. We add to this model the ideas of household production, so as to emphasize right from the beginning the importance of time use. We assume that for most readers this chapter will contain little new information, but for completeness and easy reference we shall repeat those theories. The unit of the analysis is the individual. In empirical work on demand systems, however, it is usually the household that is taken as a unit for data collection. In Chapter 3 we investigate this discrepancy between theory and practice of the demand analysis and see whether we can narrow the gap. From a viewpoint of economic policy the well-being of individuals within the household, and not average household wealth, is the object of concern. So it is important to study the intrahousehold allocation of resources. In this chapter we shall also introduce a game theoretic approach to household decision-making and analyse its outcomes. In Chapter 4 we analyse how the institutional and social setting may affect household choices. We start with a historical survey of the role and position of households in society. After that we concentrate on models describing the influ-. ence of different tax and social security systems on household choices. Rationing limits the free choice of individuals. Governments may cause rationing in some markets, but rationing can also have different roots. We shall study the effects of rationing on our models in general terms in this chapter, and more specific applications follow in later chapters. A consumer's past may place him or her in the current period with a stock of habits: the consumer may even be addicted to certain goods. His or her current preferences are affected by these factors and by the behaviour of some other members of society, his/her reference group. Another point of interest in Chapter 4 is the effects of uncertainty. In order to make an optimal decision the consumer should be well informed about current and future possibilities. Uncertainty arising from incomplete information and uncertainty of events will affect the optimal decision-making process. In Chapter 5 some (static) household labour supply models are introduced. In particular, we shall pay attention to the differences between male and female labour supply. The tax and social security structure can cause non-convex multi-dimensional budget sets for the household, which makes the analysis more complicated, but still traceable. Chapter 6 deals with household production, volunteer labour and leisure activities. The value of household production is discussed and several methods to estimate this value are discussed. Chapter 7 emphasizes the role of children on household expenditure and time use. In the same chapter we shall also discuss the use of equivalence scales and the ways in which they are derived.

Starting with Chapter 8, the models describe dynamic aspects of household behaviour. In Chapter 8, household formation and dissolution is studied. Duration (or hazard rate) models are frequently used to analyse these processes. A short introduction to these models can be found in Appendix A. In this chapter they are applied to the timing of births, divorce and remarriage. Chapter 9 deals with dynamic aspects of household consumption, with the role of savings and debts, and with typical household investments: durable goods. We shall look in Chapter 10 at some dynamic aspects of labour market behaviour. We start with a brief review of some life-cycle labour supply models and present a model of job search. Again, hazard rate models will be used. Then we discuss how the job search model can be extended to describe simultaneous job search of husband and wife in a household. Finally, the retirement decisions of the partners are studied. Another dynamic aspect of household behaviour concerns investment in human capital, which is discussed in Chapter 11. The individual can influence his or her earning capacity by investments in education and health. Investments in health are surrounded by many uncertainties, even more than investments in education, but health seems to be an important determinant of well-being. The last chapter, Chapter 12, looks at the final results of all these efforts to increase utility. What is the relationship between utility, well-being and happiness, and between utility, income and poverty? Answers to these questions depend greatly on how happiness and poverty are defined. We shall first discuss the relationship between poverty, income and income distribution. Then we shall shed light on how income, utility and happiness are related.

CHAPTER 2

The Neo-Classical Model and Some Extensions

2.1 Introduction

In Chapter 1 a theoretically 'ideal' model of household behaviour was outlined. However, in empirical work, such a complicated model cannot be used. A lack of sufficiently detailed data and computational limitations would make it impossible to analyse the different aspects of behaviour simultaneously. In addition, to do this is not always desirable either. We use a model as an abstract representation of reality which focuses on a particular question we are interested in and neglects other aspects.

In this chapter we discuss three versions of the neo-classical model of consumer behaviour. All of them are static models. We start with the simplest version. Then we introduce labour supply. Finally, we discuss Becker's so-called 'New Home Economics' model. This chapter serves as an introduction to models in subsequent chapters that describe the behaviour of multi-person households. Here we concentrate on a single consumer and the fact that s/he is a member of a household is not important as yet. Whether the consumer is one individual or whether s/he represents a whole household remains undecided.

The assumptions underlying the neo-classical model of economic choice are quite restrictive, and indeed there are many examples where the model has failed to pass empirical testing. The assumptions of the model are made explicit in Section 2.2, so the reader can judge its limitations. In Section 2.3 some points of criticism against the neo-classical model are formulated. In Sections 2.4 and 2.5, respectively, paid market labour and labour within the household are introduced into the model. Section 2.6 summarizes the chapter.

2.2   The simplest neo-classical model of consumer behaviour

Why do consumers buy what they buy and how do they react to changes in the prices of the consumer goods and to a change in their income? The neo-classical theory does not explain how consumer preferences come about, but it is quite capable of answering questions regarding consumers' responsiveness to price and income changes. Table 2.1 gives a foretaste of the kind of answers the neo-classical model can help us to obtain.

The reactions are usually measured as *elasticities*: the change in demand caused by a 1 per cent change in price or income. For example, a 1 per cent rise in income would have caused demand for food to rise by 0.78 per cent in India and by 0.48 per cent in the UK. If the price of food had risen by 1 per cent, demand would have decreased by 0.74 per cent in India and by 0.29 per cent in the UK.

The *assumptions* of the neo-classical model are as follows:

1. Human beings experience 'utility' from the consumption of goods and services.[1]
2. Human beings are capable of comparing bundles of goods available for consumption and can decide whether or not the first bundle, A, is at least as good (≥) as the second bundle, B, or not. The ordering of their preferences is consistent in the following sense:

   - reflexive (A ≥ A for all bundles A);
   - transitive (if A ≥ B and B ≥ C, then A ≥ C); or
   - complete (either A ≥ B, B ≥ A, or both (that is, A = B)).

3. Given income and prices, the consumer will buy the best bundle of goods s/he can afford (rationality).
4. Full information on income, prices and qualities is available; there is no uncertainty.
5. Goods and services can be bought in arbitrary small or large amounts.
6. If the quantity of one good in a bundle is increased, keeping amounts of the other goods constant, the consumer prefers this bundle to the original one (non-satiation).
7. If the consumer is indifferent with respect to two bundles, a linear combination of the two will be preferred. This assumption is equivalent to the assumption of a convex indifference curve.

The neo-classical model in formulae

The assumptions mentioned above can be translated into a mathematical model. This facilitates the analysis of their implications. Let q_i denote the consumed quantity of good i, $i = 1, \ldots, N$, so that $(q_1, \ldots, q_N)$ represents a bundle of consumer goods. We use a utility function $U(q_1, \ldots, q_N)$ to represent

12

Table 2.1 Price and income elasticities

Category	Elast.	Food	Clothing	Housing	Medical Care	Transp. Comm.	Recreation	Education	Other
India	inc.	0.78	0.96	1.25	1.85	1.80	2.16	1.10	1.89
	pr.	-0.74	-0.72	-0.92	-1.33	-1.28	-1.54	-0.81	-1.34
Hungary	inc.	0.61	0.96	1.16	1.32	1.31	1.35	1.08	1.32
	pr.	-0.48	-0.72	-0.86	-0.96	-0.95	-0.98	-0.80	-0.96
Israel	inc.	0.58	0.96	1.16	1.30	1.29	1.33	1.08	1.30
	pr.	-0.43	-0.72	-0.86	-0.95	-0.94	-0.96	-0.80	-0.95
UK	inc.	0.48	0.96	1.15	1.26	1.26	1.29	1.08	1.27
	pr.	-0.29	-0.71	-0.85	-0.92	-0.92	-0.94	-0.80	-0.93
Germany	inc.	0.43	0.96	1.14	1.25	1.25	1.27	1.08	1.26
	pr.	-0.21	-0.71	-0.85	-0.92	-0.92	-0.93	-0.80	-0.92
USA	inc.	0.37	0.96	1.14	1.24	1.24	1.26	1.08	1.25
	pr.	-0.12	-0.71	-0.85	-0.91	-0.91	-0.92	-0.79	-0.92

Source: Theil, Chung and Seale (1989).

preferences. Bundle A is preferred over bundle B if and only if $U(q_1^A, \ldots, q_N^A) > U(q_1^B, \ldots, q_N^B)$. The utility function $U(.)$ is assumed to be increasing in each of its arguments (non-satiation), and strictly concave, with continuous first- and second order derivatives. The strict concavity (implying decreasing marginal utility) can be shown to follow from Assumption 7.

The rational consumer chooses $(q_1, \ldots, q_N)$ such that $U(q_1, \ldots, q_N)$ is maximized subject to the restrictions

$$\sum_{i=1}^{N} p_i q_i \leq y \tag{2.1}$$

$$q_i \geq 0 \quad \text{for} \quad i = 1, \ldots, N,$$

where p_i is the price of good i, and y is income. The first restriction says that total expenditure can not exceed income. The non-satiation assumption implies that the consumer will exhaust available income so that the restriction will be binding. Therefore we shall work with the equality $\Sigma p_i q_i = y$ from now on. The second set of restrictions merely state that consumed quantities cannot be negative.

Let us now look at a specific example with preferences represented by the so-called Stone–Geary utility function:

$$U(q_1, \ldots, q_N) = \sum_{i=1}^{N} \alpha_i \ln(q_i - \gamma_i), \tag{2.2}$$

with $\alpha_i > 0$ and $\Sigma \alpha_i = 1$. We focus on this specification because it is simple and convenient for introductory purposes. In the following chapters we shall encounter more flexible (and more complex) specifications. Since the function $\ln(x)$ is defined for $x > 0$ only, we must have $q_i > \gamma_i$. Therefore, we can interpret γ_i as a subsistence level for good i and, consequently, $\Sigma p_i \gamma_i$ as a subsistence income level. Note that:

$$\frac{\partial U}{\partial q_i} = \frac{\alpha_i}{q_i - \gamma_i} > 0 \quad \text{and} \quad \frac{\partial^2 U}{\partial q_i^2} = -\frac{\alpha_i}{(q_i - \gamma_i)^2} < 0, \tag{2.3}$$

that is, utility is increasing and concave in q_i.

We first solve the maximization problem, ignoring the non-negativity constraints. The Lagrangian function for the case with a general utility function is given by:

$$\mathcal{L} = U(q_1, \ldots, q_N) + \lambda(y - \sum_{i=1}^{N} p_i q_i), \tag{2.4}$$

with the scalar variable λ being the Lagrange multiplier. The solution, $(q_1^*, \ldots, q_N^*, \lambda^*)$ is derived from the set of $N + 1$ equations:

$$\begin{cases} \dfrac{\partial \mathcal{L}}{\partial q_i} = \dfrac{\partial U}{\partial q_i} - \lambda p_i = 0, \quad i = 1, \ldots, N \\ \\ \dfrac{\partial \mathcal{L}}{\partial \lambda} = y - \displaystyle\sum_{i=1}^{N} p_i q_i = 0. \end{cases} \tag{2.5}$$

The conditions imply that in the solution:

$$\frac{\partial U/\partial q_i}{\partial U/\partial q_j} = \frac{p_i}{p_j}, \tag{2.6}$$

That is, for any combination of two goods, the ratio of their marginal utilities equals the ratio of their prices. For the Stone–Geary utility function, optimal demand can be written as:

$$p_i q_i = p_i \gamma_i + \alpha_i (y - \sum_{i=1}^{N} p_i \gamma_i); \tag{2.7}$$

see Exercise 2.1. Equation (2.7) has a nice and natural interpretation. The expenditure on good i is the sum of the expenditure on the subsistence level $(p_i\gamma_i)$ and a share α_i of the income that remains after all subsistence quantities have been purchased $(y - \Sigma p_i \gamma_i)$. The demand system in Equation (2.7) is known as the Linear Expenditure System (LES); expenditures are linear functions of income and prices.

Exercise 2.1

(a) Show that for the Stone–Geary utility function, Equation (2.5a) implies

$$p_i q_i = p_i \gamma_i + \frac{\alpha_i}{\lambda}, \quad i = 1, \ldots, N. \tag{2.8}$$

(b) Sum the above equation over i and use Equation (2.5b) to show that:

$$\lambda = \left(y - \sum_{i=1}^{N} p_i \gamma_i \right)^{-1} \tag{2.9}$$

Exercise 2.2

It is sometimes more convenient to write a demand system in terms of quantities (q_i) or budget shares $(w_i \equiv p_i q_i / y)$ rather than expenditures $(p_i q_i)$. Write down these alternative representations for the LES.

We now specify the example somewhat further. Suppose that $N = 3$, $\gamma_1 = \gamma_2 = \gamma_3 = -1$, $p_1 = p_2 = p_3 = 1$ and $y = 1$. If $\alpha_1 = \alpha_2 = \alpha_3 = 1/3$, then $q_1 = q_2 = q_3 = 1/3$. Clearly, the non-negativity constraints $q_i \geq 0$ are non-binding. However, if $\alpha_1 = 1/2$, $\alpha_2 = 1/3$ and $\alpha_3 = 1/6$, for example, then $q_1 = 1$, $q_2 = 1/3$ and $q_3 = -1/3$, which is clearly not an admissible solution. In Chapter 4 we shall show how a solution can be obtained in such a case. For the time being we shall consider cases where the non-negativity constraints are non-binding (*interior solutions*).

Duality

The functions that describe the optimal quantities as a function of income and prices are called *Marshallian* or *uncompensated demand functions*; we use the general notation $q_i = g_i(y; p_1, \ldots p_N)$. The utility level at the optimal quantities (that is, the highest possible utility level by definition) is, of course, found by substituting the optimal quantities into the utility function $U(q_1, \ldots, q_N)$. The resulting expression, a function of y and $(p_1, \ldots, p_N)$, is referred to as the *indirect utility function*. For the LES example it is given by:

$$V(y; p_1, \ldots p_N) = \sum_{i=1}^{N} \alpha_i \ln(\alpha_i) - \sum_{i=1}^{N} \alpha_i \ln(p_i) + \ln(y - \sum_{i=1}^{N} p_i \gamma_i); \quad (2.10)$$

see Exercise 2.3. To emphasize the distinction between the indirect utility function $V(y; p_1, \ldots p_N)$ and the utility function $U(q_1, \ldots, q_N)$, the latter is often referred to as the *direct utility function*.

The uncompensated demand equations can be retrieved from the indirect utility function using *Roy's identity*:

$$q_i(y; p_1, \ldots, p_N) = -\frac{\partial V/\partial p_i}{\partial V/\partial y}. \quad (2.11)$$

For a proof, see, for example, Deaton and Muellbauer (1980).

Exercise 2.3
(a) Derive Equation (2.10).
(b) Check that application of Equation (2.11) to Equation (2.10) yields Equation (2.7).

The *cost function* gives us the costs that have to be made (that is the income that is required) to attain a certain utility level, u, given prices $p_1, \ldots p_N$. From the definition of the indirect utility function it follows that the cost function, denoted as $c(u, p)$, must be the inverse of the indirect utility function with respect to income, y.

Exercise 2.4
Check that the cost function of the LES is given by:

$$c(u, p) = \sum_{i=1}^{N} p_i\gamma_i + \exp(u - \sum_{i=1}^{N} \alpha_i\ln(\alpha_i) + \sum_{i=1}^{N} \alpha_i\ln(p_i)). \quad (2.12)$$

Note that here costs are equal to the costs of all subsistence quantities $p_i\gamma_i$ plus an additional amount which increases with prices and with the utility level.

The definition of the cost function implies that it can also be obtained as follows. Choose $(q_1, \ldots, q_N)$ such that $\Sigma p_i q_i$ is minimized subject to the restriction $U(q_1, \ldots, q_N) \geq u$. The solution, a function of u and $(p_1, \ldots p_N)$, is known as the *Hicksian or compensated demand functions*; we use the general notation $q_i = h_i(u; p_1, \ldots, p_N)$. The cost function is then obtained as $c(u; p_1, \ldots, p_N) = \Sigma p_i h_i(u; p_1, \ldots, p_N)$.

Exercise 2.5
(a) Write down the Lagrangian of the cost minimization problem in case of a Stone–Geary utility function.
(b) Show that the value of the Lagrange multiplier in the solution is now given by:

$$\mu = \exp(\sum_{i=1}^{N} \alpha_i\ln(\alpha_i) - u - \sum_{i=1}^{N} \alpha_i\ln(p_i)). \quad (2.13)$$

(c) Derive the compensated LES demand functions.
(d) Show that substitution into $\Sigma p_i q_i$ yields Equation (2.12).

Finally, it can be shown that the compensated demand functions can be retrieved from the cost function using *Shephard's lemma*:

$$h_i(u, p_1, \ldots, p_N) = \frac{\partial c(u, p_1, \ldots, p_N)}{\partial p_i}. \quad (2.14)$$

Viewing the consumer's problem in terms of the maximization of utility subject to an upper bound on income is referred to as the *primal approach*. A description in terms of cost minimization subject to a lower bound on utility is known as the *dual approach*. The relationship between both approaches and the concepts described here are summarized in Figure 2.1.

Some definitions

We now define a number of concepts we shall encounter at various places in the book.

A function is called *homogeneous of degree k* in $x_1, \ldots, x_N$ if

$$\varphi(\alpha x_1, \ldots, \alpha x_N) = \alpha^k \varphi(x_1, \ldots x_N) \quad (\alpha > 0). \quad (2.15)$$

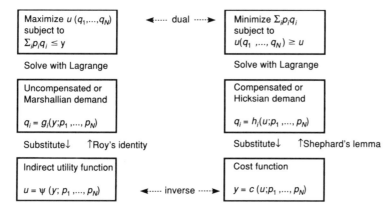

Figure 2.1   Utility maximization and cost minimization

Exercise 2.6
(a) A cost function should be homogeneous of degree 1 in prices. Explain why.
(b) An uncompensated demand function should be homogeneous of degree zero in prices and income. Explain why.

Preferences are called *homothetic* if utility, u, is a monotonic increasing function of φ, with φ being a homogeneous function of degree one. So:

$$u = f(\varphi(q_1, \ldots, q_N)), \qquad (2.16)$$

with

$$\frac{\partial f}{\partial \varphi} > 0 \text{ and } \varphi(\alpha q_1, \ldots, \alpha q_N) = \alpha\varphi(q_1, \ldots, q_N). \qquad (2.17)$$

Exercise 2.7
Show that with homothetic preferences:
(a) $c(u, p) = f^{-1}(u)\,\theta(p)$, where $\theta(p)$ is homogeneous of degree one in prices.
(b) Uncompensated demand functions are of the form $q_i = (y/\theta(p)).(\partial\theta(p)/\partial p_i)$.
(c) All income elasticities equal 1.

Another important concept that is often used in relation to preferences is *separability*. If preferences are separable, the commodities can be partitioned into groups, so that preferences within the group can be described independently of the quantities in other groups (Deaton and Muellbauer, 1980, p. 122). For example, if three groups can be formed, then:

$$U(q_1, \ldots, q_N) = F(\varphi_1(q_1, \ldots, q_k), \varphi_2(q_{k+1}, \ldots, q_m),$$

$$\varphi_3(q_{m+1}, \ldots, q_n)), \tag{2.18}$$

where F is an increasing function and φ_1, φ_2 and φ_3 are subutility functions. If a subset of goods appears only in a subutility function, it means that the quantities purchased within that group can always be written as functions of group expenditure and prices within the group only. Separability, as in Equation (2.18) is usually called *weak separability*. If the subutility functions are combined additively, preferences are *strongly separable*, that is:

$$U(q_1, \ldots, q_n) = F((\varphi_1, \ldots, q_k) + \varphi_2(q_{k+1}, \ldots, q_m)$$

$$+ \varphi_3(q_{m+1}, \ldots, q_n)). \tag{2.19}$$

Demand systems and integrability conditions

Utility itself cannot easily be observed (although an attempt will be made in Chapter 12), but observing quantities, income and prices is simple in principle. Therefore, research on consumer demand often starts with directly specifying a (Marshallian) demand system rather than a utility function. The question arises as to whether the mathematical formulation of demand functions is always consistent with a preference structure as formulated in Assumptions 1 to 7. The answer is no. Besides $q_i \geq 0$ for all i, four conditions should be fulfilled by the demand equations, the so-called *integrability conditions*. The term integrability conditions comes from the fact that integration of the Hicksian demand functions should lead to a concave linearly homogeneous cost function. The conditions are:

1. Additivity, which means that the demand system should satisfy the budget constraint for all values of income and prices:

$$\sum_{i=1}^{N} p_i q_i(p_1, \ldots, p_N, y) = y. \tag{2.20}$$

2. Zero degree homogeneity of Marshallian demand functions in income and prices. This means that an equal percentage change in income and prices should not effect demand:

$$q_i(p_1, \ldots, p_N, y) = q_i(kp_1, \ldots, kp_N, ky). \tag{2.21}$$

3. Slutsky symmetry. The Slutsky matrix, the $N \times N$ matrix with typical elements:

$$s_{ij} \equiv \frac{\partial h_i}{\partial p_j} = \frac{\partial g_i}{\partial p_j} + \frac{\partial g_i}{\partial y} q_j, \quad i, j = 1, \ldots, N, \qquad (2.22)$$

should be symmetric. Note that this is the matrix of second order derivatives of the cost function $c(u, p)$ with respect to prices, as $h_i(u, p)$ is the first order derivative of $c(u, p)$ with respect to p_i. Since the order of differentiation is immaterial in obtaining a second order derivative of a differentiable function (the cost function, in our case), it must be that $s_{ij} = s_{ji}$ for all i and j.
4. Slutsky negativity: the Slutsky matrix should be negative semi-definite. This condition is tantamount to concavity of the cost function. A necessary condition for this to hold is that $s_{ii} \leq 0$ for all i.

For a detailed discussion and proofs we refer to Deaton and Muellbauer (1980) or Varian (1992).

Exercise 2.8
(a) Derive Equation (2.22) using the identity $h_i(u; p) = g_i(c(u, p); p)$, where p stands for $(p_1, \ldots p_N)$.
(b) Check the integrability conditions for the LES.

Applications

Demand functions are interesting because they can tell us how a consumer reacts on changes in income and prices. If his or her income rises (and prices remain constant) s/he can obviously buy more, but how will s/he spend the extra money? If one or more prices increase (while income is constant), where will s/he cut down his or her expenses?

Recall that the consumer's optimal choice is given by the Marshallian demand system $q_i = g_i(y, p)$. As noted before, the effect of a change in an independent variable, z (one of the prices or income), on demand is usually expressed by the corresponding elasticity:

$$E_z^i = \frac{\partial q_i / q_i}{\partial z / z} = \frac{\partial q_i}{\partial z} \frac{z}{q_i}, \qquad (2.23)$$

the relative (or percentage) change in demand, divided by the relative (or percentage) change in z.

A good with a positive income elasticity is called a *normal* good. If its income elasticity is negative, the good is called *inferior*: an income rise will result in a decreased demand. A normal good with an income elasticity exceeding 1 is called a *luxury*, if it is between 0 and 1 it is referred to as a *necessity*. The relationship between demand and income is known as the *Engel curve*.

Summarizing:

$$\begin{cases} E_y^i \geq 0 = \text{normal good} \\ \\ E_y^i < 0 = \text{inferior good.} \end{cases} \qquad \begin{cases} 0 \leq E_y^i \leq 1 \qquad = \text{necessity} \\ E_y^i > 1 \qquad\qquad = \text{luxury} \end{cases}$$

When the price of a commodity goes up, how will demand react? To analyse the effect, we rewrite the Slutsky equation as:

$$\frac{\partial g_i}{\partial p_j} = \frac{\partial h_i}{\partial p_j} - \frac{\partial g_i}{\partial y} q_j, \quad i, j = 1, \dots, N. \tag{2.24}$$

As Equation (2.24) suggests, the effect of a price change can be decomposed in two parts:

1. Since good j has become more expensive relative to the other goods, a reallocation of income such that Equation (2.6) will hold again will be necessary to reach again a new utility maximum. This reaction is called the *substitution effect* of a price change. For $i = j$, it is always negative; that is, less of good i will be bought when its price rises.
2. Since *real income* decreases, the consumer will buy less of all *normal* goods and more of all *inferior* goods. This is the *income effect*.

For $i = j$, the total effect of a price rise is negative for normal goods, as both terms in Equation (2.24) are negative. For inferior goods, the first term is negative while the second is positive. In theory, it is possible that the total effect is positive. In such a case the price rise will result in an increased demand for the good. Such a good is called a *Giffen good*.

For $z = p_i$, E_z^i is called the *own-price elasticity* of good i. As we have seen, it is always negative, except for Giffen goods. For $z = p_j$ ($j \neq i$), E_z^i is called a *cross-price elasticity*. It tells us how the demand for good i responds to a change in the price of good j. It is positive when i and j are *substitutes* (for example, coffee and tea) and negative for *complements* (for example, coffee and cream).

In Table 2.1, only 'own' price elasticities were presented. Since elasticities are independent of the units of measurement, they are well-suited for international comparisons. The elasticities in Table 2.1 are not based on observations of individual households, but derived from (aggregate) per capita data. From the table it follows that, in all countries, housing, medical care, transportation, education and recreation are luxury goods, $(E_y > 1)$ and the other categories are necessary goods $(0 < E_y < 1)$. On an individual level, this is not necessarily true. In the category 'food' we observe great differences between the income elasticity in India and countries such as the UK and Canada. If income rises by 1 per cent in India, food expenditure will rise by 0.78 per cent, but not necessarily for everybody. The richer people in India will spend less than 0.78 per cent of their income rise on food and the poorest will probably spend almost all their extra income on food. So it is important to know *whose* income is changing when we want to predict reaction in demand; aggregates may not predict well enough. The demand for medical care, transportation and recreation is *elastic*, $E_p < -1$, and the demand for food, clothing and housing is *inelastic*, $-1 < E_p < 0$.

Reduced form versus structural form

A relationship between expenditure (or quantities or budget shares for that matter) on the one hand, and income and prices on the other might also simply be written as:

$$p_i q_i = a + by + c_1 p_1 + c_2 p_2 + \ldots + c_N p_N. \tag{2.25}$$

In some cases one is merely interested in the statistical relationship between these variables. Once the coefficients have been estimated, the income and price elasticities can be calculated straightforwardly without any reference whatever to utility theory. In such a case the demand equation is called a *reduced form* equation. It has no direct interpretation in terms of a behavioural model. A relationship between expenditure, income and prices as in Equation (2.7) is referred to as a *structural form* equation.

Note that the complete reduced form demand system (with N equations, one for each good) has N constant terms, N income coefficients and N^2 price coefficients. The complete structural demand system, on the other hand, has only $N - 1$ independent αs (since $\Sigma \alpha_i = 1$) and N γs. Hence, the utility model apparently imposes restrictions on the reduced form parameters. Many empirical studies have been performed to test these restrictions, with mixed results.

Finally, we show some estimation results for the LES model, based on cross-section data on one-person households; see Table 2.2.

Exercise 2.9
(a) Explain why γ_7 could not be estimated.
(b) Determine the income elasticity of 'food' at $y = 15\,000$, $y = 30\,000$, $y = 60\,000$ and $y = 120\,000$ for the LES model in Table 2.2. Comment on the results. Draw the Engel curve for food.

2.3 Criticisms on the neo-classical model of consumer behaviour

In Section 2.2 we listed seven assumptions on which the neo-classical model is based. By displaying what the assumptions are, a way is opened to judge

22

Table 2.2 LES parameter estimates for one-person households

n	1 Food	2 Clothing	3 Housing	4 Other fixed expenditure	5 Education & recreation	6 Transport	7 Other expenditure & savings
$p_n \tau_n$	4 186	577	3 891	1 332	1 541	830	0^1
α_n	0.0656	0.0345	0.1947	0.1384	0.0883	0.0816	0.3989

Notes: Amounts are in Dfl. All parameters estimates are significant on a 0.01 level; $p_7\tau_7$ was fixed at 0 for identification.

Source: Howe (1975).

the model. Economists, psychologists, anthropologists and other practitioners of the social sciences have formulated their criticisms with respect to the model. Their objections vary in character. Some are very fundamental, such that trying to 'repair' the model does not seem to make sense. In those cases one should offer a completely different approach. Others show the need for some adjustments of the original model. Here we will mention some of the points that are put forward.

The model describes the behaviour of one person
Households often consist of more than one person and the question arises, who is 'the consumer'? What happens within the household before one of the household members buys something? In Chapter 3 an extension of the model towards a household model of choice will be presented.

Human beings are consumers, but consumption is not the only 'utility creating' item. Time use should be incorporated in the models
By concentrating only on consumption the role of time use is neglected in the neo-classical model. A simple extension of the model is treated in Section 2.4, where the consumer can choose between two kinds of time use: working in the labour market for a fixed wage rate, or spending time at home as leisure time. Leisure is supposed to affect utility positively. Income is no longer fixed: it is determined by the decision about how much time to spend on working.

The role of time use need not be restricted to labour and leisure only. The consumer has all kinds of productive activities within the household that cannot be considered as pure leisure. In Section 2.5 we shall pay attention to the household production theory – Becker's New Home Economics model – in which these household activities are made explicit.

The model is static, as if the past and future of the consumer and his or her changing environment are irrelevant
In reality, the consumer is faced with a continuously changing environment. Prices, technologies, wage rates and government policies change over time. In the past the consumer may have bought durables that s/he can still use, s/he may have borrowed money that s/he still has to pay back, and s/he may have gone back to education in order to find a better job. In the current period s/he is taking decisions that will affect his or her future. The composition of the household may change as well. Chapters 8 to 12 will focus on the dynamic aspects of household behaviour.

The model assumes full information on income and prices (in the present and future)
In reality, the consumer is faced with uncertainty about his or her future income and about current and future prices. The problems with uncertainty can be met partly by introducing the concept of expected utility (Section 4.6). But to get an idea about the probability distribution of uncertain variables

(income, prices, wages, qualities), the consumer needs information. Usually, getting information has a price in terms of time and/or money. It generally makes sense for the consumer to search to some degree for information on prices in order to pay less, and on job offers to find a better-paid or more pleasant job.

It is assumed that goods and services can be bought in arbitrary small or large amounts, but that is not always true. The model makes no distinction between expenditure and consumption
Durable goods are a counter-example: one cannot buy a little bit of car, for example. Moreover, it is not the car that is consumed, but its services. Special attention will be paid to durables in the household, in particular to their role in home production. Since durables last for several periods, they form a link between past and future. Durables are discussed in Chapter 9.

The model does not take into account the rules and regulations of the outside world
The consumer is usually not free to choose the number of hours s/he wants to work. A simple example is the fact that sometimes s/he can either take a job and work 40 hours per week, or leave it. It may even happen that there are no jobs available. This means that the consumer's original optimal choice is not attainable. Other forms of rationing may affect demand. In Section 4.4, rationing will be discussed.

The government interferes by imposing taxes on income and sales, by supplying subsidies, free services and a social security system. In many countries, shops open and close at fixed times, and children have to go to school at fixed hours. These opening hours may interfere with the optimal time use of the consumer.

One of the basic assumptions of the neo-classical model is the rationality of the consumer
For every activity, the consumer chooses the best combination out of a range of possibilities. However, behaviour depends on traditions and habits, and the consumer may reflect on the social group s/he belongs to. Consumers sometimes buy impulsively and they are influenced by advertisements. In principle, habit formation and social reference group effects can be absorbed in the model, as will be done in Chapters 9 and 4, respectively. Some psychological aspects of consumer behaviour will be paid attention to in Chapter 4.

Many of the theoretical objections that are mentioned here can be overcome by changing parts of the model. In this way we can improve the model and emphasize different aspects of household behaviour. Hypotheses based on these models can be tested in principle, by using observations on actual behaviour.

2.4 The introduction of time in the neo-classical model

According to the first assumption of the neo-classical model (see page 11), *human beings experience 'utility' from the consumption of goods and services.* Implicit in this assumption is that income and labour time are fixed. Once we realize that leisure is also appreciated by consumers, the allocation of time becomes important. In this section, Assumption 1 is replaced by:

> *Human beings experience 'utility' from the consumption of goods and services and from leisure time.*

The more hours of labour the consumer supplies, the more income s/he earns, and the more s/he can spend on consumer goods, but the less leisure s/he enjoys. Initially we shall assume that, at a given market wage rate (predetermined mainly by education and job experience), the consumer can choose exactly the number of hours s/he wants to work, and the job is presumed to be available. Of course, in practice, the number of hours worked can be quite different from the preferred number of hours. Non-voluntary unemployment is an obvious example. This issue will be addressed further in Chapter 5.

Here we introduce the simplest neo-classical model that includes labour supply (or, equivalently, leisure demand) as a choice variable. In a model with labour supply, the consumer maximizes:

$$U(q_1, \ldots, q_N, l)$$
$$s.t.$$
$$\begin{cases} T = t_w + l \\[2mm] \displaystyle\sum_{i=1}^{N} p_i q_i = \mu + w t_w \\[2mm] t_w \geq 0,\ l \geq 0,\ q_i \geq 0, \end{cases} \qquad (2.26)$$

where
l = leisure time
t_w = labour time
T = total time available
w = consumer's wage rate
μ = non-wage income.

An important difference from the previous model is that we now have to deal with the additional time constraint $t_w + l = T$: the time spent on labour plus the time spent on leisure must be equal to the total time available. The two equality constraints can be combined into one:

$$\mu + wT = \sum_{i=1}^{N} p_i q_i + wl. \qquad (2.27)$$

The left-hand side of Equation (2.27) is called *full income*. It is the amount of money the consumer could (theoretically) earn if s/he spent all his or her time in the labour market. Full income is spent on consumer goods and leisure time, the price of leisure being the wage rate of the consumer. So the *opportunity costs* of leisure are *wl*. The optimal amount of leisure depends on the shape of the utility function (preferences), the prices of consumer goods, the wage rate and non-wage income (or 'unearned income'). In most societies, a substantial proportion of individuals choose not to work in the labour market. Thus, in the labour supply model, the corner solution $t_w = 0$ is particularly relevant. We relegate the discussion of corner solutions to Chapter 5.

The expansion of the neo-classical model to labour supply discloses a completely new area of research. The model can be used to study the interaction between the labour market and markets of goods and services. Questions such as: 'What is the effect of a wage rate increase on consumption and labour supply?' or 'What is the effect of an increase in the cost of living?' can be answered once the model's parameters have been estimated. Here we shall only make some general remarks for the case with one (composite) consumption good. We also assume that both leisure and consumption are normal goods.

An *increase in the price of the consumption good*, again, has an income and a substitution effect. For the consumption good itself (that is, the 'own price effect'), both effects point in the same direction: to a decrease in demand. For leisure (the 'cross price effect'), it is different. The total effect depends on the relative strength of the income and substitution effects. If the income effect is the stronger, demand for leisure will decrease and labour supply will increase, but if the substitution effect dominates, labour supply will diminish. It all depends on the preferences of the consumer.

An *increase in the market wage rate* will increase full income and decrease the relative price of consumption as compared to leisure. For consumption, both effects point in the same direction: towards increased consumption. For leisure, this is again different. On the one hand, leisure demand will increase because of the rise in full income, but on the other, it will decrease because the relative price of leisure has increased. Whether the first effect dominates the second or not is an empirical matter. It is possible, for example, that the substitution effect is stronger at low wage levels and the income effect stronger at higher wage levels. In that case the labour supply curve is forward-bending for lower wages and backward-bending for a higher range of wages; see Figure 2.2.

An *increase in non-wage income* has an income effect only, since there is no change in relative prices. More leisure and more consumption will be demanded, resulting in less labour supply and less labour income.

labour time

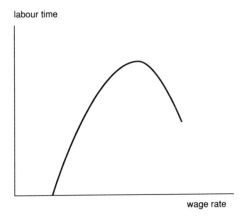

wage rate

Figure 2.2 Forward- and backward-bending labour supply

Exercise 2.10

Consider a consumer with preferences represented by

$$U(q_1, \ldots q_N, l) = \sum_{i=1}^{N} \alpha_i \ln (q_i - \gamma_i) + \beta \ln (l - \gamma_l),$$

with $\Sigma \alpha_i + \beta = 1$.

(a) Derive the corresponding labour supply function and leisure demand equations.

(b) Can labour supply be backward-bending in this model?

2.5 The 'New Home Economics' theory

In agricultural societies, households can be considered as small production units. Households in such societies depend to a large extent on home and agricultural production. In the past this was also true for Western countries (for a historical survey, see Chapter 4). Since the Industrial Revolution, the role of households is most Western countries has changed drastically. The agricultural sector has become less important and households have become both the suppliers of specialized labour for the market and consumers of the goods produced by the market.

In the neo-classical model of Section 2.4, these two functions of households can be recognized: households supply labour and households consume the products supplied by the market. However, in reality, the production role of households, although not visible in the neo-classical model, is still important. It may have become less important since the market and the public sector have taken over many tasks of the households, but it has never disappeared.

The New Home Economics theory, as it was introduced by Becker (1965), emphasizes the productive role of households. According to Becker, market goods and services can only generate utility if they are combined with the consumer's time. For example:

• Having a ticket for the cinema does not generate utility. The consumer needs time to go to the cinema, watch the film and return home.
• Having money for food does not generate utility. Time is needed for buying food, preparing the meal and for consuming it. Only this combination of food and the consumer's time generates utility.

It has been suggested that *unpleasant* household activities can be considered to be productive, and *pleasant* activities to be leisure. We shall not use these criteria, because of their subjective nature. Pleasure should be considered as a positive contribution to utility and aversion as a negative contribution, as Winston (1982) suggested. Final commodities and pleasure (or dislike) are created in a joint production process. Another criterion for defining productive activities is the *third party* standard. It dates from Reid (1934). All activities that could be taken over by another person without quality loss, should be considered productive. There should be a market substitute for the activity. Although this may seem a suitable measure, it still has a subjective element. Some people may think that child care can be taken over by another person (day-care centre, crèche or a private nanny), others may consider this a lower-quality, incomplete substitute. Another problem is that 'education' is not productive according to this standard. Still, it cannot be considered as leisure. Investments in human capital can be very productive in the long run. Chapter 11 is dedicated to investments in human capital. In Becker's view, all activities in the household are productive, even sleeping and watching TV.

The production process in the household requires inputs (time of household members and market goods) and generates one or more outputs (commodities). This notion is formalized by the introduction of *production functions*. The commodities that result from these production processes in turn generate utility. Again, we change the first assumption of the neo-classical model:

Human beings experience utility from the commodities that are produced in the household with a combination of market goods and household time.

Normally, there are several techniques available to produce a final commodity. We shall give an example: the commodity 'eating a meal' can be produced at home starting from scratch (going shopping, preparing the meal, eating it at home and washing the dishes). It is also possible to go shopping and buy a frozen meal, that only needs to be heated. Another alternative is to get a meal delivered at your home (pizza service or other meal service). Finally, one could go to a restaurant and eat there. Although the final commodity, 'eating a meal', is not exactly the same in each case, this example shows that several 'technologies' exist to reach (almost) the same goal.

People with a high wage rate may choose less time-intensive, but financially more costly, technologies, more often than people with a lower wage rate. The more elaborate household production models specify different technologies and describe the consumer's optimal choice among them. Household production will be discussed in more detail in Chapter 6.

In Gronau's (1980) household production model a distinction is made between work, leisure and household labour time (or 'household production time'). We present it here, as it is both relatively simple and instructive. Household utility depends on two commodities: consumption goods (c) and leisure time (l). The household can obtain consumption goods in two ways. First, it can produce them at home. This only requires time as input (and no market goods). The production process at home is represented by the production function $z = f(h)$ with $f' > 0$ and $f'' < 0$. The second way to obtain consumption goods is to become a wage-earner and use the earnings to purchase consumption goods on the market. So, market goods and home-made goods are perfect substitutes. Given these assumptions, the model becomes:

$$\text{maximize } u = U(c, l)$$
$$\text{s.t.} \qquad z = f(h)$$
$$c = x + z$$
$$t_w + h + l = T$$
$$x = y_0 + t_w w$$

where:

x	= expenditures on market products	w	= wage rate
z	= home products	t_w	= paid labour time
l	= leisure time	$f(.)$	= household production function
y_0	= unearned income	h	= household production time
c	= consumption		

A graphical representation of the model is given in Figure 2.3a. The curved line represents the production function. Note that it runs from right to left: if the consumer is at point T, then all available time is spent on leisure. At point B, BT is spent on household production, at the expense of leisure. Between B and T the slope of the production function is larger (in absolute value) than the slope corresponding to the wage rate w (that is, $f'(h) > w$). Therefore, between B and T it is more efficient to produce consumption through household production than through paid labour and next purchasing the goods on the market. Beyond B (going from right to left) this is no longer the case. The consumer will then also work on the market, as his or her productivity there is larger then his or her productivity at home (that is, $f'(h) < w$). As a consequence, the opportunity set is bounded by ST to the right of B and by RS to the left of B.

We consider two kinds of outcome. A consumer with preferences as indicated by the indifference curves in Figure 2.3a will spend BT on household production, AB on paid labour and OA on leisure time. The household

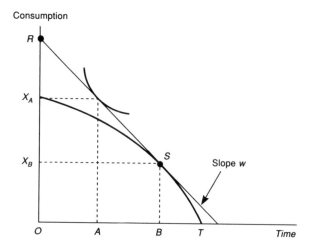

Figure 2.3a   *Household production, leisure and labour supply*

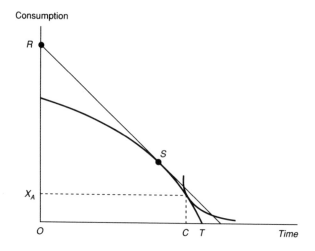

Figure 2.3b   *Household production, leisure and no labour supply*

production is OX_B. The labour earnings, X_AX_B, are used to buy consumption goods, so that total consumption equals OX_A. In point A the marginal rate of substitution between leisure and consumption equals the wage rate: $(\partial U/\partial l)/(\partial U/\partial c) = w$. Figure 2.3b shows the case for a consumer with a relatively strong preference for leisure. In this case, the indifference curve is a tangent to the opportunity set to the right of B. The consumer will spend CT on household production, OC on leisure, and she will not work in the market. In point C the marginal rate of substitution between leisure and consumption equals the transformation rate between production and household production time: $(\partial U/\partial l)/(\partial U/\partial x) = f'(h)$.

Note that a consumer who has a very low productivity at home such that $f'(0) < w$ will not spend any time on household production. For the special case without opportunities to work in the labour market ($w = 0$), the model describes the world of Robinson Crusoe. The economy has one producer and one consumer, and Point C represents the simplest case of general equilibrium.

The model generates two simple predictions, which are easily checked using the figures. The first is that for a consumer with a paid job, a rise in the wage rate will decrease the amount of time spent on household production. The second prediction is that an increase in unearned income will leave it unaffected.

Gronau applied this model to Israeli data and estimated the parameters of the production function. These can, in turn, be used to estimate the value of household production. We shall return to further applications of household production models in Chapter 6.

2.6 Summary

In the simplest neo-classical model, a consumer maximizes utility subject to a budget constraint. As a description of reality, this model is easy to criticize. However, many of the objections that have been put forward can be accounted for by changing and extending parts of the model. In the present chapter we have focused on two such extensions: the inclusion of labour supply and the inclusion of time spent on productive activities within the household.

While the simplest neo-classical model is often too simple a description of real-world individual economic behaviour, we shall adhere to the general idea that individuals maximize or minimize something subject to constraints. In subsequent chapters we shall try to find out more about what it is that people attempt to optimize and what the constraints they are facing when doing so look like.

Note

1. Application and testing of the theory has not been confined to human behaviour, however; see, for example, Kagel *et al.* (1995).

CHAPTER 3

Household versus Individual Economic Behaviour

3.1 Introduction

Traditionally, the economic theory of consumer demand has taken the individual as a unit of analysis. Empirical work on demand systems, on the other hand, is usually based on data that take the household as the unit for data collection. In this chapter we shall investigate this discrepancy between the theory and practice of demand analysis, and possibilities of narrowing the gap.

From a viewpoint of economic policy, it is the well-being of individuals – rather than the average well-being of individuals within a household – that is the ultimate object of concern. Several studies have reported results indicating that well-being is by no means equally distributed within households. Rosenzweig and Schultz (1982), for example, find that in India, infant mortality is less among boys than among girls. They argue, on the basis of anthropometric indicators, that boys receive preferential treatment. Alderman and Gertler (1989) report that the income and price elasticities of the demand for health care in Pakistan are larger for girls than for boys, which suggests that the good health of girls is considered to be less of a necessity than the health of boys. Using data from a variety of cultural and economic settings, Thomas (1990) finds evidence that a change in household resources is unlikely to be gender neutral. Given the evidence that intrahousehold inequality of well-being may be substantial, the importance of studying intrahousehold allocation can hardly be overestimated.

Why do many people prefer living in a household with others? From an economic perspective, three types of explanation may be put forward. First, there are psychic benefits in terms of love and companionship which may be much larger if people live within the same household than if they do not. A second explanation relates to the existence of economies of scale in a household of several persons. Living together is often beneficial from a financial point of view, in particular with regard to housing expenditure, but also with respect to the use of (durable) consumer goods such as a car or a washing machine. The literature that attempts to measure these scale economies will be discussed in Chapter 7. Living together also facilitates the possibilities of having and raising children. A third reason (which will be discussed in detail in Chapters 5 and 6) arises from the possibility of specializing if household members have different skills and labour market wages.

In principle, each household member may compare the maximum utility that can be reached within the joint household with the utility that would be reached in a one-person household. The utility attainable outside the household is sometimes referred to as the *threat point*. If this utility level cannot be reached within the joint household, an individual may threaten not to participate.

The discussion shows that there is a connection between intrahousehold allocation of resources on the one hand and the formation, existence and dissolution of households on the other. The latter issue will be discussed in Chapter 8, but it is useful to keep in mind the interrelationship between both issues.

3.2 A game theoretic approach to household decision-making

In this section we present a theoretical framework for analyzing issues of intrahousehold allocation. We confine ourselves to households with two decision-makers (which is, of course, not necessarily identical to a two-person household). This restriction does not only simplify the exposition, it also corresponds to the predominant household type in Western societies of a couple, with or without children, with the two adults taking most of the household's economic decisions.

Sharing a loaf of bread

The decision-makers will be indicated by the indices m (male) and f (female). For convenience we shall sometimes use the term 'husband' for m and 'wife' for f. We start by analysing a primitive example. Both m and f are hungry and have to reach agreement on how to share a loaf of bread (with weight Y). The bread is the only resource they have available. The consumption by partner i is denoted by x_i, so the division (allocation) must satisfy $x_m + x_f \leq Y$. We assume that both partners are so hungry that this budget constraint will be binding. The set of possible outcomes is visualized by the line AB in Figure 3.1. If both partners were completely selfish, m's preferred allocation would be Point B (where he receives everything and she receives nothing), and f's preferred allocation would be the opposite, Point A. However, we shall assume that both exhibit some degree of

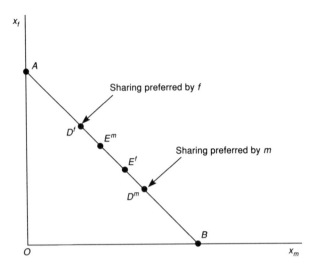

Figure 3.1   Sharing a loaf of bread

altruism, and that the preferred allocations are represented by points D^f for partner f and by D^m for partner m. We also assume that the utility level of partner i increases when the allocation gets closer to D^i. Of course it is possible that D^m and D^f coincide. This will then also be the actual allocation, but clearly this is not a very interesting case from a game theoretic perspective.

The central question now is how the bread will actually be divided. It seems reasonable to assume that the actual outcome will be somewhere between D^m and D^f. If not, other allocations would be possible which would increase the utility level of both partners. All allocations between (and including) D^m and D^f are *Pareto optimal*: in those cases there does not exist another allocation that would improve the utility level of one partner without decreasing the utility level of the other. But which allocation between D^m and D^f will be chosen? All that we shall say about it for now is that the final outcome is likely to be a reflection of something that is related to influence, persuasiveness and power.

Let us also consider briefly the case where the preferred allocations are E^i, $i = m, f$. So the husband wants his wife to eat more than he himself, and vice versa. Note that in this case, giving the larger share to a partner is altruistic in terms of consumption, although it is egoistic in terms of utility.

A more complicated case

Let us now turn to the case where the preferences of m and f can be represented by the utility functions $U^m(x_m, x_f, x_h)$ and $U^f(x_m, x_f, x_h)$, respectively. The variable y_i is the income of the decision-maker, i. It is put into the pool of joint household income, but decision-maker i remains in control over y_i should s/he decide to leave the household. The variable x_i represents private goods of person i ($i = m, f$), that is, goods that are consumed exclusively by person i; x_h represents public goods, that is, goods that are consumed jointly, such as housing. The utility functions are well-behaved, in the sense defined in Section 2.2.

The fact that the private consumption of partner j enters the utility function of partner i does not necessarily imply that partner i is altruistic. For example, suppose that a wife likes her husband to wear expensive suits, whereas he himself is little interested in the way he dresses. Then male clothing (x_m) increases the wife's utility, but it is not clear whether this should be considered to be altruism by the wife. An explicit way to model *altruism* is to suppose that the utility Z^i of partner i is an increasing function of the utility (rather than the consumption) of partner j. Thus:

$$Z^i(x_m, x_f, x_h, U^j(x_m, x_f, x_h)); \ \partial Z^i/\partial U^j > 0. \tag{3.1}$$

But Z^i has the same arguments as the original utility function U^i. Therefore Z^i is indistinguishable from U^i (as long as U^j is not observed directly). We conclude that the utility functions $U^m(x_m, x_f, x_h)$ and $U^f(x_m, x_f, x_h)$ are consistent with egoistic as well as altruistic preferences.[1]

As an example, we consider the case where x_m and x_f represent male and female leisure, respectively, and x_h represents joint household consumption. We choose this example not least because much of the literature on household decision-making focuses on labor supply decisions. The utility functions in our example are of the Cobb–Douglas type:

$$U^m(x_m, x_f, x_h) = \alpha_m \log x_m + \alpha_f \log x_f + (1 - \alpha_m - \alpha_f) \log x_h \tag{3.2}$$

$$U^f(x_m, x_f, x_h) = \beta_m \log x_m + \beta_f \log x_f + (1 - \beta_m - \beta_f) \log x_h. \tag{3.3}$$

The budget constraint is now written as:

$$p_m x_m + p_f x_f + p_h x_h = y_m + y_f + (p_m + p_f) T \equiv Y. \tag{3.4}$$

T is the total time each decision-maker has available; y_m and y_f should here be interpreted as non-labor incomes, and p_m and p_f as wages. Y is the household's full income (see page 26). For simplicity, we ignore the constraints $0 \leq x_i \leq T$, $i = m, f$.

The *dictatorial allocation* of the ith partner is defined as the solution of maximizing $U^i(x_m, x_f, x_h)$ subject to the household budget constraint in Equation (3.4). It is the allocation that would occur if individual i had complete control over household resources. In our example, the leisure demand functions in case of male dictatorship are given by:

$$x_i = \frac{\alpha_i}{p_i} \cdot Y, \qquad i = m, f, \tag{3.5}$$

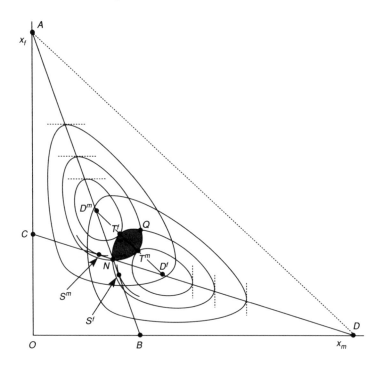

Figure 3.2   Preferences and solution concepts

and in the case of female dictatorship by:

$$x_i = \frac{\beta_i}{p_i} \cdot Y, \qquad i = m, f. \tag{3.6}$$

(We use the normalization $p_h = 1$.)

A convenient graphical representation of Equations (3.2) and (3.3) is obtained by eliminating x_h from the utility function by using the budget constraint in Equation (3.4), and then drawing indifference contours in the (x_m, x_f) space; see Figure 3.2.

The curves around the dictatorial point D^f are indifference curves of individual f; the curves around the dictatorial point D^m are indifference curves of individual m. The farther away an indifference contour of individual i is from the dictatorial point D^i, the lower is the utility level.

Some explanation may be useful on the difference between the indifference contours in Figure 3.2 and the more usual indifference curves as in, for example, Figure 9.4 (see page 164). First, an indifference curve as in Figure 9.4 is based on a utility function with two arguments, whereas the indifference contours are based on a three-argument utility function. The indifference contours are obtained after substitution of the household budget constraint in Equation (3.4) into the utility function. Thus, all points within the triangle OAD in Figure 3.2 exhaust the budget, whereas in Figure 9.4 the budget is exhausted only at the points that are on the budget line. Since the specification in Equation (3.2) requires that $x_m \geq 0$, $x_f \geq 0$ and $x_h \geq 0$, all contours are within the bounded set $\{(x_m, x_f)/x_m \geq 0, x_f \geq 0, Y - p_m x_m - p_f x_f \geq 0\}$.

What is m's optimal demand for x_m, given that x_f assumes some given value, say $\bar{x}_f$? The solution, which is sometimes referred to as m's reaction curve, is obtained by maximizing

$$U^m(x_m, x_f, x_h) = \alpha_m \log x_m + \alpha_f \log x_f + (1 - \alpha_m - \alpha_f) \log x_h, \quad (3.7)$$

subject to the two restrictions:

$$\begin{cases} p_m x_m + p_f x_f + p_h x_h = Y \\ x_f = \bar{x}_f. \end{cases} \quad (3.8)$$

The solution of the problem is given by:

$$x_m = \frac{\alpha_m}{p_m(1 - \alpha_f)} [Y - p_f \bar{x}_f] \quad (3.9)$$

Equation (3.9) is a so-called conditional demand equation, which will be discussed further in Chapter 4. In the present example, the conditional demand for x_m is linear in $\bar{x}_f$. In Figure 3.2, it is represented by the line *AB*. It connects all tangency points of horizontal lines with m's indifference curves. Analogously, *CD* is the conditional demand function for x_f of decision-maker f, given x_m.

The set of Pareto optimal allocations – the *contract curve* – can be visualized easily in Figure 3.2. Consider point Q. Clearly, Q is not Pareto optimal. If we move from Q counter-clockwise along f's indifference curve, for example, f's utility remains constant, whereas m's utility increases. Given f's utility level, m's utility is maximized at allocation T^f, at which f's indifference curve is at a tangent to one of m's indifference curves. Since the contract curve is the set of all tangency points of m's indifference curves with those of f, it satisfies:

$$\frac{\partial V^m/\partial x_m}{\partial V^m/\partial x_f} = \frac{\partial V^f/\partial x_m}{\partial V^f/\partial x_f}, \quad (3.10)$$

where $V^i \equiv V^i(x_m, x_f) = U^i(x_m, x_f, Y - p_m x_m - p_f x_f)$. Thus, in our example,

$$V^m(x_m, x_f) = \alpha_m \log x_m + \alpha_f \log x_f + (1 - \alpha_m - \alpha_f) \log (Y - p_m x_m - p_f x_f), \quad (3.11)$$

and

$$V^f(x_m, x_f) = \beta_m \log x_m + \beta_f \log x_f + (1 - \beta_m - \beta_f) \log (Y - p_m x_m - p_f x_f). \quad (3.12)$$

Applying Equation (3.10) to derive the contract curve yields:

$$\frac{x_f}{x_m} \cdot \frac{\alpha_m x_h - (1 - \alpha_m - \alpha_f) p_m x_m}{\alpha_f x_h - (1 - \alpha_m - \alpha_f) p_f x_f} =$$
$$\frac{x_f}{x_m} \cdot \frac{\beta_m x_h - (1 - \beta_m - \beta_f) p_m x_m}{\beta_f x_h - (1 - \beta_m - \beta_f) p_f x_f},$$

(3.13)

which can be simplified to:

$$(\alpha_f - \beta_f) p_m x_m + (\beta_m - \alpha_m) p_f x_f + (\alpha_m \beta_f - \alpha_f \beta_m) Y = 0. \qquad (3.14)$$

Thus, in this case, the contract curve is a linear segment in the (x_m, x_f) plane. An alternative way to represent it algebraically is:

$$p_m x_m = [\lambda \alpha_m + (1 - \lambda) \beta_m] Y$$
$$p_f x_f = [\lambda \alpha_f + (1 - \lambda) \beta_f] Y,$$

(3.15)

for $0 \leq \lambda \leq 1$. (To see the equivalence, solve λ from Equation (3.15a) and substitute the solution into Equation (3.15b)). Now the marginal budget shares are weighted averages of the marginal budget shares in the corresponding male and female dictatorial Equations (3.5) and (3.6).

A comparison of Equations (3.5) and (3.6) with Equation (3.15) leads us to the conclusion that, *without further information*, the dictatorial models and the Pareto-optimality model are indistinguishable empirically. Stated differently, for the Cobb–Douglas specification of individual utility functions, using a joint household utility function is consistent with the two partners having different preferences combined with a Pareto-optimal outcome of the decision process. If we were to use the more general Stone–Geary functions for the specification of Equations (3.2) and (3.3), then the implied demand equations for Pareto-optimal outcomes would not be of the Stone–Geary type. However, the distinction between the two models would then rest entirely on the assumed functional form. It is generally recognized that the distinction of competing models solely on the basis of functional form is too shaky a basis for inference.

Equation (3.13) also follows immediately from the first order conditions for maximizing $V^i(x_m, x_f)$ subject to $V^j(x_m, x_f) = U_0$ $(j \neq i)$, where U_0 is some given utility level. Alternatively, Equation (3.13) can be obtained by maximizing the function:

$$\tilde{U} = W \{U^m(x_m, x_f, x_h), U^f(x_m, x_f, x_h)\}, \qquad (3.16)$$

subject to the budget constraint, Equation (3.4). Here, W may be interpreted as a 'social welfare function' or a 'family welfare function'; it is increasing in both its arguments. Note again that without further information there is no way in which this problem can be distinguished from the direct maximization of a household utility function with arguments x_m, x_f and x_h subject to Equation (3.4).

A special form of Equation (3.16) is:

$$\tilde{U} = \lambda U^m(x_m, x_f, x_h) + (1 - \lambda) \, U^f(x_m, x_f, x_h)\}, \tag{3.17}$$

with $0 \leq \lambda \leq 1$. Here, λ indicates which point on the contract curve is actually chosen by the household. The extreme cases $\lambda = 0$ and $\lambda = 1$ correspond to female and male dictatorship, respectively. Thus λ measures the relative bargaining strength of both partners.

Threat points

The discussion until now has taken the existence of the household as given. Suppose that T^i is the threat point of individual i, that is, at T^i, i's utility level equals the utility level that may be obtained outside the household. Then the shaded area in Figure 3.2 is the set of allocations at which both individuals are better off than outside the household. In that case, only the intersection of this set and the contract curve should be considered as the set of potential equilibria. In this case the household's behaviour can be described by:

$$\max \tilde{V} = W \{V^m \, (x_m, x_f), V^f \, (x_m, x_f)\}$$
$$s.t. \ V^m \, (x_m, x_f) \geq \varphi^m \tag{3.18}$$
$$V^f(x_m, x_f) \geq \varphi^f,$$

where φ^i is the utility corresponding to the threat point T^i of partner i. If a point on the contract curve outside the shaded area is reached, one of the individuals will prefer the outside option and behave non-cooperatively.

A special case of Equation (3.18), the Nash bargaining model, has been studied by McElroy and Horney (1981) and McElroy (1990):

$$\tilde{V} = [U^m \, (x_m, x_f, x_h) - \varphi^m] \cdot [U^f(x_m, x_f, x_h) - \varphi^f]. \tag{3.19}$$

The threat point utilities φ^i will generally depend upon p_i, and y_i, since these variables are obviously important for the utility level that can be reached outside the household. In addition, they will depend on variables describing marriage opportunities (for example, age-specific sex ratios) and the legal, fiscal and social security settings relevant for household formation and dissolution (for example, the additional welfare benefits in case of a divorce). For this model, McElroy and Horney have derived a Nash generalization of the Slutsky conditions.

Which allocation will be chosen?

The question that arises is, which allocation will be the ultimate outcome of the decision process? Note that all points within the triangle OAD satisfy the household budget constraint. One point that seems to be a natural candidate for the solution is the intersection point, N, of the reaction curves AB and CD, the Nash equilibrium (note the difference with the Nash bargaining solution mentioned earlier, which corresponds with a point on the contract curve $D^m D^f$). Point N may be thought of as the point of convergence of an iterative process, where decision-maker m reacts to changes in x_f made by f, and decision-maker f reacts to changes in x_m made by m. Figure 3.2 clearly illustrates a well-known property of the Nash equilibrium, N, namely that it is generally not Pareto optimal. As has been argued by Manser and Brown (1980), it seems more appropriate in a household context to employ models which only yield Pareto optimal outcomes. However, even if one adopts Pareto optimality as a maintained hypothesis, the question remains about which Pareto optimal point will ultimately be chosen. Since it is hard to put forward theoretical arguments in favour of one Pareto optimal solution or another, the answer to this question seems to be an empirical matter. It seems likely that the outcome will be a reflection of something like the division of power within the household, which in turn may be related to the household's and partners' characteristics. Addressing the issue empirically requires, at least conceptually, that the outcome of the decision process as well as the utility functions of both decision-makers can be measured. The actual observed allocation is the natural candidate as a measure of the ultimate outcome of the decision process, assuming that the decision process has converged. One kind of information that may be used to elicit the preferences of a decision-maker are responses to subjective questions. In Kooreman and Kapteyn (1990), subjective survey data on how many hours a respondent would like to work were used to identify the respondent's dictatorial point. This approach requires a very careful design of the questionnaire and phrasing of questions.

Exercise 3.1
Derive the algebraic representation of Point N in Figure 3.2.

Chiappori (1988, 1992) has paid a fair amount of attention within the context of household labour supply to Pareto optimal outcomes generated by solving a maximization problem of the form:

$$\tilde{V} = W\{V^m(x_m), V^f(x_f)|w_1, w_2, y\}, \tag{3.20}$$

with $x_m = (L_m, Z_m)$ and $x_f = (L_f, Z_f)$. Here L_i, Z_i and w_i denote the leisure, the private consumption and the wage rate of the ith partner, $i = m, f$, and y is the total non-labour income of the household.

On the one hand Equation (3.20) is more general than Equation (3.16), since the social welfare function is allowed to depend on prices (wages) and non-labour income. This is motivated by the fact that the bargaining strength of the spouses may depend on these variables. This introduces price-dependent preferences into the model. On the other hand, Equation (3.20) is more restrictive than Equation (3.16) since in Equation (3.20) x_m is weakly separable from x_f. Assuming maximization of this function subject to the budget constraint, Chiappori derived a set of restrictions that should be satisfied by household labour supply. The restrictions do not overlap with Slutsky conditions because of the appearance of prices and income in the function $W(.)$. If in Equation (3.20) we remove the dependency on prices, then stronger conditions can be derived directly from the familiar separability conditions.

Although Chiappori's analysis is ingenious, it is hard to believe that leisure or consumption of spouses are separable. For instance, spouses may want to have a meal together every now and then. In that case L_m, Z_m, L_f and Z_f will be arguments of both utility functions, so that the separability assumption cannot hold.

Finally, we mention that game theoretic models of household behaviour have been developed for the case of discrete choices. Originally, these models were introduced as an alternative to simultaneous probit models (Bjorn and Vuong, 1984, 1985). Bresnahan and Reiss (1991), Kooreman (1994) and Hiedemann (1993) present extensions and empirical applications to household labour force participation and retirement decisions (see also Chapter 10).

3.3 Analysing intrahousehold allocation using household data

It will be clear intuitively that the empirical analysis of intrahousehold allocation requires data that provide more detail than just consumption on a household level. However, the possibilities for drawing inferences on intrahousehold allocation having data available on a household level alone are not completely absent.

Consider two households, one with a boy and one with a girl. If the two households are exactly identical in all other respects, a difference in the expenditure pattern of the two households may be attributed to the gender difference of the children. This idea has been exploited in papers by Deaton (1989) and Subramanian and Deaton (1990), who use regression analysis to control for factors other than gender that affect the household's expenditure pattern. In particular, they look at the differences in expenditure on *adult goods*, such as tobacco, alcohol and adult clothing. In a household with children, a fraction of income will be used to meet the children's needs for food, clothing, health care and other items, and the amount available for the adult goods will be smaller than in a household without children. For adult goods, the addition of a child to the household acts exactly like a reduction of income. The reduction in expenditure on adult goods should therefore be proportional to the marginal propensities to spend on these adult goods. Moreover, in the absence of *gender bias*, the reduction in expenditure on adult goods should be independent of whether the child is a boy or a girl.

To formalize these ideas, consider an Engel-curve of the form:

$$p_i q_i = f_i (y, n_m, n_f, z), \tag{3.21}$$

where $p_i q_i$ are the expenditures on good i; y is household total expenditure; n_m is the number of boys in the household within a particular age group; and n_f is the number of girls in the household within the same age group; z represents all other factors affecting expenditure on good i. If $i = 1, \ldots, I$ are adult goods, then:

$$\tau_{ij} = \frac{\partial(p_i q_i)/\partial n_j}{\partial(p_i q_i)/\partial y}, \qquad j = m, f \tag{3.22}$$

should be negative (since the addition of a child acts as a decrease in income), and independent of i. If τ_{ij} is also independent of j, there is no indication of boys and girls being treated differently. However, if for example τ_{im} is more negative than τ_{if}, then there is some evidence that boys get more than girls.

On the basis of this procedure, Deaton (1989) and Subramanian and Deaton (1990) found weak evidence of discrimination in favor of boys, using data from Thailand and India, respectively. In studies using data from the Ivory Coast and Peru, no evidence of gender bias was found (Deaton (1989) and Dobbelsteen (1996), respectively).

3.4 Analysing intrahousehold allocation using individual data

Although the previous paragraph illustrates that there exist some possibilities to investigate intrahousehold allocation using household level data, data collected at the level of individual household members is the preferred type of information for studying issues of intrahousehold allocation. Intrahousehold data collection, however, entails a number of problems, in addition to those that are encountered in the collection of more conventional household data (such as measurement errors and representativeness). First of all, a number of goods and services should be identified which primarily affect the well-being of an individual household member. In this respect, it is important to recognize that the allocation of welfare is not identical to the allocation of goods and services; recall the earlier example of a wife who likes her partner to wear an expensive suit. The example shows that the answer to 'who gets what' in terms of goods and services may provide little information about 'who gets what' in terms of welfare. However, consumption of food, drink and health care services are examples where a direct positive relationship between consumption and well-being of the individual that receives these goods and services will be undisputed. Indeed, food, drink and health care are the expenditures items on which intrahousehold data collection usually focuses.

Health status is usually measured on the basis of a set of anthropometric indicators. Height and weight of individuals are the ones most frequently used, not least because it is relatively easy to collect these data. Among nutritionists, 'height for age' is considered a long-run measure of nutritional and health status, and 'weight for height' is particularly useful for the description of current health status. 'Skinfold thickness for height' is an alternative short-run health measure.

One interesting study on intrahousehold allocation that uses anthropometric indicators as a measure of health status is the paper by Thomas (1990). One of his findings, based on regression analysis, is that a mother's education has a greater effect on the health of her daughters than of her sons. The education of the father, on the other hand, has a larger effect on the health of his sons than on that of his daughters. If education is an indicator of a partner's bargaining strength within the household (and there is some empirical evidence that this is indeed the case; see below), the finding might be caused by boy preference of fathers and girl preference of mothers. However, it may also reflect differences in the 'technology' of child rearing. For example, if fathers spend more time with sons and mothers with daughters, then a parent may be more efficient in the rearing of a child of his or her own gender than in the rearing of a child of the other gender. Another study indicating that there may be other explanations for health differences than gender preferences is the paper by Pitt *et al.* (1990) in which panel data of 400 households from Bangladesh were analysed. Men have a greater participation in activities which require much physical activity. As is quite common in low-income societies, productivity and the earned wage are positively related to health status. The implication is that the objective of equalizing health status among household members may be in conflict with the objective of maximizing household income, and thus the total amount of food available to the household. Pitt *et al.* (1990) inferred from their estimates that households are adverse to inequality in health outcomes.

It was noted earlier that the outcome of decision processes within a household is likely to be a reflection of the division of power within that household, which in turn may be related to the household's and partners' characteristics. One of the few empirical studies in which such a relationship is investigated is the paper by Ott (1991b). This author used a sample of German wives, who were asked to respond to the question, 'Who is in fact the more powerful partner in your marriage: your husband, yourself, or do you think you are about equal?'. Ott estimated an ordered Probit model with the response to this question being the dependent variable; see Table 3.1.

Table 3.1 Balance of power within marriages

Variable	Coefficient estimate	t-value
Constant 1	−0.585	−5.9
Constant 2	1.101	10.7
Own house	−0.169	−2.3
Children have left home	0.280	1.6
Wife has high education	0.419	2.0
Wife has own income	0.162	2.0
Husband's income	−0.127	−2.5
n = 1101		

Notes: Ordered probit model for housewives – Dependent variable:

more powerful part in marriage $\begin{cases} 1\text{-husband} \\ 2\text{-both about equal} \\ 3\text{-wife} \end{cases}$

Source: Ott (1991b).

The table indicates that the variables 'children have left home', 'wife has high education' and 'wife has own income' have a positive effect on the wife considering herself more powerful. Note, however, that the table provides little information on the causal relationship; for example, the wife having an income of her own may well be a consequence of the wife being more powerful.

In the economic psychology and marketing literature a lot of research has been done into the relative influence of husband and wife in purchasing decisions (the relationship with the individual and household characteristics is usually considered to be of secondary importance). We mention a study by Woodside and Motes (1979), who asked both partners about their perceptions of relative influence in the purchasing decision for a number of products; see Table 3.2. Note the small discrepancies between the husbands' and wives' perceptions of their relative influence.

A related issue is the way the household manages its budget in practice. Pahl (1990 and earlier work) has described four systems:

(a) The *whole-wage system*, in which one partner, usually the wife, manages all household finances, except for the personal spending money of the other partner;

(b) The *allowance system*, in which one partner, typically the husband, gives the other an amount of money for some expenditure items, while the rest of the money remains under his control;

(c) The *pooling system*, in which both partners have access to all the household money and both are responsible for managing the common pool and for expenditures drawn from it;

(d) The *independent management system*, in which both partners separately have access to money, neither having access to all the financial resources of the household.

Table 3.2 Influence pattern in purchases of four commodities as perceived by husbands and wives

Influence pattern	Car H/W	Washer H/W	Rug H/W	TV set H/W
Husband has more influence than wife	58/58	23/21	12/14	46/44
Both spouses have equal influence	39/39	41/42	50/48	44/45
Wife has more influence than husband	03/03	36/37	38/38	09/11

Note: The numbers are percentages of husbands' (first value) and wives' (second value) perceptions of influence.

Source: Adapted from Woodside and Motes (1979).

For a sample of 102 married couples with at least one child, in Kent in 1982–3, Pahl found that the pooling system was used by about half the households. A quarter used the allowance system, a sixth the whole-wage system and a twelfth the independent management system.

Note that on the level of a single household there is not necessarily a relationship between adopting one of these systems and the outcome of the decision process in terms the models described above. For example, if a household adopts the whole-wage system with the wife managing the household finances, it may still be the case that she acts according to her husband's preferences. On the other hand, it seems plausible that there is some relationship between the type of management system that is used and the division of power within the household; see Dobbelsteen (1996).

3.5 Summary

For a long time the household has been a black box in microeconomics. It was treated as an entity, both in economic theory and in data collection. What was going on within the household was apparently not considered to be an interesting subject for economic analysis. However, we know that preferences as well as control over resources sometimes differ substantially between household members. Even if we are only interested in explaining behaviour at the household level, this may have important implications for empirical analyses. For example, a model of household demand that has total household income as an explanatory variable is likely to be misspecified, as the incomes of different household members generally have different effects on total household demand.

We have argued that game theory provides a useful framework for analysing intrahousehold issues. Among other things, it generates a clear definition of bargaining power, a concept that has been central, but not always well defined, in the sociological literature on intrahousehold issues. We have also seen that for a truly powerful test of game theoretic models we need specific data on each of the players in the household game. One way of obtaining such information is to use responses to subjective questions. Another way might be to use data on the behaviour and preferences of divorced or widowed people.

Note

1. Adam Smith (1759) has been viewed as the founder of 'egoism' in economic models: 'We are not ready to suspect any person of being defective in selfishness' (p. 446). However, he also recognizes the existence of altruism within the family: 'After himself, the members of his own family, those who usually live in the same house with him, his parents, his children, his brothers and sisters, are usually the objects of his warmest affections. They are naturally and usually the persons upon whose happiness or misery his conduct must have the greatest influence' (p. 321).

CHAPTER 4

Households in Their Institutional and Social Setting

4.1 Introduction

In the previous chapters it was assumed that household members make a rational choice, that is, they maximize utility given their preferences, incomes or wage rates of both partners, and constraints they are facing. In this chapter we shall pay attention to the household's institutional and social setting, which is partly responsible for the constraints and which sometimes even affects household preferences and decisions.

The laws of a country, the economic organization, social structure, traditions and so on together determine the limits within which the consumer can make his or her own choices. An individual household cannot change the laws of the land. Only gradually can consumers as a group change the institutional and social setting. This is what, in theory happens in a democratic system. However, in the short run the individual household has to accept factors such as the tax system, the social security system, the educational system, the opening hours of shops, and the labour market regulations as they are.

A government can try to influence the behaviour of households by changing the framework within which households can make their choices. For instance, if a government would like to influence the labour market participation of married women, it could (a) use the tax and social security system to make participation more (or less) attractive; (b) set up and subsidize child day-care centers; or (c) make the costs of such centres deductible from the pre-tax income of the parents.

A government can also try to affect household choices in a more direct way by acting upon the preferences of households. Education is an important means of influencing preferences, especially in the long run. In the short run it seems more difficult to affect preferences, but, like private enterprises, governments can use a whole marketing mix of economic and psychological instruments to reach their goals.

Besides economic variables, sociological variables may also affect household choices. A household is not an isolated decision unit. It belongs to a society and within this society it belongs to a certain social group, or it may wish to become a member of another group. Preferences are partly determined by the traditions and the revealed preferences of that group.

Ignorance and uncertainty will make it difficult for a household to make an optimal choice. The household cannot know the qualities and prices of all goods and it cannot know the qualities and wages of all jobs, so how does it react?

These and other factors will be discussed in the next sections. We start, in Section 4.2, with a short historical survey of the changing roles of households in society. In Section 4.3 the effects that different tax systems have on household decisions are discussed. In Section 4.4 we analyse choices when households are rationed, and in Section 4.5 the interdependence of the preferences of different households. The effects of uncertainty and risk will be discussed in Section 4.6. All models discussed in this chapter assume that the consumer makes a rational choice. Do real consumers always act rationally? Economic models are often rejected by sociologists, psychologists and anthropologists with the argument that 'the consumer' is not at all rational. In Section 4.7 we pay attention to the rationality assumption.

4.2   The changing roles of households

To a certain extent the economic organization of the household is determined by the structure of society. The function of the household and the allocation of tasks over the household members is influenced by a combination of economic, social, cultural and legal factors. In a short historical survey we shall discuss how households have changed as society has changed. We shall concentrate on three aspects of the household: its size, its functions and the relationships between household members.

Society structure and household size

The household size is affected by the number of births, life expectancy, the stability of the household, the number of generations living together and the number of indoor servants and relatives. It has always been strongly connected with economic factors. In the past the average life expectancy was much lower than it is now. In Europe it almost doubled between 1850 and 1950, from 37 to 72. After 1950 it has remained stable. However, the average life expectancy for the world as a whole is still much lower. In 1985 it was around 60. Most of the rise in life expectancy has been a result of a diminishing rate of infant mortality (death within one year after birth), as a result of better health care. Funds for health care became available as a result of the improvement of the economic situation of many households. Infant mortality was 9.4 per 1000 births in Europe in 1985, the world average being 77 per 1000 births.

Whether or not three or more generations live together in one household is also partly determined by economic factors. In the industrialized Western countries, the elder generation usually lives apart from their adult children. The elderly are economically independent, they have their pensions and there is a social security system.

In agricultural communities the elderly often stay with their children (also in the Western world). From an anthropological point of view, an important factor related to average family size is the mobility of family property. The families of nomads are usually small. One of the explanations may be that they have to carry their belongings with them and second that their property is not their main source of income (Goode, 1963), since they are hunters or simply gather food from nature. In such communities, there are seldom more than two generations living together. In the Western world there are hardly any nomad communities left: they long ago became farmers.

For farmers, land is crucial as a source of income. Therefore the situation of households is quite different in agricultural societies. The household members all work on the farm, where there is always a need for labour. Land, farm and cattle are very important for the production of food, housing and clothing. These factors affect the household size strongly. Often these households are big. The land and farm is usually not divided among the children when the parents die. One son (or daughter) inherits everything. However, unmarried brothers and sisters stay on the farm, as do workers. Also, grandparents stay on the farm, so we often find what are called 'extended' families. For the poorer tenant-farmers the situation is quite different. They often live in bad conditions and their families are smaller. The Western world is no longer predominantly an agricultural society. That does not mean, of course, that there are no farmers. However, the volume of work done by farmers accounted for only 8 per cent of total employment in the countries of the European Economic Community (EEC) in 1985 (Eurostat, 1988). Moreover, agriculture's share of the gross domestic product (GDP) is still falling in all industrialized countries. It accounted for only 3 per cent of total GDP in the countries of the EEC in 1985. Outside the Western world there are still many agricultural societies. Most developing countries still have a structure that could be indicated as such, although the industrial sector is developing fast in several countries, in particular in Asia and South America.

After the Industrial Revolution in the nineteenth century, Western countries developed into industrialized societies. During this transition, family property became less important as a basis for income formation. We now observe a stronger separation between consumption and production units. Households supply labour to factories and use their earnings to buy the products of farms and factories. In an agricultural society, households are more or less self-supporting, but in the industrialized society 'the market' becomes more important. Households become consumers who buy most of the things they need in the market. The production role of the household becomes less prominent, but this does not mean that it disappears completely (as we shall see in Chapter 6). In the agricultural society the extended families took care of the elderly and the sick, and they fed their unemployed relatives. These families were the social security of the community, but this security disappeared after the Industrial Revolution. Gradually, starting around the beginning of the twentieth century, a system of social security was created and pensions for the elderly were introduced. As a result, the elderly were able to live independently of their children and it has now become rare to find more than two generations living together in a Western industrialized society. The improvement of the economic situation of households resulted in much better health care, a decrease in child mortality and longer life expectancy. The introduction of contraceptives has made it easier for parents to decide about the number of children they prefer. The small, 'nuclear' family is now more or less standard in the Western world, although extended families are still found in agricultural areas. In 1993 the number of people employed by the industrial and agricultural sectors in the European Union (EU) accounted only for 29.0 and 5.3 per cent of the labour force respectively and their contributions to the Gross Domestic Product (GDP) for 30.3 and 2.4 per cent. In Japan the industry contributed 44.2 per cent and agriculture 2.1 to the GDP, in the USA industry around 26 per cent and agriculture less than 2 per cent.

This means that these societies have become more and more 'service economies'. A real boom in the tertiary sector (the service sector) took place between 1975 and 1985, and thus now dominates economic activity in terms of both the value and the number of jobs in the EU and it is still growing. Its share of both gross domestics product (GDP) and employment was over 65 per cent in 1993 in the EU countries.

Husband and wife

The rights and duties of husband and wife with respect to each other and towards their children are embedded in the cultural values and legislation of a country. These laws are often a reflection of the thoughts and ideas of the majority of the people, and the function of a marriage is strongly connected with the type of society. In mobile, nomadic societies with their small families, the choice of a partner was a personal affair and affection could play an important role in this choice. In agricultural societies this personal choice was only a secondary consideration: the marriage was primarily an economic affair, often arranged by the parents of the partners. The relationship between partners was more formal and appreciation for each other often had to do with the way the other partner fulfils his or her duties. This is nicely illustrated by the following quotation from Collins (1868):

> *The woman I found my eye on, was the woman who kept house for me at my cottage. . . . Selina, being a single woman, made me pay so much a*

week for her board and services. Selina being my wife, couldn't charge
for her board and would have to give me her services for nothing. That
was the point of view I looked at it from. Economy – with a dash of love.

When economic factors are so important in a partner's choice one can
expect marriage to be a contract for life, independent of emotional aspects.
From this point of view one would expect households to be very stable in
agricultural societies, but this is not necessarily true. Since agricultural societies are usually poor, health may not be good and the early death of one
of the partners will bring about the end of the marriage. Divorces are very
unusual in these societies. Still, the average duration of marriages in agricultural societies is not very different from what it is at present in Europe
and the USA. In modern Western society, affection, sexuality and romance
are important ingredients for a marriage and in many cases marriage no
longer seems to be a contract for life. At present one out of three marriages
ends in divorce.

Children

The position and role of children is different in different communities. One
of the common features of (former) agricultural societies is the extended
family. The agricultural household requires a longer economic dependency
and infancy of children, than do the mobile nomad and the modern household. In the developing countries the extended family, with the authority of
the elderly, is still very common. Children in agricultural societies and early
industrializing countries have to work from an early age. The parents need
their children's labour contribution, and they also need their children as a
kind of insurance against poverty in old age. In the industrialized Western
countries this is no longer a reason for having children, because most governments have now set up social security systems which provide financial support to the elderly. It has also become quite common for people to build up
a pension during their working career. In most Western countries child labour
has gradually been abolished as the economic need for children has dimin-
ished. Now the emphasis is on affection and development of the child: the
meaning of children for parents is more psychological and emotional. Still,
economic factors influence the timing and number of births, and children
have a great effect on the consumption and time use patterns of the household. These factors will be discussed in Chapters 7 and 8.

4.3   Income tax policy, sales tax and subsidies

Income tax policy

In most countries the government plays a dominant role in redistributing
income and ensuring the welfare of its citizens. The authorities collect taxes

and premiums, and spend money on public goods, subsidies and social security. Income tax and sales tax create income for the government and it
limits the opportunity sets of households. Different tax systems can do this
in different ways. As a result, such a system affects the optimal decisions
with respect to expenditure and labour supply of households. We shall illustrate this with an example.

Taxing households or individuals?

In some countries household income is taxed, and in others taxes are levied
on individual incomes. In the numerical example of Exercise 4.1 below we
show how different net household income under these two regimes can be.
Because this example is only illustrative, the currency is not specified. One
could think of ECU's.

Exercise 4.1
Assume the income tax rate is:

| 0% on the first 10 000 | 25% of $10\,000 \leq y < 30\,000$ |
| 35% of $30\,000 \leq y < 60\,000$, | 50% of all income over 60 000 |

Assume that the gross wage rate of m is $w_m = 30$ and m works 1600
hours a year; the wage rate of f is $w_f = 20$ and f works 800 hours a
year. Show that, if partners are taxed individually, net household income will be 51 200, but when the authorities tax household income
instead, net income will be 46 500.

The effects that the tax system may have on labour supply is even more
interesting. Consider the household discussed in Exercise 4.1. Again, m works
1600 hours and $w_m = 30$, but f does not work, hence household income is
48 000. If, in this situation, f considers labour market participation, then f's
net wage rate depends greatly on the tax system. If partners are taxed individually, f's net wage for the first 500 hours is 20, but if household income
is taxed, f's contribution to household income reduces to $0.65 \times 20 = 13$
per hour. Since labour supply usually depends positively on the net wage
rate, f's labour supply is expected to be less in the household-based tax
system than in the individual-based system.

To compensate for this effect of the household-based tax system, one could
think of a higher level of tax-free income for two-earner families. If the
two-earner family of Exercise 4.1 starts with a 20 000 zero tax zone they
would still pay more under the household-based tax system than in the individual-based system. But the differences are less extreme.

Hausman and Ruud (1984) estimated the effect of another form of com-

Table 4.1 An international comparison of the relative importance of income sources, taxes and benefits

	Average value of income components as percentage of average gross income					
	USA	UK	West* Germany	Sweden	Norway	Israel
Market incomes	90.8	81.7	83.3	70.8	84.9	90.6
Cash benefits	8.0	17.2	16.5	29.2	14.1	8.3
Private transfers and other cash income	1.2	1.1	0.2	0.0	0.9	1.0
Gross income	**100**	**100**	**100**	**100**	**100**	**100**
Income and payroll tax	21.0	16.9	22.5	29.7	25.3	28.7
Net income	**79.0**	**83.1**	**77.5**	**70.2**	**74.7**	**71.3**

(*) The data were collected before the unification of West and East Germany

Source: O'Higgins, Schmaus and Stephenson (1990).

pensation for the progressive structure of the household income tax system on labour supply in the USA: a 10 per cent tax deduction for two-earner couples. This deduction should reduce the effects of what they call the *marriage tax*. We shall return to this subject in Chapter 5.

The social security system, just like the income tax system, can either consider the individual adult, or the household as a unit. The consequences are similar. The tax and social security system change the income and consequently also the welfare distribution of households. Since different countries have different tax policies, the impact of governments on income distributions are not identical. O'Higgins, Schmaus and Stephenson (1990) compared the relative importance of income sources, taxes and benefits of six countries. Their results are shown in Table 4.1. The table shows only average results, but the effects are different for different income classes. The effect of taxes on the distribution of income across households will be discussed in Chapter 12.

How can we analyse these differences in income tax systems? In a model *without* labour supply (as in Section 2.2), an income tax system will simply shift the budget line downwards. The shape of the consumption possibility curve is not affected as long as prices are independent of income. However, in a model *with* labour supply (as in Section 2.3), the gross wage rate is a datum and net wages depend on the tax structure. A progressive income tax system changes the shape of the budget restriction: kinks appear when gross income enters a new tariff zone. In Figure 4.1 we consider two individuals, I and II. We assume that both earn a gross wage of w an hour, but I has unearned income Y_0^I, whereas II has unearned income Y_0^{II}. Assuming that both earned and unearned incomes are taxed, the kinks will appear in different places.

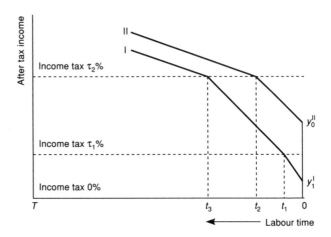

Figure 4.1   Convex budget sets, progressive income tax

For I the net wage rate for the first hours is w; when working t_1 hours I's total income is $Y_0^I + t_1 w$ and s/he enters the $\tau_1\%$ zone. Then his/her net wage rate becomes $(1 - \tau_1)w$. If s/he works more than t_3 hours his/her net wage becomes $(1 - \tau_2)w$. The net wage rate for the first hours of consumer II is $(1 - \tau_1)w$ and at t_2 II's income level is $Y_0^{II} + t_2 (1 - \tau_1)w$ and s/he enters the τ_2 zone. Because labour income and non-labour income are jointly responsible for total income, non-labour income is contributory to the shape of the kinked budget line.

How can we find the individual's optimal consumption choice in such a situation? The kinks point outwards, so the budget set is still convex. But if the optimum is on one of the kinks, the indifference curve is no longer tangent to the budget line. This means that the traditional analysis is no longer valid. The general principle used in the analysis of convex budget sets with kinked frontiers is to have the consumer choose his or her most preferred labour/consumption combination on each budget segment, determine the corresponding utility levels and then determine the point with the highest utility level (Hausman, 1979b; Pudney, 1991). It may frequently occur that the optimal choice of the consumer is located on one of the kinks. If we have a well-behaved strict quasi-concave utility function, the optimum is unique and can be found in an easy, straightforward way.

For instance, for consumer I in Figure 4.1, we first derive optimal labour supply t_w^*, when the net wage rate is w and non-labour income is Y_0^I. If t_w^* is less than or equal to zero, the consumer supplies zero hours. If $0 < t_w^* < t_1$ s/he will supply t_w^* hours, but if $t_w^* \geq t_1$ we have to look for an optimum at the next segment of the budget line. Here the net wage rate is $w(1 - \tau_1)$. Again we derive optimal labour supply. If $t_w^* < t_1$ then $t_w^* = t_1$, but when $t_1 \leq t_w^* < t_3$, the consumer will supply t_w^* and if $t_w^* \geq t_3$ we move to the next segment. Then we look for the optimal number of hours t_w^*, when the net wage is $w(1 - \tau_2)$. If $t_w^* < t_3$, then $t_w^* = t_3$, or else it is t_w^*.

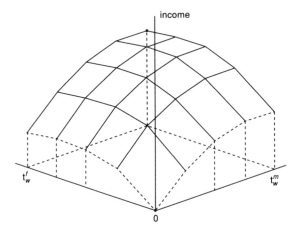

*Figure 4.2   Budget set for a two-earner household, when house-
hold members are taxed individually*

Exercise 4.2
Why can one expect clustering of observations around convex kinks?

If the individual is a member of a multi-person household, we have to
consider the income tax laws for two-earner families. If *household income*
is taxed, the net wage rate of the wife depends on the income earned by
herself and her husband, and vice versa. Figure 4.2 shows the shape of the
budget set when the partners are taxed individually. In Chapter 5 we shall
present a household labour supply model under such a tax regime.

Indirect taxes

Sales taxes, excise taxes and value added taxes will change prices for all
consumers in the same way; they do not depend on household income or
composition. Governments may impose different tax rates on different kinds
of product. They may prefer to put a lower rate on food and a higher rate
on luxury goods, on products that cause pollution (such as cars), or on products
that are bad for your health (such as alcohol and tobacco). In this way the
relative price structure is partly determined by the government, and the consumer, making an optimal choice, will adjust his or her behaviour.

Wasserman *et al.* (1991) examined whether excise taxes on tobacco affect
the decision 'to smoke or not to smoke' and whether they affect the number
of cigarettes that smokers buy. They compared the effect of these indirect
taxes with the effect of government regulations with respect to non-smoking
zones in, for example, public buildings and airplanes. Using a two-step model

they find that price changes have their greatest effect on the decision whether or not to become a smoker, rather than on the number of cigarettes people consume once they have chosen to smoke. Their regulation index has only a statistically significant effect on the number of cigarettes smoked, not on the decision to become, or not to become, a smoker.

Transfers in kind

Instead of supporting households with an income transfer, governments can decide to support certain households with transfers 'in kind'. For example, they do not provide money to buy food, but give people food; they do not give money to pay the rent, but they provide accommodation. In reality, governments often create a system in which poor households need to pay less for certain goods up to a certain maximum quantity.

Some of the subsidies supplied by governments depend on *household* income, others on the *individual* income levels. Here, again, the system could discourage labour market participation, because an income gain causes a subsidy loss, and welfare does not increase as much as the extra earnings would suggest (the so-called 'poverty trap'). Rent allowance and food stamps are usually based on total household income and family composition.

Exercise 4.3
Show, by using a diagram, that a cash transfer equal to the value of the in-kind transfer, will add as least as much ($\geq$) to household utility as the in-kind transfer does.

According to the outcome of Exercise 4.3, it would be better for households to receive money transfers instead of in-kind transfers. So why do governments choose in-kind transfers? One explanation is paternalism: the government assumes it knows what is good for its people.

Food stamps are an example of a price reduction for only a limited amount of goods. Such a subsidy will usually, but not always, restrict consumers in their choices. If a consumer buys so much of the subsidized good, that s/he passes the subsidy limit, the transfer is called *inframarginal*. Then the transfer in kind is equivalent to a cash transfer. This is illustrated in Figure 4.3 (Moffitt, 1989). If food is not subsidized, the budget constraint is represented by DE, | slope DE | = 1, but if food is subsidized up to the amount K, the budget line is DGF, | slope DG | < 1, | slope GF | = 1. Assume that the preferences of Consumer I are such that his or her optimum is on GF, then the transfer is inframarginal for him/her and equivalent to cash, because an increase of income with amount B would leave him or her in the same location. For Consumer III, the cash equivalent of food stamps is only C,

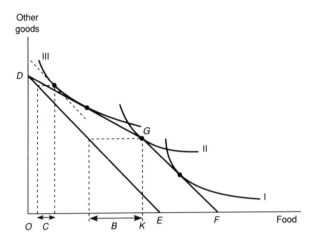

Source: Moffitt (1989).

Figure 4.3 A budget constraint with a price subsidy for food, restricted to a maximum quantity.

and *C* is smaller than *B*. The cash equivalent ratio of food stamps is *C/B* for Consumer III.

Exercise 4.4

Derive the cash equivalent of the subsidy for Consumer II in Figure 4.3.

Food stamps are not only equivalent to cash when the transfers are inframarginal, but also when the stamps could be traded (*trafficking*, as it is called). The revenues will usually be less than the face value of the stamps. The trafficking of rent subsidy seems to be impossible. The welfare effects of rent allowances will be discussed in Chapter 12.

In 1982, Puerto Rico cashed out food stamps to the recipients. The government paid the full bonus amount in cash, irrespective of whether the household had used the full bonus before. Moffitt (1989) examined this conversion. Earlier studies (Cooper and Katz, 1977) suggested that the cash equivalent of foods stamps was as low as 0.39, but Moffitt's findings are quite different. He found almost no cash out effects. In part this arose because the maximum benefit levels in Puerto Rico were sufficiently low, so that most households are on part *GF* of the budget constraint of Figure 4.3. Indirect evidence on trafficking could explain the lack of a cash out effect for the remaining households.

Public goods

In some cases, governments may decide to provide goods as a public service, either free of charge, or at a low charge. Choices made by consumers are highly affected by this system, as is their welfare level. For example, if education is a public service, free, or almost free of charge, families with children benefit from it most. In the long run the whole of society benefits from it, because human capital is one of the main factors of production.

4.4   Rationing

The institutional setting within which the consumer can make his or her optimal choice can be such that restrictions exist regarding the quantities of consumer goods. Some of these restrictions have the nature of equalities: consumption equals some predetermined amount and it can neither be more nor less than this. An example is compulsory payment of health insurance premiums for some households in The Netherlands.

In other cases, the restrictions take the form of inequalities. An obvious example of a lower bound on consumption is a non-negativity constraint. An example of an upper bound is the case where expenditure on housing is restricted from above because the mortgage a bank is willing to provide is limited. Note that in case of inequality constraints it is in fact the consumer who decides whether the constraint will be binding or not. Therefore, this type of rationing is sometimes referred to as *endogenous rationing*. In contrast, the equality constraint case is referred to as *exogenous rationing*.

Exogenous rationing: theory

We consider an individual who maximizes a utility function $u(q_A, q_B)$ subject to the budget constraint $p'_A q_A + p'_B q_B = y$ and the additional constraints $q_A = \bar{q}_A$. The vectors q_A and q_B denote the quantities consumed of goods 1, ..., K and $K + 1$, ..., N respectively; p_A and p_B are corresponding price vectors, and y is income. The problem now is to derive equations that give optimal demands for q_B, given $\bar{q}_A$, p_A, p_B and y: the *rationed or conditional demand equations*.

It is fairly easy to derive the rationed demand when preferences are *weakly separable* (see Chapter 2) between q_A and q_B. In that case, $U(q_A, q_B)$ can be written in the form $U^* (q_A, \varphi(q_B))$ and since $\bar{q}_A$ is a constant, the problem is equivalent to:

$$\text{maximize } \varphi(q_B)$$
$$s.t. \ p_B q_B = y - p_A \bar{q}_A.$$

If preferences are not weakly separable, but the direct utility function is known, the problem can readily be solved by using the Lagrange method:

the primal approach (see Exercise 4.5 on page 62). If the direct utility function is not known explicitly, as is the case in the Indirect Translog model or the Almost Ideal Demand system, for example, this direct approach is, of course, not applicable. In principle, however, the solution can be derived directly from the unconditioned demand system, as follows.

Deriving rationed demand functions from unrationed demand functions

Let $q_i = g_i(y, p_A, p_B)$ for $i = 1, \ldots, N$ be the unconditional demand system, that is, the solution of maximizing $u(q_A, q_B)$, subject to the budget constraint only. Then the optimal values for q_B, conditional on $q_A = \bar{q}_A$, are given by:

$$q_i = g_i(\bar{y}, \bar{p}_A, p_B), \quad i = K + 1, \ldots, N, \tag{4.1}$$

where $\bar{p}_A$ and $\bar{y}$ are defined by:

$$\bar{q}_i = g_i(\bar{y}, \bar{p}_A, p_B), \quad i = 1, \ldots, K \tag{4.2a}$$
$$\bar{y} = y - (p_A - \bar{p}_A)'\,\bar{q}_A. \tag{4.2b}$$

So, one first solves the K *shadow* (or *virtual*) prices $\bar{p}_A$ and the *shadow income* $\bar{y}$ from the $K + 1$ Equations (4.2a) and (4.2b), and next substitutes them into Equation (4.1). The following proof of this result uses the dual approach and was first given by Neary and Roberts (1980).

As we recall from Chapter 2, the *cost function without rationing* is defined as:

$$c(u; p_A, p_B) = \min_{q_A, q_B} [p_A' q_A + p_B' q_B \mid u(q_A, q_B) \geq u]. \tag{4.3}$$

The *restricted or conditional cost function* can be defined as:

$$\begin{aligned} c^R(u; p_A, p_B \mid q_A = \bar{q}_A) &= \min_{q_B} [p_A' q_A + p_B' q_B \mid u(\bar{q}_A, q_B) \geq u] \\ &= p_A' \bar{q}_A + \min_{q_B} [p_B' q_B \mid u(\bar{q}_A, q_B) \geq u]. \end{aligned} \tag{4.4}$$

We assume that there exists a vector of shadow prices $\bar{p}_A$ such that $\bar{q}_A$ is optimal at prices $(\bar{p}_A, p_B)$, that is:

$$\bar{q}_i = \frac{\partial c(u; \bar{p}_A, p_B)}{\partial \bar{p}_i}, \quad i = 1, \ldots, K. \tag{4.5}$$

(For conditions that ensure the existence of shadow prices, see Van Soest *et al.* (1993)). Since $\bar{q}_A$ is optimal at $(\bar{p}_A, p_B)$ we also have:

$$c(u; \bar{p}_A, p_B) = \bar{p}_A' \bar{q}_A + \min_{q_B} [p_B' q_B \mid u(\bar{q}_A, q_B) \geq u]. \tag{4.6}$$

Subtracting (4.6) from (4.4) yields the following relationship between the rationed and unrationed cost functions:

$$c^R(u; p_A, p_B \mid q_A = \bar{q}_A) = c(u; \bar{p}_A, p_B) + (p_A - \bar{p}_A)' \bar{q}_A. \qquad (4.7)$$

The rationed compensated demands for goods $K + 1, \ldots, N$ given $q_A = \bar{q}_A$ follow from applying Shephard's lemma to the restricted cost function:

$$q^R_i = \frac{\partial c^R}{\partial p_i} = \frac{\partial c(u; \bar{p}_A, p_B)}{\partial p_i} + \sum_{j=1}^{K} \frac{\partial c(u; \bar{p}_A, p_B)}{\partial \bar{p}_j} \cdot \frac{\partial \bar{p}_j}{\partial p_i} - \sum_{j=1}^{K} \bar{q}_j \cdot \frac{\partial \bar{p}_j}{\partial p_i} =$$

$$\frac{\partial c(u; \bar{p}_A, p_B)}{\partial p_i}, \qquad i = K + 1, \ldots, N. \qquad (4.8)$$

As in the unrationed case, we find the corresponding uncompensated demands by first solving u from the cost function, in this case:

$$c^R(u; \bar{p}_A, p_B \mid q_A = \bar{q}_A) = y,$$

and substituting the solution into (4.8). Using (4.7) we find the solution for u to be:

$$u = \Psi [y - (p_A - \bar{p}_A)' \bar{q}_A; \bar{p}_A; p_B], \qquad (4.9)$$

where $\Psi(y, p)$ denotes the indirect utility function corresponding to $c(u, p)$. This completes the proof.

Endogenous rationing: theory

We now consider an individual who maximizes a utility function $u(q_A, q_B)$ subject to the budget constraint $p'_A q_A + p'_B q_B = y$ and the additional constraint $q_A \geq \bar{q}_A$. (Here we shall confine ourselves to the case of lower bound inequalities.)

If the direct utility function is known, the problem can be solved in primal form using the Kuhn–Tucker method. The Kuhn–Tucker theorem states that a solution, q, is characterized by the following set of equations:

$$\frac{\partial U(q_1, \ldots, q_N)}{\partial q_i} + \mu_i - \lambda p_i = 0 \qquad i = 1, \ldots, N$$

$$\sum_{i=1}^{N} p_i q_i = y$$

$$\mu_i(q_i - \bar{q}_i) = 0 \qquad i = 1, \ldots, N$$

$$\mu_i \geq 0 \qquad i = 1, \ldots, N$$

$\lambda > 0$

$$q_i \geq \bar{q}_i \qquad\qquad i = 1, \ldots, N. \qquad\qquad (4.10)$$

If the direct utility function is not known explicitly, the dual approach allows us again to derive the solution as follows from the unrestricted equations. It works as shown here.

The solution satisfies the equations:

$$q_i = g_i(\bar{y}, \bar{p}_1, \ldots, \bar{p}_N), \qquad\qquad i = 1, \ldots, N$$
$$\bar{p}_i \leq p_i$$
$$\bar{q}_i \leq q_i$$
$$\sum_{i=1}^{N} (p_i - \bar{p}_i)(q_i - \bar{q}_i) = 0, \qquad\qquad (4.11)$$

with

$$\bar{y} = y - \sum_{i=1}^{N} (p_i - \bar{p}_i)\bar{q}_i. \qquad\qquad (4.12)$$

As an example, we consider the case of non-negativity constraints (that is, $q_i \geq 0$, so $\bar{q}_i = 0$) for the Linear Expenditure System with three goods. Note that $\bar{y} = y$ in this example. In principle, seven different 'regimes' are possible: either no non-negativity constraint is binding (one case); the non-negativity constraint is binding for one good (three cases); or they are binding for two goods (three cases). Consider the regime $q_1 = 0$, $q_2 > 0$ and $q_3 > 0$, for example. This occurs if:

$$\bar{p}_1 q_1 = \bar{p}_1\gamma_1 + \alpha_1(y - \bar{p}_1\gamma_1 - \bar{p}_2\gamma_2 - \bar{p}_3\gamma_3) = 0$$
$$\bar{p}_2 q_2 = \bar{p}_2\gamma_2 + \alpha_2(y - \bar{p}_1\gamma_1 - \bar{p}_2\gamma_2 - \bar{p}_3\gamma_3) > 0$$
$$\bar{p}_3 q_3 = \bar{p}_3\gamma_3 + (1 - \alpha_1 - \alpha_2)(y - \bar{p}_1\gamma_1 - \bar{p}_2\gamma_2 - \bar{p}_3\gamma_3) > 0$$
$$\bar{p}_1 \leq p_1$$
$$\bar{p}_2 = p_2$$
$$\bar{p}_3 = p_3. \qquad\qquad (4.13)$$

Substituting the last three conditions into the first three, we obtain:

$$p_1\gamma_1 + \alpha_1(y - p_1\gamma_1 - p_2\gamma_2 - p_3\gamma_3) \leq 0$$
$$p_2\gamma_2 + \left(\frac{\alpha_2}{1 - \alpha_1}\right)(y - p_1\gamma_1 - p_2\gamma_2 - p_3\gamma_3) > 0$$
$$p_3\gamma_3 + \left(\frac{\alpha_3}{1 - \alpha_1}\right)(y - p_1\gamma_1 - p_2\gamma_2 - p_3\gamma_3) > 0. \qquad\qquad (4.14)$$

Note that the left-hand side of the first equation is nothing but the unrationed demand equation for Good 1, whereas the left-hand sides of the second two are rationed demand equations for Goods 2 and 3, given that $q_1 = 0$. For $\gamma_1 = \gamma_2 = \gamma_3 = -1$ and $p_1 = p_2 = p_3 = y = 1$ the conditions reduce to:

$$\alpha_1 < \frac{1}{4}$$

$$\alpha_2 < \frac{1}{3} - \frac{1}{3}\alpha_1$$

$$\alpha_2 < \frac{2}{3} - \frac{2}{3}\alpha_1. \tag{4.15}$$

Figure 4.4 indicates which values of α_1 and α_2 yield the seven possible regimes.

Exercise 4.5

Assume that a consumer's preferences can be represented by the Stone–Geary utility function:

$$U(q_1, \ldots, q_N) = \sum_{i=1}^{N} \alpha_i \ln(q_i - \gamma_i) \qquad \text{with } \Sigma\alpha_i = 1,$$

and that his or her budget is Y.

(a) Is U weakly separable?

If the consumer is obliged to buy the quantity z_1 of Good 1 (with $z_1 > \gamma_1$), the expenditure on the other goods ($i = 2, \ldots, N$) is:

$$p_i q_i = p_i \gamma_i + \left(\frac{\alpha_i}{\sum\limits_{j=2}^{N} \alpha_j} \right) (y - p_1 z_1 - \sum_{j=2}^{N} p_j\gamma_j).$$

(b) Interpret this formula.

(c) Derive the result using the primal approach.

(d) Derive the result using the dual approach.

Deaton (1981) applies the model to time series data, but he uses a more flexible model than the Stone–Geary model of Exercise 4.5. He assumes that, for the majority of households, 'housing' is rationed. Households remain in houses that are too small or too large relative to their current needs. Deaton estimates both the rationed and the unrationed model. He finds that the rationed model explains the budget shares better than the free model. For further details we refer the reader to Deaton (1981).

For many popular forms of demand systems it has been shown to be diffi-

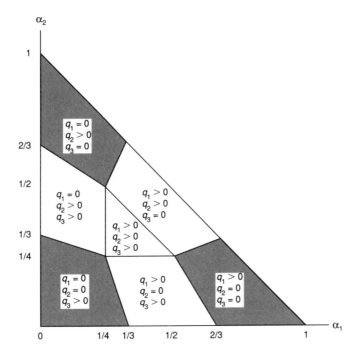

Figure 4.4 Endogenous rationing; seven possible regimes

cult to derive virtual prices analytically. The problem is simplified substantially when the 'ration' is zero; see Lee and Pitt (1986). In Chapter 5, rationing is analysed within a labour supply context.

4.5 Interdependent preferences and habit formation

In the neo-classical model on consumer behaviour, preferences are exogenous. However, preferences may be affected by the family composition of the consumer, by habits, by the behaviour of other households and by advertisements. We shall pay attention to demographic effects in Chapter 7. Here we shall analyse habit formation and the interdependence of preferences.

Households notice the activities of their friends, relatives and colleagues, observe what they buy and sometimes ask them for information on products. According to the French philosopher Baudrillard (1970), households not only communicate with language, but also by means of their consumption. He considers consumption to be a signal to other households. By showing other households what you consume, you show them more or less who you are. Either you can try to distinguish yourself from other households, or try to show that you belong to a certain group. This may cause a change in preferences towards the consumption pattern of some households and away from others. The group of households which affect the preferences of a specific household is called its 'reference group'. Of course, household '*n*' is not only affected by household '*m*', but vice versa. We are not only 'Keeping up with the Joneses'; the Joneses are also keeping up with us. The phenomenon was pointed out by Duesenberry (1949) and analysed by Gärtner (1974), Pollak (1976), and Alessie and Kapteyn (1991).

Habits are formed by experiences in the past. Addiction can be considered as an extreme form of habit formation. The consumption history of an individual partly determines his or her preferences in the current period, and not only for alcohol, drugs and tobacco. Habit formation is called *myopic*, if the consumer does not recognize the impact of his current consumption on his future preferences. Alessie and Kapteyn (1991) estimated a model with myopic habit formation and interdependent preferences. We shall discuss this model below. Other economists assume that consumers anticipate the effect of current consumption on future preferences as well and estimate models based on this assumption for alcohol, cigarette and drug addiction. See, for example, Becker and Murphy (1988), Chaloupka (1991), and Becker, Grossman and Murphy (1994).

Alessie and Kapteyn started with the cost function of Deaton and Muellbauer's (1980) Almost Ideal Demand system:

$$\log C_n\,(t,\,u_n\,(t),p(t)) \,=\, \log a_n(t,\,p(t)) \,+\, u_n(t)b(p(t)), \tag{4.16}$$

where n and t are the consumer and the time index, respectively. For short, we write:

$$\log C_n \,=\, \log a_n \,+\, bu_n, \tag{4.16*}$$

where b and a are:

$$b \,=\, \beta_0 \, \prod_i p_i^{\beta_i}$$

$$\log a_n \,=\, \alpha_{0n} \,+\, \sum_i \alpha_{in} \log p_i \,+\, 1/2 \sum_i \sum_j \gamma_{ij} \log p_i \log p_j$$

$$\sum_i \gamma_{ij} \,=\, \sum_j \gamma_{ij} \,=\, 0 \text{ and } \gamma_{ij} \,=\, \gamma_{ji},\, \sum_i \alpha_{in} \,=\, 1 \text{ and } \sum_i \beta_i \,=\, 0.$$

The indices i and j indicate goods. The demand functions, represented by the budget shares w_{in} are derived with Shephard's lemma (see Chapter 2):

$$w_{in} \,=\, \alpha_{in} \,+\, \beta_i(\log x_n \,-\, \log a_n) \,+\, \sum_j \gamma_{ij} \log p_j, \tag{4.17}$$

where x_n denotes income.

The demographic effects (see also Chapter 7 for the use of equivalence scales) are adopted in the αs in order to get the budget share of a standard consumer. The role of *preference interdependence* is specified as follows. A 'mean perceived budget share' m_{in} of Good i is introduced. The perception depends on the actual budget share w_{in} and also on the consumption by other people, indicated with index $k \neq$ n. It is defined as follows:

Table 4.2 The AIDS model with habit formation and interdependent
preferences; some parameter estimates

	Income parameter	Persistence parameter	Conspicuousness parameter
1. Food	−0.033*	−0.072	0.002
2. Housing	−0.011**	0.311	0.037
3. Clothing & footwear	0.013*	0.515*	0.203*
4. Medical care	−0.017*	0.623*	0.328*
5. Education entertainment	0.032*	0.622*	0.221
6. Transport & other	0.016	0.470*	0.002

Notes: $x^2(23)$ = 29.39; * = Significant 5% level; ** = Significant 10% level.

Source: Alessie and Kapteyn (1991).

$$m_{in} = \sum_{k=1}^{N} z^i_{nk} \, w_{ik}; \qquad \text{with } \sum_{k} z^i_{nk} = 1. \qquad (4.18)$$

The non-negative 'reference weight' z^i_{nk} denotes the relative importance Consumer n attaches to the consumption of Good i by Family k. If Consumer n is not at all interested in what others do, these zs will be zero, except for $k = n$. The weights may change over time. Many of the zs will be zero, because n does not know Household k.

If the perceived budget share depends also on the household's own consumption of Good i in the past, this can be interpreted as habit formation. The effects of habit formation and interdependency of preferences are incorporated in the parameter α_{in} by expressing it as a linear function of the mean perceived budget share of the previous period. This includes n's own consumption of Good i one period ago, so that the effects of habit formation can be estimated with this model.

After making some (necessary) simplifying assumptions the habit formation, or *persistence* parameters and the preference interdependence, or *conspicuousness* parameters are estimated. The results are presented in Table 4.2. The higher the conspicuousness parameter of Good i, the more one's consumption is influenced by the consumption of others. The category 'medical care' is most conspicuous, followed by 'education and entertainment' and 'clothes + footwear'. Habit formation is most important for the categories 'clothing', 'medical care' and 'education', followed by 'transportation' and 'housing'. Food consumption is not (significantly) affected by the reference group and nor by the consumer's history. For further details, see Alessie and Kapteyn (1991).

Consumers are not necessarily short-sighted, as is assumed in the myopic model. If a consumer takes the effects of his or her current consumption on future preferences into account, s/he is even more rational than in the previous model: s/he is farsighted. Becker and Murphy (1988) formulated a theory of rational addiction. It involves, of course, a dynamic utility function like that to be introduced in Chapter 9, which incorporates a 'learning by doing process' that results in a stock of 'consumption capital'. The stock grows with current consumption, so consumption is considered as a form of investment. For details, we the reader refer to the literature mentioned above.

4.6   The effects of uncertainty on demand

One of the assumptions of the neo-classical model is that the consumer knows his or her environment, s/he knows the institutional and social setting, s/he knows the prices and qualities of all goods that are available in the market, s/he knows the labour market and so on. In reality, complete information is usually lacking and the consumer may even have inaccurate ideas about the market. This could result in choices that would not have been made if the consumer had had full information. In order to diminish ignorance and to allow for making better choices, time and money can be spent on obtaining this information. As Stigler (1960) indicated more than 35 years ago:

> *Ignorance is like subzero weather: by a sufficient expenditure its effects upon people can be kept within tolerable or even comfortable bounds, but it would be wholly uneconomic entirely to eliminate all its effects. And, just as an analysis of men's shelter and apparel would be somewhat incomplete if cold weather is ignored, so also our understanding of economic life will be incomplete if we do not systematically take account of the cold winds of ignorance.*

At certain costs consumers can diminish their ignorance, but uncertainty cannot be eliminated completely, since it is inherent in many events. Nobody knows whether there will be an earthquake or thunderstorm next month, or whether his or her car will be damaged tomorrow. The only information that one may get is about the probability of the occurrence of such events. Uncertainty is a reason for people to insure themselves against risks that cannot be avoided.

Search for information

The search for information concerns two main subjects, the price/quality ratio of goods and services and the wage/quality ratio in the job market. First we shall pay attention to information about prices. Neither households nor sellers know exactly the quality and price of all goods available in the market. If there are differences in the price/quality ratio it may be worthwhile to look for the best deal. However, this information is not free. Households can become members of a consumer organization in order to get information, they may buy reports on tests, but it will cost them money. It will also cost them time to get the information. Some go 'window shopping' just to see for themselves what is available in the market. This will cost them a lot of time and also some money (for example, transportation costs). The total costs of this search are financial expenditure and time costs. The expected gain of collecting this information is a lower price (or better quality), but the costs should not exceed the gain. To quote Linder (1970): 'Only unintelligent buyers acquire complete information'. The gain of the search effort depends on the distribution of prices of the good that the household intends to buy. The higher the price and the greater the variety of prices, the higher the expected gain from a search effort. It is also important to know how long the consumer is going to use the good s/he buys. If it is a durable, s/he will enjoy its good quality (or regret its bad quality) for a long time, and so information becomes more important.

Suppose the distribution of prices for Good X is $F(p)$; $F(p)$ represents the cumulative distribution of prices. The more often the household inquires at different shops, the lower will be the expected minimum price it will find.

Exercise 4.6

Suppose n inquiries are made at random and n prices are known: $p_1, \ldots, p_n$. Show that the probability that the minimum value of this set of prices is less or equal to a given price $\bar{p}$ is: $Pr[\min(p_1, \ldots, p_n) \leq \bar{p}] = 1 - (1 - F(\bar{p}))^n$.

According to Exercise 4.6, the distribution of the minimum price after n searches, $G(p)$ is:

$$G(p) = Pr[p_{\min} \leq p] = 1 - (1 - F(p))^n.$$

The expected minimum price after n searches is found with the corresponding density function $g(p)$:

$$E[p_{\min}] = \int p \cdot g(p) dp.$$

Exercise 4.7

Suppose prices vary between p_1 (lowest) and p_h (highest). Show that

$$E[p_{\min}] = p_1 + \int_{p_1}^{p_h} (1 - F(p))^n dp. \tag{4.19}$$

(*Hint*: Use partial integration and notice that $F(p_h) = 1$ and $F(p_1) = 0$.)

For example, if the distribution of prices is uniform on the [0, 1] interval then it follows from Exercise 4.7 that:

$$E[p_{min}] = \int_0^1 (1 - p)^n dp = \frac{1}{n + 1}.$$

This means that the expected price in the first trial is 1/2, the expected minimum in two trials is 1/3 and so on. The expected (marginal) gain in the nth−search effort is $\left(\frac{1}{n} - \frac{1}{n + 1}\right) = \frac{1}{n(n + 1)}$, so the gain decreases quickly when n increases. This value should be compared with the marginal costs of the nth search. The rational consumer should stop his or her search activities when marginal costs exceed marginal gains. The 'intelligent' consumer will not continue until s/he has complete information.

Here we concentrated on the price, given the quality, but a household may be more interested in the utility of a price–quality combination. It may compare the utility gain of another search with utility forgone by putting money and time into this search.

The situation in the job market is not very different from the market of goods and services. Given a certain quality of the job, there will be a distribution of wages. Once this distribution is known, an individual getting a certain wage offer knows how this wage compares to the other wages. The expected gain of another search effort should be compared with the expected costs. Job search is discussed in Chapter 10.

Uncertainty of events

When a household has to decide about the allocation of its budget, sometimes it cannot be sure about the utility of the expenditure. For example, a household can buy fire insurance for its home, but the house will probably not burn down and the money is wasted. However, if there is going to be a fire the utility of the insurance premium is high.

Exercise 4.8
Suppose the value of a house is 200 000 Euro, the insurance costs 300 Ecu and household income is 50 000 Euro a year. The estimated probability of a fire is 1/1000. What is the expected household budget left for other expenses if it takes the insurance, and what if it does not?

By looking at the expected budgets of Exercise 4.8 it seems wiser not to insure. However, in our models it is not the budget that is important for the household, but the utility level. Therefore, one should compare the expected utility levels of the insured and the non-insured situations.

Let V be the indirect utility function of income of the household in Exercise 4.8. Then the expected utility of the insured household is:

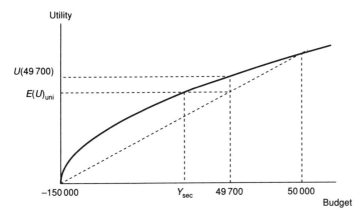

Figure 4.5 Risk aversion in uncertain circumstances

$$E[U_{ins}] = U_{ins} = V(49\ 700).$$

The expected utility of an uninsured household is:

$$E[U_{uni}] = 0.999V(50\ 000) + 0.001V(-150\ 000).$$

When preferences are strictly convex; that is, when V is strictly quasi-concave (as in Figure 4.5), the household will decide to take out fire insurance, because the expected utility of the risky situation is lower than $V(49\ 000$ Ecu). This kind behaviour is called *risk aversion*. For the consumer in Figure 4.5, even a secure income of less than 49 700 Ecu is preferred to the risky situation of no insurance, as long as it is not less than Y_{sec}. For a further discussion of the concept of risk aversion, see Section 9.4.

4.7 Economic psychology, rational behaviour and the consumer's choice

In Section 4.6 we discussed the fact that a household searches for information about products and jobs at certain costs. By doing so it learns about its environment. However, many firms are happy to provide information about their products. They hope that if the household decides to buy, it will buy their brand. Advertisement is a form of communication in which the seller takes the initiative. First, the advertiser wants to attract the attention of the consumer with a combination of written or spoken language, images and sound. After the seller has caught his or her attention, the consumer should become interested in the product, even desire it, and finally buy it. But in commercials, it is not simply product information (properties, quality and price) that is being offered. More important nowadays are the symbols that are used in commercials (Engel *et al.*, 1986). These symbols represent a world of abstract feelings, for instance freedom, wealth, youth or health, things that are not for sale, but desired by many. Do such commercials change a consumer's preferences, or do they only suggest non-existing properties of the good they offer? In microeconomic models we do accept that individuals are learning, but it is assumed that when similar households are exposed to the same information, their reactions will be similar. In economic theory we do not attempt to explain the differences in character structure, although preference heterogeneity can be taken into account.

Neo-classical economic theory does not deal with explanation preferences of consumers: it accepts preferences as they are revealed by actual choices. It may study the effects of different kinds of advertisement on the demand for a product, but not the mental process that causes a change in demand. In economic psychology, human thought processes are studied and this implies the use of subjective data obtained directly from the individual (Antonides, 1991). This approach provides an opportunity to study the individual perception of economic goods. Most of these psychological aspects are hard to incorporate into microeconomic models, but some can be.

When making a choice, does a consumer really weigh one possibility against another? Is what s/he chooses really what will satisfy him or her best? How is it posible that s/he sometimes regrets what s/he did? Do his or her choices reveal his/her preferences? Are goods and services determining his/her happiness; and does a person become happier when his/her income rises? These and other questions are asked by economists who have their doubts about the neo-classical theory of consumer behaviour. In this section we shall mention some of the alternatives that are suggested by them.

According to Scitovsky (1976), economists should listen to and learn from psychologists in order to understand the motivation of consumers. Scitovsky argues that human beings are, on the one hand, trying to lower their arousal level, thus relieving discomfort, but on the other hand they need and seek out physical and mental stimuli. However, these stimuli go hand-in-hand with a high level of activity and a rise in the arousal level. They are making their way between strain and boredom. Scitovsky also argues that needs are not inborn, they are developed in a learning process.

Learning processes are to some extent incorporated in economic models. Individuals learn from information. Information enlarges the set from which they can make a choice and it increases the amount of human capital. Ideas about the search for physical and mental stimuli on the one hand and for rest and comfort on the other have also found a place in micro-models. By analysing activities (for example, Becker, 1965; Winston, 1982) instead of pure consumption, and by including habit formation and preference interdependency, we have embodied some of Scitovsky's ideas.

In the neo-classical model, income restriction limits the consumer in satisfying his or her needs. When income increases, the consumer's maximum utility level rises. Do consumers experience it this way? Van Praag (1968) asked consumers in a direct way about their appreciation of different income levels and translated these verbal evaluations of income into numbers on an

[0,1] scale (see also Section 12.5). These numbers were then interpreted as welfare (or utility) indicators. He found that the opinion on what income level is 'good' (or 'bad') depends highly on the consumer's own income, his reference point. Once people get used to a higher income level, the extra utility, which may have been there shortly after an income rise, vanishes. This phenomenon is called *preference drift*. It has also been found that extra utility partly vanishes when the incomes of the reference group of a household rise as well; this is called *reference drift*.

In neo-classical theory it is not assumed that utility levels of different households, or of one household in different time periods, are comparable. The utility level only represents preferences, it is an ordinal function, not necessarily cardinal. Van Praag assumes that if two different households indicate that they both have 'a good income', this means that they perceive the same utility level, although their levels of income may be quite different. In the neo-classical model such an assertion is not made.

According to Elster (1983), human beings have the ability to adjust to circumstances in such a way that they can even manipulate their needs to a certain extent. Needs that cannot be met are suppressed by the consumer and excluded from his preference scheme (for example, if I am not rich enough to buy a pleasure boat, I put pleasure boats out of my mind, or start thinking that they are dangerous and boring; my preferences are adjusted to the possibility set).

On the other hand, once a choice has been made, the consumer will look (only) for positive affirmative information on the product of his or her choice, to avoid a situation in which the comparison between the performance of a product and prior expectations could lead to dissatisfaction. This theory of *cognitive dissonance* was developed by Festinger (1957).

The consumer, knowing how easily s/he is led to do things that provide short-run satisfaction, may install rules on his or her behaviour (that may even cost him or her money), just to be sure that long-run goals can be met. For example, s/he is willing to pay for the services offered by Weight Watchers, or for a saving program that does not allow him or her to use his/her own money before a certain date, for example, Christmas. As Elster (1986) puts it: to bind oneself is to carry out a certain decision at time t_1 in order to increase the probability that one will carry out another decision at time t_2. This type of behaviour is related to the concept of time preference; see Section 9.3.

4.8 Summary

The consumer may not always seem as rational as the neo-classical model suggests. However, as a general framework, the neo-classical model is still the best model we have. The objective function may sometimes be too simplistic, so that individuals do not seem to be maximizing it, but since many of the ideas about behaviour and human thought that originate from psychology have been adopted in economic models, they become more and more realistic. The influence of the social and institutional setting on household choices can certainly be analysed with the neo-classical framework, as we showed in the previous paragraphs. The model should not be used for problems for which it is not well equipped, however, as, for example, brand choice.

CHAPTER 5

Household Labour Supply

5.1 Introduction

In Chapter 2 we distinguished three kinds of time use: paid labour, household labour and leisure. Although these categories seem to be well-defined, it is still sometimes difficult, if not impossible, to determine which label should be attached to an activity. Even for the category *paid labour* it can be a point of debate. The time we need for travelling to and from our job: does it belong to the category paid labour? Unpaid overtime at work, do we consider these hours as hours spent on paid labour? The choices made in different research projects vary with the questions that are to be answered. Different choices can be made by researchers. The same kind of problem arises when the wage rate is used in economic research. Should we use the gross or net wage rate, the marginal or average rate, and how should we deal with income in kind? Again, choices have to be made and the reader should always be aware of those choices.

In this chapter on household labour supply we shall start in Section 5.2 with some facts about labour market participation of men and women in some Western countries, followed by an overview of the historical development. The existence of a segmentation of the labour market into 'male' and 'female' jobs is discussed, and some special features of the part-time and contingent work force. In Section 5.3, we shall introduce a neo-classical model with one joint household utility function in which consumption and leisure of both partners appear as choice variables. We leave the game theoretic approach of Chapter 3 in order to simplify the analysis of demographic effects and rationing on labour supply. The results are interdependent labour supply functions. In Section 5.4 we shall present a more sociological view of labour market behaviour. Opinions of the reference group could play an important role in the labour market participation decision of individuals, in particular for married women with children. As we saw in Chapter 4, the government can encourage or discourage the participation decision with its tax and social security laws. In Section 5.5 we shall analyse the effects of the social security and tax system on household labour supply a little further. Finally, in Section 5.6 we shall pay attention to the interaction between the formal and the informal labour markets. The dynamic aspects of household labour market behaviour are not dealt with in this chapter; they are analysed in Chapters 10 and 11.

5.2   Some facts about household labour participation

There is a great difference between the observed labour market behaviour of men and married women, but only a small difference between that of men and women living singly. Although a little over 50% of the population of the European Union (EU) consists of women, they account for only 37 per cent of total employment (Eurostat, 1988). In the USA and Japan these rates are 43 per cent and 40 per cent respectively. On average, 13 per cent of the working population in the EU countries has a part-time job: 67 per cent of these are married women, and the remaining 33 per cent is divided almost equally between men and single women. No more than 20 per cent of the working married women have a full-time job.

In Table 5.1 the activity rates – the percentage of the population that is actively working – in the EU, the USA and Japan are shown. Employment or participation rates are usually measured as a percentage of the labour force, or the age group 15 to 65, but the activity rate has the whole population as its basis. Long school enrollment, early retirement, low participation rates and high unemployment all have negative effects on the activity rate. In all countries, more men than women perform paid labour.

The historical development of the activity rates of seven European countries has been studied in Pott-Buter (1993). The first data are from the year 1846. The author warns us that the reliability of the data is questionable, especially for the older data. Even nowadays there are still problems with the different methods of measurement in the different countries.

Male activity rates have been fairly stable in all countries studied. They vary roughly between 50 per cent and 65 per cent, the highest rates being observed between 1920 and 1950. Female activity rates are also quite stable, but have risen gradually since the 1970s. However, there are great differences between the seven countries. Sweden and Denmark have had a female activity rate of around 50 per cent since 1985, while in the other countries it has varied between 34 per cent and 41 per cent (in 1990).

Young children and aged people usually do not perform paid work. They may be active as volunteers, or in home production, but not usually in the labour market. Only people whose age is between 15 and 65 can potentially belong to the labour force. In Tables 5.2 and 5.3, the development of the participation rates of male and female labour in this age group are shown for the seven countries that were studied by Pott-Buter.

In general, the labour market participation of (married) women is less

Table 5.1   Rate of activity[1], male and female, in the EU, USA and
Japan in 1993 (per cent)

	EU	USA	Japan
Total	45	50.2	53.1
Men	53.7	56.4	64.3
Women	36.6	44.4	42.2

[1]) Rate of activity = active population/total population.

Source: OECD (1995).

Table 5.2   Male labour force participation rates, 1960–90

	Belgium	Denmark	France	Germany	Netherlands	Sweden	UK
1960	88	100	95	95	98	98	99
1971	84	91	88	92	85	89	94
1973	83	90	86	90	83	88	93
1975	82	90	84	87	82	89	92
1977	80	91	84	85	80	88	92
1979	79	90	83	86	78	88	91
1981	79	88	81	84	81	87	90
1983	77	88	78	83	77	86	88
1985	75	87	77	82	76	84	89
1987	73	88	76	83	79	86	88
1988	72	90	75	82	79	84	87
1989	72	90	75	82	80	85	87
1990	73	90	75	82	80	85	86

Notes: percentage of the male population, aged 15–64.

Source: Pott-Buter (1993).

than that of men. On average, working women work fewer hours than working men. But there are more differences between working men and women,
for instance in the kinds of job they have. In 1930, 76 per cent of all women
in the Dutch labour force were to be found in a mere seven jobs out of the
371 occupations distinguished: domestic servant, agricultural worker, cleri-
cal work, shop assistant, seamstress, primary school teacher and nurse (Pott-
Buter, 1993, p. 71).

Currently, in the seven countries listed in Table 5.3, women are employed
principally in the 'caring professions' (nurse, teacher, welfare worker); in
junior white collar posts (clerk and secretary); and in sales (cashier, sales-
woman) and service occupations (cook, cleaner).

The division of labour over the industrial sectors is also different for men
and women. For both men and women there have been changes: the agricultural sector has gradually occupied fewer people; the industrial sector has
remained fairly stable; and the other sectors have been growing. Tables 5.4

Table 5.3 Female labour force participation rates: 1960–90

	Belgium	Denmark	France	Germany	Netherlands	Sweden	UK
1960	36	44	47	49	26	51	49
1967	39	55	47	48	27	55	50
1971	40	59	49	49	30	61	51
1973	41	62	50	50	31	63	53
1975	43	64	51	51	31	68	56
1977	45	65	53	51	31	70	57
1979	46	70	54	52	33	73	58
1981	48	72	54	53	38	75	57
1983	49	74	54	53	40	77	57
1985	49	75	55	53	41	78	61
1987	51	77	56	54	49	79	63
1988	51	78	56	55	51	80	64
1989	52	77	56	56	51	81	65
1990	52	78	57	56	53	81	65

Notes: percentage of the female population, aged 15–64.

Source: Pott-Buter (1993).

and 5.5 show that relatively few women are occupied in the agricultural and industrial sectors.

When looking at the data on labour market behavior there are two important differences between male and female data. First, when there are two partners in a household, the average number of hours worked by males is higher than by females. Second, the average male wage rate is higher than the average female wage rate. If it is assumed that wages are determined by the value of the marginal productivity of labour, the wage differences may be explained by differences in productivity. In Chapter 11 we shall pay attention to this human capital approach and shall look at the expected returns on investments in human capital. Although differences in educational level and experience are very important factors, they are not capable alone of explaining the total wage difference.

Labour market segmentation

A second explanation for wage differences is that the labour market consists of two segments. These segments are referred to as the primary and secondary markets, and it is assumed that the mobility between the two segments is very limited. The 'good' jobs are found in the primary sector, and the 'bad' jobs in the secondary sector. Good and bad jobs could be replaced by 'good' and 'bad' professions, or 'good' and 'bad' industries. The behaviour of employers and workers considering entry, mobility and stability patterns would differ strongly for each sector (see also section 5.6 of this chapter). If, in fact, entrance to the 'good' jobs or professions is rationed (Cain, 1976) this may explain part of wage differences. A segmentation between typical

Table 5.4 Breakdown of the total labour force by three sectors, seven countries, 1880–1990 (percentages)

	Belgium			Denmark			France			Germany			Netherlands			Sweden			UK		
	a	b	c																		
1880	43	35	22	54	26	21	48	31	21	42	36	22	–	–	–	68	17	15	13	49	38
1890	42	37	21	49	28	23	45	34	21	36	39	25	33	30	37	62	22	16	11	49	40
1900	23	38	39	40	29	31	44	34	22	–	–	–	31	34	35	55	28	17	9	51	40
1910	22	44	34	38	29	33	43	35	22	34	40	27	28	33	36	45	32	23	8	52	40
1920	15	47	38	37	30	33	38	39	23	30	42	27	24	34	33	44	35	21	10	43	47
1930	17	48	35	32	31	37	36	39	25	29	41	30	21	49	32	40	36	24	6	46	48
1940	–	–	–	32	30	48	36	37	27	26	42	32	–	–	–	34	38	28	–	–	–
1950	12	49	39	27	32	48	26	38	36	29	39	32	19	37	44	25	43	32	6	37	57
1960	9	47	45	19	37	45	22	38	40	14	49	37	12	40	48	14	42	43	4	34	62
1970	5	42	53	11	35	52	13	40	47	8	48	43	7	38	55	8	38	54	3	44	53
1980	3	34	63	7	31	62	9	35	56	5	44	51	5	31	64	6	31	64	3	36	62
1990	3	28	69	6	28	66	6	30	64	3	40	57	5	27	68	3	29	67	2	30	69

Notes: a (first column) = agricultural sector.
b (second column) = industrial sector.
c (third column) = other sectors.

Source: Pott-Buter (1993).

Table 5.5 Breakdown of the female labour force by three sectors, seven countries, 1880–1990 (percentages)

	Belgium			Denmark			France			Germany			Netherlands			Sweden			UK		
	a	b	c	a	b	c	a	b	c	a	b	c	a	b	c	a	b	c	a	b	c
1880	55	26	19	46	19	35	40	27	33	44	24	35	–	–	–	50	6	44	44	3	53
1890	44	23	23	44	20	36	32	30	38	41	24	35	21	16	63	49	7	44	44	2	54
1900	10	40	50	41	23	36	43	32	25	–	–	–	19	17	64	45	10	45	45	1	53
1910	8	44	48	35	17	48	43	33	24	47	23	30	21	18	65	37	12	51	46	1	54
1920	10	39	51	29	16	55	46	29	25	43	25	32	14	21	65	32	19	49	33	2	65
1930	14	37	51	25	14	59	41	29	30	40	24	36	14	20	66	17	21	52	38	1	61
1940	–	–	–	29	18	53	40	27	43	38	28	44	–	–	–	13	24	63	–	–	–
1950	7	39	54	24	20	62	27	24	49	41	22	37	18	18	64	7	26	67	24	2	74
1960	8	30	62	14	24	62	19	26	55	20	34	46	4	23	73	9	24	77	19	1	80
1970	3	27	71	7	22	71	8	24	58	12	34	55	3	17	80	5	19	77	28	2	71
1980	2	17	82	5	15	80	6	24	70	7	28	65	3	11	86	3	15	82	20	2	78
1990	1	14	84	3	15	82	3	23	74	3	24	72	3	10	87	2	14	84	16	1	83

Notes: a (first column) = agricultural sector.
b (second column) = industrial sector.
c (third column) = other sectors.

Source: Pott-Buter (1993).

female professions (such as nursing and administration) and male professions (technical jobs, construction) may also be responsible for some of
the wage differentials. The theories of dualist development (Lewis, 1954) and
of labour market segmentation (Piore, 1979) assert that in some countries
these theories describe and explain wage differences better than the perfect
competition theory. Whether wage differences and other job characteristics
are explained by differences in productivity or by segmentation of the labour
market, should be tested. Magnac (1991) tested a specification hypothesis of
a four-sector labour market model using labour supply data in Colombia.
The hypothesis was rejected, although the study underlines the inequality of
wage functions across sectors. A wage function shows the relationship between wage and years of schooling and work experience. (Wage functions
are discussed in Chapter 11.) For a summary of segmented labour market
theories, see Cain (1976) or Niesing (1993). Dual labour market theories
seem to be more popular in the USA than in Europe. The difference in the
structure of US and the European labour markets may be related to the
greater involvement in labour market problems of the governments of Europe.

Part-time jobs and contingent workers

In the USA, part-time and contingent workers[1] represent a kind of 'second-
class' labour force, with little protection and few career planning possibilities; see, for example, DuRivage (1992). Employment in the temporary help
industry, an important subset of the entire contingent workforce, grew quickly
during the the 1980s in the USA as well as in Europe. In the USA temporary agencies and employee leasing firms placed 1.3 million workers daily in
1991. In Europe, career planning and human capital investments by employers
in part-time workers is very limited. Women more often than men have
part-time jobs and this could explain part of wage differences. Neo-classical
theory assumes that this part-time work is the result of optimal choice. But,
according to Tilly (1992) this is not true for 20 per cent of the part-time
working women in the USA; they would like to work more hours. In 1988,
the rate of part-time employment for the non-agricultural sector in the US
was 18.4 per cent, consisting of 13.7 per cent 'willing' and 4.7 per cent
'reluctant' part-time workers. These people face restrictions from the demand side of the labour market.

Before trying to analyse the differences in labour market behaviour between men and women, let us first look at the advantages and disadvantages
of work. In the first place, work creates income, status and social contacts
but it takes time and a person's energy. Time spent in the labour market
cannot be used for household production, child care or leisure activities. If
the value of an hour spent on household production, child care or on a
leisure activity is higher than the (marginal) wage rate, this hour should not
be spent in the labour market. In Chapter 6 we shall discuss household
production and in Chapter 7 child care.

5.3   Neo-classical household labour supply models

Unrationed labour supply models

Suppose household utility depends on joint household consumption and leisure of both partners: $U^h(x, l_m, l_f)$. We shall analyse two utility functions
that may represent household preferences: the LES and the AIDS models.
   In the LES model the household solves the problem:

maximize $U^h(x, l_m, l_f) = \alpha \log (x - \bar{x}) + \beta_1 \log(l_m - \gamma_m) +$
         $\beta_2 \log (l_f - \gamma_f)$, with $\alpha + \beta_1 + \beta_2 = 1$
s.t. $Y = x + w_m l_m + w_f l_f = y_0 + w_m T + w_f T$,   (5.1)

where

l_j = leisure time of j	w_j = marginal wage rate of j
t_j = labour time of j	y_0 = unearned income
x = household expenditures	Y = full income
$\bar{x}$ = subsistence level	T = total time available per period
γ_j = subsistence level of leisure of j	$j = f, m$.

The parameters α, β_1 and β_2 can be interpreted as the relative importance of
consumption and m's and f's leisure in the household utility function. If
$\beta_1 < \beta_2$, m's leisure adds less to household utility than does f's leisure.
Since there is no distinction between household labour time and leisure in
this model, m's and f's leisure may be used for household production. We
shall discuss this aspect of leisure in Chapter 6.

Exercise 5.1
Show that the demand for leisure functions of m and f in Equation
(5.1) become:

$l_m = \gamma_m + \beta_1\{(w_m + w_f)T - \bar{x} - w_m\gamma_m - w_f l_f + y_0\} / w_m$
$l_f = \gamma_f + \beta_2\{(w_m + w_f)T - \bar{x} - w_m\gamma_m - w_f l_f + y_0\} / w_f$ (5.2)

Exercise 5.2
What is the functional form of (male) labour supply $t_m = f(w_m)$; and
what is the functional form of the relationship between t_m and w_f:
$t_m = g(w_f)$?

The LES model results in rather restrictive labour supply functions (see
Exercise 5.2). One usually prefers a more flexible model, which allows for
forward- and backward-bending labour supply curves, so that the data on

Table 5.6 Labour supply elasticities

	No. of children	Male labour supply is unrationed	Male labour supply is rationed
Male		−0.2863	
Female	0	0.4274	0.6489
	1	0.1074	0.0889
	2	−0.1926	−0.3010

Source: Blundell and Walker (1982).

actual behaviour will determine the shape of the labour supply functions. Blundell and Walker (1982) modeled the joint determination of household labour supplies and commodity demands using a generalization of the Gorman Polar cost function[2] to represent preferences. The labour supply functions can be either forward or backward-bending. They find that the labour supply elasticity, $\dfrac{\partial t/t}{\partial w/w}$, for male workers evaluated at the average hours worked (39.6 per week) is −0.2863. (The elasticities are given in Table 5.6.) This means that if wages rise by 1 per cent, labour supply will decrease by almost 0.3 per cent. The labour supply elasticity of women depends greatly on the number of children in the household. Explanations for this phenomenon can be found in Chapters 6 and 7, which cover household production and effects of children on household decisions.

Deaton and Muellbauer's AIDS model (see Chapter 4), as used by Kooreman and Kapteyn (1986) allows for labour supply functions that can be forward-bending (supply increases when the wage rate increases) in some ranges of wages, and backward-bending (supply decreases when the wage rate increases) in others. Like Blundell and Walker, they use the dual approach. Their cost function $C(u, w_m, w_f) = \text{minimum} (w_m l_m + w_f l_f + px \mid v \geq u)$ for two-earner families is specified as:

$$C(u, w_m, w_f) = \exp (\alpha + \beta u), \tag{5.3}$$

with

u = utility

$\alpha = a_0 + a_m \log w_m + a_f \log w_f + a_x \log p +$

$\qquad \frac{1}{2}b_{mm} \log^2 w_m + b_{mf} \log w_m \log w_f + b_{mx} \log w_m \log p +$

$\qquad \frac{1}{2}b_{ff} \log^2 w_f + b_{fx} \log w_f \log p + \frac{1}{2}b_{xx} \log^2 p$

$\beta = c_0 (w_m)^{c_m} (w_f)^{c_f} p^{c_x}$

a_i, b_{ij} and c_i are parameters, $i = m, f, x, j = m, f, x,$

$\sum_i a_i = 1, \sum_j b_{mj} = 0, \sum_j b_{fj} = 0$ and $\sum_i b_{ix} = 0.$

> **Exercise 5.3**
> Derive the compensated and uncompensated demand for leisure
> functions, using the cost function of Equation (5.3) (see Chapter 2).
>
> **Exercise 5.4**
> Show that labour supply can be forward-bending in some ranges of
> wages and backward-bending in others (see also Figure 5.1).

The effect of family composition on labour supply is modeled by allowing
a_1, a_2 and a_3 to depend on family size and the presence of young children:

$$a_i = a^0_i + a^1_i \log N + a^2_i D, \quad i = m, f, x, \tag{5.4}$$

where:

N = family size, $D = 0$, if no children under the age of 5 are present,
$D = 1$, if children under the age of 5 are present.

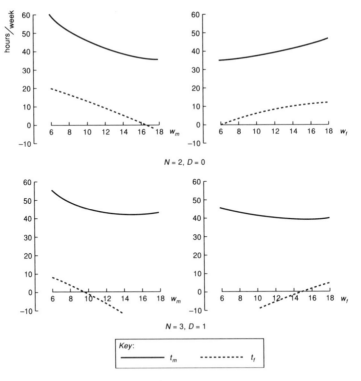

Notes: N = Family size; D = 0, no children under 5; D = 1, family with
children under 5.
Source: Kooreman and Kapteyn (1985).

Figure 5.1 Labour supply functions, two-earner families

The estimation resulted in the labour supply functions that are represented in Figure 5.1. These figures show that m's optimal labour supply is backward-bending in the lower ranges of w_m and forward-bending in the higher ranges. Female labour supply decreases with increasing w_m, but it increases with increasing w_f. Female labour supply reacts strongly to family size and composition, as was found by Blundell and Walker. In particular, the presence of young children makes females work less outside the home.

Model (5.3) was estimated using a sample of two-earner families only. When one-earner families are included in the sample, rationing theory is used, because in one-earner households $t_f = 0$ is given. The quantity rationing of labour for these households may change the results, as we shall see in the next section.

A rationed household labour supply model

Exercise 5.5

Apply the theory of Section 4.4 to sh4ow that male-rationed demand for leisure for model (5.3), given $t_f = \bar{t}_f$, is:

$$\frac{w_m l^R}{\bar{Y}} = a_m + b_{mm} \log w_m + b_{mf} \log \bar{w}_f + b_{mx} \log p$$
$$+ \log \bar{Y} - c_m \bar{\alpha}, \qquad (5.5)$$

where

$\bar{w}_f$ = virtual price of female labour, $\bar{l}_f = T - \bar{t}_f$ and
$\quad \bar{Y} = Y - \bar{l}_f(w_f - \bar{w}_f)$,
Y = full income and $\bar{\alpha}$ is defined as in Equation (5.3), but with w_f replaced by $\bar{w}_f$.

The female's rationed share is:

$$\frac{\bar{w}_f \bar{l}_f}{\bar{Y}} = a_f + b_{ff} \log \bar{w}_f + b_{mf} \log w_m + b_{fx} \log p +$$
$$c_f \log \bar{Y} - c_f \bar{a}. \qquad (5.6)$$

Kooreman and Kapteyn studied the case where the wife does not participate in the labour market, so $\bar{l}_f = T$. Then $\bar{Y} = w_m T + \bar{w}_f T + y_0$. This would be the full income if female wage rate equals $\bar{w}_f$. However, more general situations of under- and over-employment can be studied with this model if information on desired hours is available.

When putting this model into practice, we get a switching regime model: we have two groups of households, one where both partners work and one where only the male partner works. We write that female optimal labour supply as:

$$t_f^* = T - l_f^* = T - g_f(w_m, w_f, p, y_0).$$

However, it can only be realized if $l_f^* < T$. If $l_f^* > T$, then $l_f = T$.

So let $l_f^* = g_f(w_m, w_f, p, y_0)$, then:

$$\left. \begin{array}{l} l_f = l_f^* \\ \text{and} \\ l_m = g_m(w_m, w_f, p, y_0) \end{array} \right\} \quad \text{if } l_f^* < T \qquad (5.7)$$

$$\left. \begin{array}{l} l_f = T \\ \text{and} \\ l_m = g_m(w_m, \bar{w}_f, p, y_0) \equiv l_m^R \end{array} \right\} \quad \text{if } l_f^* \geq T. \qquad (5.8)$$

An extra problem arises for the wage rate of non-working females. Their wage rate is unknown and should be estimated. Usually information from a working female is used (such as age, educational level, experience and so on), but one should be aware that working women are probably a selective sample of all women, because their characteristics may be special. So a correction for selectivity should be made when predicting the wage rate of non-working women; see Heckman (1979).

Kooreman and Kapteyn's estimation results for this model are slightly different from those based on the sample of two-earner families. Again, we show the graphs of the male and female labour supply functions (see Figure 5.2). Only for the families without children ($N = 2$), male rationed and unrationed labour supply are quite different. The estimated parameters are more accurate, because of the larger sample (one-earner families are now included). An interesting result is that the average shadow wage $\bar{w}_f$ for non-participating women, is one and a half times as high as the average pre-dicted wage $\hat{w}_f$ for non-participating women. This is something one might have expected. When checking $\bar{w}_f$ and $\hat{w}_f$ in individual cases the relationship $\bar{w}_f > \hat{w}_f$ holds in 76 per cent of the cases. When $\bar{w}_f < \hat{w}_f$ this could be inter-preted as a case of non-voluntary unemployment.

5.4   A sociological view on household labour supply

The approach to human behavior in the social sciences varies widely with the discipline. While economists assume that choices are made rationally, (given the consumer's preferences and restrictions, s/he makes a 'best' choice), sociologists assume that human behaviour is more determined by the group s/he belongs to, its history and its culture (see, for example, several contri-butions in Sussman and Steinmetz (1987)). The group largely determines an individual's preferences and is responsible for some of the restrictions as

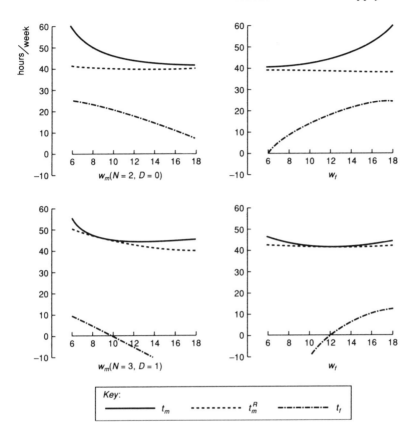

Source: Kooreman and Kapteyn (1986).

Figure 5.2 Rationed and unrationed labour supply functions

well. Individuals are supposed to play certain roles, for which they are educated. With respect to labour supply this means that, if it is the opinion of
the group that a married woman should 'stay at home, do the housekeeping
and take care of the children', it will be difficult for a person with a dissenting opinion to make a dissenting choice. The probability that she will work
is less than when other women work as well. Deviant behaviour could be
punished by the group. If 'the working mother' does not fit into the picture,
it may be more difficult for her to find people (relatives or friends) who are
willing to look after her children occasionally. The mother herself may feel
that she is not taking good care of her children and feel guilty.

The opinion of society is more or less reflected in its laws. In countries
such as France, Germany and The Netherlands, during the first half of this
century women were dismissed from their jobs as soon as they married, the
so-called 'marriage bar' (Pott-Buter, 1993). Until 1990 female teachers in
France were forbidden by law to be married. No such formal prohibition

existed in England, but in practice local authorities prevented teachers who married from continuing to teach. This practice was abandoned in 1944 (Tilly and Scott, 1987). The general ban on married women in public employment in Great Britain was lifted in 1946. In The Netherlands it lasted until 1957 before obligatory dismissal on marriage was abandoned for women in tenured posts in government service. It will be clear that during those days there were no, or very few, day-care centers for young children. The lack of a sufficient number of such centers has long remained an extra restriction on female labour market participation.

In empirical studies, the notions about the roles of men and women are often measured by the opinion that the respondents and close friends, relatives and neighbours have about the division of labour in the household. Since the beginning of the 1970s these opinions have changed in Europe as well as in the USA. In particular, the more highly educated (see Scanzoni and Fox, 1980) and younger people (see Antill and Cotton, 1988) have more egalitarian notions about the roles of men and women.

Although the theory of exchange has its basis in economics, sociologists rather than economists first applied the theory to the problem of the division of labour within the household. According to Blood *et al.* (1960) the endowment and resources of partners are an important spring for their behaviour in the relationship. In economics, game theorists picked up this idea to model the choice of a household utility function out of all possible Pareto optimal combinations of individual utility functions (see Chapter 3). In economics, power is often related to earning capacity or actual earnings. In sociology, non-financial factors can play an important role as well, but these are difficult to measure. In these models a distinction between resources that can only be used inside the household and resources that are also valuable outside the household should be made. Resources that can also be used outside the household will make the controlling partner more independent of the household.

Psychology and labour supply

Economic psychologists will emphasize the intangible advantages and disadvantages of paid and unpaid labour. The esteem related to a paid job is usually greater than the esteem connected to housekeeping. A person can derive part of his or her identity from the work s/he is doing; this holds also for housekeeping and child care. Paid jobs usually open opportunities for new social contacts. Working breadwinners are on average more content with their social contacts than people who are unemployed (Antonides and van Raaij, 1990). These factors are positive secondary effects of work. However, negative side effects also exist. Market work may be dirty, noisy, boring, tiring or stressful.

When formulating an economic labour supply model, one should try to take these factors into account and see whether they add something significant to the explanation of household labour supply and the division of paid and unpaid labour between partners. Since the factors mentioned above have no natural unit of measurement, something has to be done before they can be integrated in our economic models. Often, dummy variables are introduced, or specific scales are developed to measure the relevance of a factor for an individual. In this way the variables can be treated as other economic variables and one can test for their significance.

The following example, used by van der Lippe (1993), illustrates an attempt to measure the moral code of the social environment of a person with respect to the division of labour. The respondent is asked how his or her partner would answer the following questions (graded 1 = fully agree, . . . , 5 = absolutely disagree).

1. Women should not work as long as their children are too young to attend school.
2. It is more important for a man than for a woman to have a good job.
3. The most desirable situation in a household is that the man is the breadwinner and the wife does the housekeeping and takes care of the children.

Then the person is asked how his or her best friend would answer these questions. Finally the respondent is asked about the actual behaviour of his or her neighbours and friends. These data can be used in economic models as an indication of the interdependence of preferences, but one should be aware of the problems related to interdependency: it is not one-way traffic. If person *A* is influenced by his group, then *A* himself will probably influence these same group members.

5.5 Household labour supply when the budget set is non-convex

In Chapter 4 we analysed some of the effects of government regulations on household behaviour. The tax and social security systems affect the budget restriction of a household. A progressive tax system, as used in most countries, causes kinks in the budget line. Most Western countries also have a social security system, which provides an income to unemployed people. If the unemployment benefit comes to an end when a person finds a job, the budget set is no longer convex, as shown in Figure 5.3. If a person can find a job for only a limited number of hours a week, his or her wage income may be less than the social security benefits, see Point *A* in Figure 5.3. This will discourage people from accepting such a job. The advantage of a system in which a person who accepts a limited job still receives part of the unemployment benefit, stimulates the acceptance of such jobs and diminishes the poverty trap (see also Chapter 12). In Figure 5.4 we illustrate a situation in which social security diminishes gradually. Income, consisting of social security plus labour income, shows a less dramatic drop (from Y_{ss} to *C*) and will already be larger than Y_{ss} when $t_w > t_1$. Non-convex budget

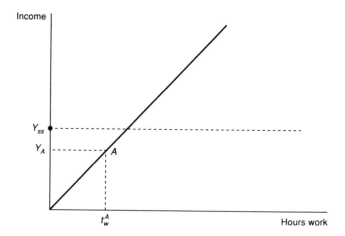

Note: Y_{ss} = social security income level.

Figure 5.3 The relationship between income and working hours, when social security stops completely on accepting a job

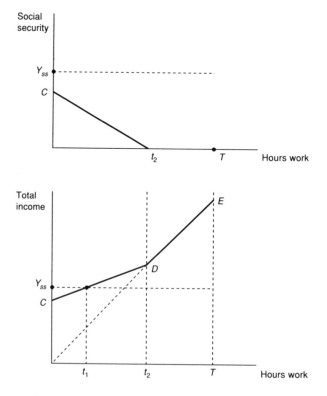

Figure 5.4 The relationship between income and working hours, when social security ends gradually on accepting a job

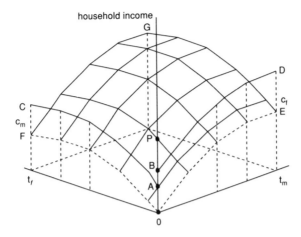

Figure 5.5 A non-convex household budget set

sets call for the calculation of local maxima of the utility function at Point $(0, Y_{ss})$, Point D (t_2, wt_2), Point E (T, wT) on the interval $[0, t_2]$ and $[t_2, T]$ and a comparison of these utility levels. Hausman paid attention to this problem in several papers (see, for example, Hausman, 1981, 1985).

The budget set for a household consisting of two adults (with or without children), in a system with unemployment benefits, becomes a surface: *OFGE*, combined with two kinked lines: *AC* and *BD* and one point: *P*, as in figure 5.5. If both partners are employed the budget set consists of the area under the manifold *OEGF*, if m is employed and f is unemployed, receiving an unemployment payment c_f, the budget line becomes *BD*; if f is employed and m is unemployed, the budget line becomes *AC*; and if both are unemployed, the household budget is represented by Point P. $(OP = OA + OB)$ Here it is assumed that a person loses the unemployment payment completely as soon as s/he accepts a job, regardless of the amount of earnings, or hours worked. The unemployment benefits c_m and c_f usually depend on the employment history of m and f, so they are not necessarily equal. The budget set is non-convex.

The tax system of a country can make the marginal net wage rate of a person dependent on the earnings (as we have already seen in Chapter 4, Section, 4.3) and unemployment benefits of the partner. To analyse the interdependence of labour supply and the effect of the tax system, Hausman and Ruud (1984) introduced the indirect utility function:

$$V\ (w_m, w_f, y_0) = \exp(\beta_1 w_m + \beta_2 w_f)\ [y_0 + \theta + \delta_1 w_m + \delta_2 w_f + \\ 0.5(\gamma_1(w_m)^2 + \alpha w_m w_f + \gamma_2(w_f)^2)] \tag{5.9}$$

or, for short,

$$V(w_m, w_f, y) = \exp(\beta_1 w_m + \beta_2 w_f).y^*\ (w_m, w_f, y_0). \tag{5.9*}$$

The corresponding cost function is:

$$C(u, w_m, w_f) = u \exp(-\beta_1 w_m - \beta_2 w_f) - y^*(w_m, w_f, y_0), \qquad (5.10)$$

where, α, β_1, β_2, γ_1, γ_2, δ_1, δ_2 and θ are parameters, the ws are net wages, and y_0 is non-labour income.

Using Roy's identity, or Shephard's lemma, it follows that the labour supply equations are:

$$t_m = \delta_1 + \beta_1 y^* + \gamma_1 w_m + \alpha w_f \qquad (5.11)$$

$$t_f = \delta_2 + \beta_2 y^* + \gamma_2 w_f + \alpha w_m. \qquad (5.12)$$

The t_m and t_f represent the optimal numbers of working hours. These may not be converted into true working hours, because of demand restrictions. It is seen that the partner's wage rate appears in the labour supply function. For the tax schedules faced by couples, the maximization of utility can be broken up into maximization over convex subsets of the budget followed by maximization over the entire set of solutions. Hausman and Ruud used the 1976 wave of the Michigan Panel Study of Income Dynamics to estimate the parameters of the model.

Kapteyn *et al.* (1990) applied the model to Dutch data and first derived the direct utility function, which is needed when the budget set is non-convex: the utility level at certain points of the budget set (such as Point P in Figure 5.5) must be compared with local maxima on convex subsets. Kapteyn *et al.* derived short-run (the partner is rationed at a certain number of hours) and long-run (the partner is not rationed) labour supply functions. Figure 5.6 shows the results for families without children; the variables that do not appear in the figures are set at their sample means. Female labour supply is forward-bending, and the tax system leads to a jigsawed response. The reason for this is that each time an individual is at a kink in the budget constraint, s/he will want to stay there if the before-tax wage rate changes slightly. To stay at a kink with an increasing wage rate means a reduction of work effort. The downward-sloping parts of Figure 5.6(d) are, therefore, hyperbolas. Hausman and Ruud's estimation results also show differences between a husband's and a wife's parameter estimates , but the differences for the Dutch data are more pronounced.

5.6   Paid labour in the informal sector

When analysing labour supply in the previous sections it was assumed that the distinction between 'not working' and 'working' is the most relevant. However, in more recent literature, there is also a tendency to distinguish between 'not working', 'working in the informal sector' and 'working in the formal sector' (Lubell, 1990). The two sectors of the labour market, the

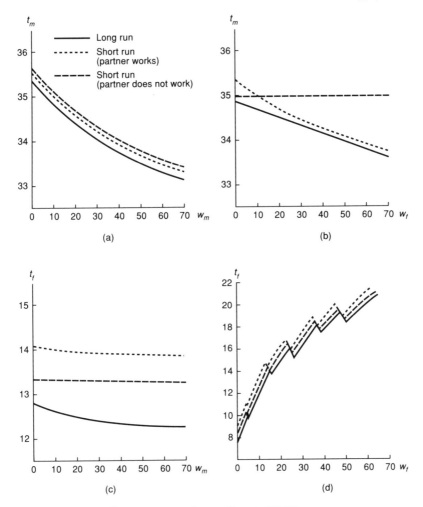

Source: Kapteyn, Kooreman and van Soest (1990).

Figure 5.6   Optimal labour supply as a function of before-tax wage rates (household without children)

formal and the informal, operate as separate markets in some ways, but they have, of course, linkages.

Definitions

What is the informal sector? There is not only one definition for the informal sector. We distinguish three groups of definitions: statistical, fiscal and juridical definitions.

1. *Statistical definitions*: labour is informal if it does not appear in the official statistics. Only labour that is registered belongs to the formal sector.

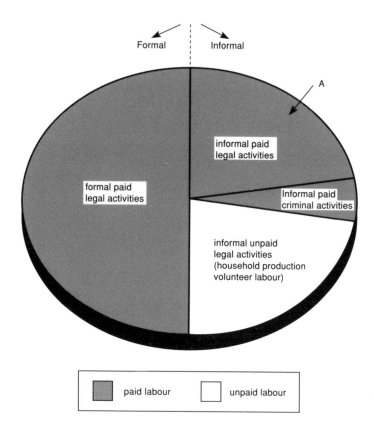

Figure 5.7   The formal and informal sectors of the economy

Productive activities that are hidden from observation, whether paid or unpaid, belong to the informal sector.

2. *Fiscal definitions*: labour is informal if the tax laws are not obeyed. This definition may be used by the treasury. It concerns activities that are usually legal by their nature, such as cleaning, construction, sewing and so on, that are income-creating, but only if all taxes and premiums for social security and so on are paid do they belong to the formal sector. Paid labour that evades one or more rules is informal.

3. *Juridical definitions*: labour is informal if it is illegal (such as selling drugs, committing burglary). Such definitions are used by the judiciary.

Economists generally use a statistical definition. Both paid and unpaid productive activities fit within this definition. We shall pay attention to (unpaid) household production and volunteer labour in Chapter 6. Here we shall address paid labour in the informal sector: segment A in Figure 5.7. We exclude criminal activities (like trading drugs and robbery) from the analyses, and concentrate on legal activities that belong to the informal sector.

Paid informal labour

In most Western countries many informal activities will also fall within the fiscal definition. The laws that regulate the formal market are laws that can be broken. For example, laws with respect to taxes, minimum wage, length of the working week, social security, safety in the factory, work permits ('green card'), and so on. So the structure of the 'black' labour market in Western countries is derived from the structure of the formal market.

The fiscal aspect of informal paid activities is a considerable problem for the authorities. If governments do not receive taxes from the majority of income-creating transactions, the burden on the shoulders of formal economic activities becomes heavier. Van Eck and Kazemier (1988) have estimated the size of the hidden labour market for The Netherlands. According to them nearly 12 per cent of the population of over 16 years of age participate in the informal sector. It is difficult to get reliable estimates of the size of this sector, because those concerned prefer to keep it hidden. Estimates of the size of the hidden economy in the Netherlands vary between 5 per cent and 22 per cent of national income, depending on research method and data. Although the informal sector is quite important in Western countries we prefer to concentrate on the analysis of informal labour in developing countries. All economies started (long ago) with informal labour (see Section 4.2) and only gradually the formal sector developed and became important, but informal labour was the basis of all. In many developing countries the informal sector is still very important, even more so than in the West.

Labour markets in developing countries

In developing countries the urban labour markets are characterized by the coexistence of a regulated formal sector and an unregulated informal sector, while rural labour (agriculture) is mostly informal. The informal urban sector is dominated by one person firms and small enterprises that employ few apprentices or hired workers. Production generally uses simple technology and requires little capital or formal skills, and there are no or only a few barriers to entering that sector. For developing countries, the informal sector is very important, because of a lack of sufficient employment possibilities in the formal sector and the lack of a well-developed social security system. Many individuals can survive only by working in the informal sector.

Most analytical studies have analysed the relationship between the formal and informal sector within the context of labour market segmentation and dual labour markets; see, for example, Magnac (1991). Continuing rural–urban migration makes clear that the urban and rural labour markets are interrelated. If urban wages increase faster than rural wages this will lead to rural migrants seeking work in the urban labour market. The increased competition that results will affect the expected wage offer for urban residents. A non-competitive wage-setting mechanism, caused, for instance, by strong union involvement or minimum wage legislation, may prevent wage levels moving to their market clearing level.

An influential contribution to this field of study has been the Harris and Todaro (1970) model. Their objective was to explain the persistence of unemployment in urban areas of a developing country. The model distinguishes two sectors: (i) informal agricultural; and (ii) formal urban. Agriculture is assumed to be a free entry sector with a wage w_a. In the formal sector, a higher wage rate, w_f, prevails. Wages in the formal sector are above the market clearing level and employment in the formal sector is rationed: F is the total number of urban sector jobs. The labour force L is assumed to be homogeneous and sector preferences depend on wages only. Because wages in the formal sector are higher than wages in the agricultural sector, $w_f >$ w_a, any individual would prefer a formal sector job. However, since the labour force, L, is greater than the number of formal jobs, F, not everybody can get a formal sector job and some people will not even try to get one. If a person tries to find a job in the formal sector, the probability of finding such a job is only p ($p < 1$), and if s/he stays in the agricultural sector s/he is sure to earn w_a. There will be an equilibrium if the expected returns $E(w)$ on both strategies are equal:

$$E_a(w) = E_f(w) \rightarrow 1.w_a = p.w_f + (1 - p).0 \rightarrow w_a = pw_f. \quad (5.13)$$

The probability of finding a job equals the number of jobs divided by the number of job-seekers L_s:

$$p = F/L_s. \quad (5.14)$$

The labour force is divided into formal-sector job-seekers, L_s, plus agricultural workers, L_a:

$$L = L_s + L_a. \quad (5.15)$$

Exercise 5.6

If $w_f = 6$ and $w_a = 3$, $F = 200$ and $L = 1000$, show that, in an equilibrium situation, $L_s = 400$, $L_a = 600$, $p = \frac{1}{2}$ and 200 job-seekers remain unemployed.

From this exercise we learn that, without being risk-seeking or risk-averse (see Chapter 4, Section 4.6), rational job-seekers may migrate to the city as long as the unemployment rate is still below the equilibrium level.

The model does not explore the coexistence of a formal and an informal sector in urban areas. If both sectors do exist in urban areas, workers of the informal sector could be seeking a formal-sector job without being unemployed. Fields (1975) extended the Harris–Todaro model in this respect. He allowed for three strategies:

1. Remain in the agricultural sector.
2. Look for a formal-sector job from the position of being unemployed.
3. Look for a formal-sector job while being employed in the informal sector.

On-the-job search is supposed to be less efficient than full-time search: the probability (p) reduces to θp, $(0 < \theta$ 1$)$. One reason for this could be that these people have less time for searching. A second reason could be that working in the informal sector has a negative stigma, which may lower the chance of entry in the formal sector. The wage rates w_a and w_f are exogenous, and w_i, the wage in the informal sector, is endogenous. The allocation of labour is in equilibrium if the expected returns are equal:

$$E_a\,(w) = E_f\,(w) = E_i\,(w) \rightarrow w_a = pw_f = \theta pw_f + (1 - \theta p)w_i. \quad (5.16)$$

The number of formal-sector job-seekers (L_s) equals the labour force queueing up for formal-sector jobs weighted by their relative efficiency of search:

$$L_s = L_f^a = \theta L_i^a, \quad (5.17)$$

where, L_f^a denotes the individuals that choose to search for employment in the formal sector from an unemployed position (superscript $a = ex\ ante$) and L_i^a those who choose to search from the informal sector. Again, the probability (p) of finding a job equals:

$$p = F/L_s.$$

A fraction $(1 - p)$ of the unemployed job-seekers remains unemployed, and a fraction $(1 - \theta p)$ of the informal-sector seekers remains in the informal sector, so *ex post* employment (superscript p) in the informal sector is L_i^p:

$$L_i^p = (1 - \theta p)L_i^a. \quad (5.18)$$

The wage rate in the informal sector depends on the demand for the informal services, Q, and the number of participants in the informal sector:

$$w_i = \frac{Q}{L_i^p} \quad (5.19)$$

The total labour force, L, equals $L_a + L_f^a + L_i^a$ *ex ante*, but *ex post* we see that there will also be unemployed individuals:

$$L = L_a + L_f^p + L_i^p + U.$$

Exercise 5.7

If $w_f = 6$ and $w_a = 3$, $F = 200$, $L = 1000$, $\theta = {}^1/_2$ and $Q = 450$, show that, in equilibrium:
$L_s = 400$, $L_a = 450$, $L_f^a = 250$, $L_f^p = 200$, $L_i^p = 225$, $p = {}^1/_2$, $w_i = 2$ and 125 job seekers remain unemployed.

The number of unemployed has decreased compared to the Harris–Todaro model because of the extra demand, Q, for informal-sector services.

According to Fields' model, the informal-sector workers are discontented with their jobs, because many of them are searching for employment in the formal sector. The informal sector is supposed to be inferior to the formal sector, but that is not necessarily true. Pradhan and van Soest (1995) analyse labour supply behaviour and the choices between not working, working in the informal sector and working in the formal sector. First they investigate whether the informal sector is only an intermediary sector between not working and working in the formal sector, or whether it is competitive with the formal sector.

In order to distinguish between these two possibilities, the results of an ordered Probit selection model are compared with those of an (unordered) multinominal Logit selection model. In the first model, the three labour market states are ordered: participation in the formal sector, participation in the informal sector, and non-participation. An underlying latent variable (Y) can be interpreted as an indicator of formality. Non-participation includes being engaged in household production, which is associated with the lowest level of formality. The formal presentation is:

$$Y = X\beta + \varepsilon \quad \begin{cases} \text{non-participation if} & Y < \alpha_1 \\ \text{working in the informal sector if} & \alpha_1 < Y < \alpha_2 \\ \text{working in the formal sector if} & Y > \alpha_2, \end{cases}$$

where
X is a vector of individual, family and regional characteristics, β is a parameter vector, α_1 and α_2 parameters for which it is assumed that $\alpha > \alpha_1$. The error ε distribution is independent of X.

For the multinominal Logit model there is no a priori ordering. Let Y_i be the indirect utility associated with state i, then we assume that:

$$Y_i = X\gamma_i + \eta_i \quad \begin{cases} \text{working in the formal sector if} & \max \{Y_1, Y_2, Y_3\} = Y_1 \\ \text{working in the informal sector if} & \max \{Y_1, Y_2, Y_3\} = Y_2 \\ \text{non-participation if} & \max \{Y_1, Y_2, Y_3\} = Y_3. \end{cases}$$

The vector X is the same as in the ordered Probit model, but now we have three parameter vectors, γ_1, γ_2 and γ_3. The error terms η_i have an extreme value type distribution, the η_i are independent of X.

Table 5.7 Sample means by labour market state, Bolivia, 1989

	Male			Female		
	Formal	Informal	Not working	Formal	Informal	Not working
Hourly earnings in B[1]	2.39	2.58		1.94	2.01	
Hours worked p/w	49.7	52.3		38.5	46.9	
Age	36	40	39	34	39	37
Education (% per sector)						
Basic ($\leq$ 5 years)	21	35	24	9	39	29
Inter[2]	14	19	13	8	16	15
Medio[2]	29	30	33	22	20	29
Middle technical	4	3	4	9	3	5
Higher technical	3	2	3	5	1	1
Normal (teacher)	6	1	2	27	2	3
University	19	7	16	17	3	5
Other	4	3	5	3	16	13
N	3 605	1 863	881	1 439	1 972	3 882

1) In 1989 3Bs = 1$ 2) Inter = intermediate education, at completion: 8 years
Medio = number of years at completion: 12

Source: Pradhan and van Soest (1995).

These two models are non-nested and one can only test which model is closest to the data. The models are estimated using 1989 Bolivian household survey data and applied in a test developed by Vuong (1989). For male workers, the maximum likelihood of the ordered Probit model is larger than in the multinominal Logit, but the difference is too small to reject the hypothesis of equality between the expected log-likelihoods. For females, the test favored the multinominal model. So there is no reason to assume an ordering in the sectors.

For Bolivia, some interesting sample means are presented in Table 5.7. From the table we learn that, on average, the payment in the informal sector is at least as good as in the formal sector. So, if individuals who work in the informal sector are still looking for a job in the formal sector, this may be due to the effect of non-monetary returns of the formal jobs.

Pradhan (1994) also introduces a *household* labour supply model in which both partners must choose between supplying their labour to the formal sector, or to the informal sector, or not to work. It is assumed that the hourly wage that a person can earn in the two sectors is given, but there may be a difference in wage level. The simplest assumption is then to assume that the individual will choose the sector with the highest hourly earnings. This, however, is not necessarily consistent with the data. Unobserved non-monetary returns are introduced to explain why people may choose the sector yielding the lower (monetary) earnings, because the total of monetary and non-monetary returns is what counts.

A standard household labour supply model, with a quadratic household utility function $U(l_m, l_f, C)$, and time and budget restrictions, is formulated. Consumption C equals $h_m w^*_m + h_f w^*_f + Y$, where w^*_i = hourly wage rate including non-monetary returns (NMR): $w^*_i = w_i + \text{NMR}_i$, $i = m, f$. These wage rates are the maximum of formal and informal wages, including non-monetary returns. It is assumed either that the budget constraint is binding and h_m and h_f both > 0, so both partners supply labour, or that one of the $h_i = 0$ ($i = m, f$), so one partner does not supply labour (for corner solutions, see Chapter 2). In either case, the first-order conditions can be derived. The optimal w_i where $i = m, f$ for the formal and informal sectors are (implicitly) determined.

The non-monetary returns reflect the sum of the effects resulting from sector-specific preferences and rationing. The sector-specific preferences include benefits such as health insurance or status attached to participation in a specific sector. Rationing is modeled as waiting queues for jobs in a specific sector, which result in costs proportional to wages. The non-monetary returns NMR_i ($i = m, f$) are standardized equal to zero for the informal sector, and for the formal sector they are functions of individual and local market conditions.

The complete model consists of two wage equations (formal and informal wage) for each sex, one NMR equation for each sex, and two labour supply equations. The estimation results show again that the participation rates and labour supply functions of the spouses are interdependent (see Chapter 5, Section 5.3). In Figure 5.8 the hours supplied are on the vertical axis (divided by 10) and on the horizontal axis are given the husbands' and wives' wages.

Exercise 5.8
Interpret the meaning of the two surfaces of Figure 5.8, note the remarkable differences between male and female labour supply.

In Figure 5.9 we see the probabilities of participation of males and females as a function of their own wage rate and their partner's hours worked. For the males, the surface is rather flat – there is only a slight positive effect of own wage rate, but for females the surface is not at all flat. For females, the own wage rate has a positive effect on the probability of participation, and the effect is stronger if the male works fewer hours.

In Table 5.8 the estimated coefficients of the two wage equations and the non-monetary return equation for both husbands and wives are shown. An important conclusion following from these results is that returns to education are larger in the formal sector than in the informal sector. This may indicate that the formal sector requires skills obtained through the formal educational system, or that education is used as a screening device in the formal sector. Moreover, the returns on education are higher for women

99

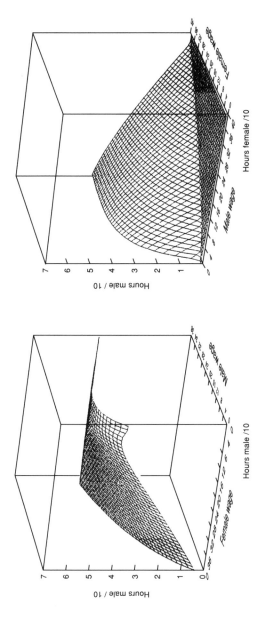

Figure 5.8 Labour supply of husbands and wives

Source: Pradhan (1994).

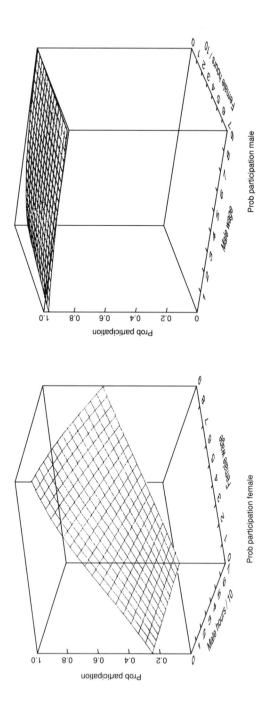

Figure 5.9   Labour market participation of husbands and wives

Source: Pradhan (1994).

Table 5.8   Some estimated coefficients of the wage and
non-monetary returns (NMR) equations[3]

	Male			Female		
	Formal	*Informal*	*NMR*	*Formal*	*Informal*	*NMR*
Intercept	−1.33*	0.65	2.40*	−2.07*	−0.82	−2.06*
Age	0.71*	0.10	−0.12	0.81*	0.43	1.11*
Age squared	−0.77*	−0.08	−0.26	−0.97*	−0.48	−1.44*
Education[1]						
Inter	0.17*	−0.06	−0.24*	0.55*	0.18	0.37
Medio	0.35*	0.17*	0.18*	0.81*	0.21*	0.40*
Midtech	0.66*	0.21	−0.05	1.12*	0.17	1.00*
Hightech	0.78*	0.31	−0.05	1.17*	0.69*	1.45*
Normal	0.58*	−0.38*	0.27*	1.28*	−0.07	2.31*
University	1.18*	0.10	−0.16	1.77*	0.33	1.13*
Other	0.58	−0.19	0.35	0.02	−0.25	−0.38

Notes: * significant, 5% level.

1) Seven dummy variables have been included to estimate the effect of education; the reference group is 'basic'.

Source: Pradhan (1994).

than for men and the non-monetary returns for formal sector employment for both males and females are positive for 'normal' education (primary school teachers). These people attach a higher status to teaching in a primary school (which is exclusively formal) than to informal sector work.

5.7 Summary

In this chapter we saw that labour market behaviour of males and females is quite different. This difference is not significant for males and females who are living alone, but we found great differences when they have a partner and children. Husbands' and wives' labour supply are interdependent. The participation rate of married women is lower than that of married men. The division of labour between partners can be explained in part by economic factors, but the traditional role of the mother, which implies that she should take care of the family, still seems to have a significant effect on the division of labour.

The labour market shows signs of rationing. This means that households sometimes have to make a second-best choice. This also holds for countries where the informal sector is very important, as is the case in most developing countries. Here, individuals who have an informal-sector job, are often still seeking a formal-sector job.

Notes

1. Contingent jobs are defined as jobs in which it is understood from the outset that employment security is strictly limited (DuRivage, 1992).
2. This cost function has the following form:

$$C(p, w, \bar{u}) = a + d_m w_m + d_f w_f + \bar{u}\, b^{1-\theta_f - \theta_m} w_f^{\theta_f} w_m^{\theta_m}, \text{ where}$$

the parameters a and b are concave functions of prices, and d_m and d_f are homogeneous of degree zero in prices.
3. In Table 5.8 we mention only the estimated coefficients of age and education; the coefficients of the other explanatory variables can be found in Pradhan (1994).

CHAPTER 6

Household Production and Leisure

6.1 Introduction

In this chapter we focus on the relationship between the time that household members spend on household production, volunteer activities and leisure. In the early neo-classical models all non-labour time was addressed as leisure, but since Becker (1965) introduced his New Home Economics theory, more attention has been paid to the productive activities in the household. Until then, production as represented in economic models seemed to be the monopoly of both private and public sectors. The fact that activities performed within the household do not appear in public statistics does not mean that they are not productive. As far back as 1941, Kuznets indicated that GNP per capita is not a good indicator for a country's welfare, since household productive activities and volunteer labour, although affecting welfare, are not included in the GNP. The fact that the products of household production are not traded and have no market price does not mean that they have no value.

Some forms of household production compare very well with market products; for example, transportation: you can use your own car, motorcycle and bicycle (private), or take a taxi, bus, train or airplane (public). In all cases you are carried from one place to another. Whether activities are performed by households, the private sector or the public sector depends on many factors. In rural parts of developing countries many people, together with relatives and friends still build their own houses. In Western countries very few people will do so. The division of labour between the household, and the private and public sectors changes over time and varies over societies; see also Section 4.2. Burns (1977) gave an indication of the size of these three sectors of the economy over the course of history. He noted their growth and shrinkage, as illustrated in Figure 6.1.

In this chapter we shall study household choices concerning home production, paid labour supply, volunteer labour supply, and leisure. When

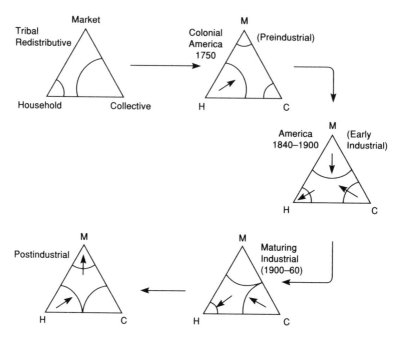

Source: Burns (1977).

Figure 6.1 Changing dominance in the economic triad

aggregated, the productive activities of households determine the lower-left corner of Burns' scheme. However, in this book we prefer to disaggregate, since we are interested in 'who does what' in the household, and why. Therefore we start analyzing, in Section 6.2, the allocation of time and the division of household labour. In Section 6.3 we shall discuss some methods that are used to estimate the value of home production. Different methods are used for different purposes. In Section 6.4 we shall pay attention to volunteer work, which is another form of productive informal labour. Finally, in Section 6.5 we shall focus on leisure and leisure activities.

6.2 Household production

The allocation of a person's time over the categories 'market work', 'household work' and 'leisure' depends greatly on the composition of the household to which the individual belongs, and on his or her position within that household; see, for example, Tables 6.1 and 6.2, both of which show data for The Netherlands in 1989. These tables show that total household labour time is the highest in households with children, and that a wife's share in it is larger than a husband's share. On the other hand, labour market participation and hours worked are the lowest for women in households with young children.

Table 6.1   Mean time allocation of women in various household types (hours/week)

Activity	Woman	Woman with children	Man & woman	Man & woman & 1 child	Man & woman & 2 children	Man & woman & 3 or more children	Total
Household labour	33.0	46.9	36.6	49.9	52.4	56.1	45.3
Paid labour	10.3	6.5	14.1	6.0	5.9	5.1	8.6
Volunteer labour	2.7	2.1	1.8	1.7	2.5	2.7	2.2
Leisure	64.3	56.8	57.5	53.7	51.2	49.4	55.1
Sleeping	57.7	55.7	58.0	56.7	56.0	54.7	56.7
	$N = 260$	$N = 78$	$N = 497$	$N = 289$	$N = 558$	$N = 196$	$N = 1878$

Source: Grift *et al.* (1989).

Table 6.2   Mean time allocation of men in various household types (hours/week)

Activity	Man	Man with children	Man & woman	Man & woman & 1 child	Man & woman & 2 children	Man & woman & 3 or more children	Total
Household labour	21.0	36.3	22.0	21.3	20.0	20.3	21.2
Paid labour	20.4	19.4	21.4	32.6	38.1	39.7	29.3
Volunteer labour	2.0	1.3	2.1	2.2	2.4	2.9	2.3
Leisure	68.8	52.4	66.1	57.1	52.9	50.7	59.8
Sleeping	55.8	58.6	56.4	54.8	54.6	54.4	55.4
	$N = 174$	$N = 11$	$N = 499$	$N = 233$	$N = 384$	$N = 140$	$N = 1441$

Source: Grift *et al.* (1989).

To analyse these differences, household production functions have to be incorporated into the models of household choice. In Section 2.5 we gave an example of such a model. Becker (1965) originally introduced Leontief production functions, with fixed technical coefficients. He allowed for the existence of several techniques, some more labour-intensive, others more capital- and/or market-good-intensive. Although the possibility of substitution between the two input factors (market goods and household labour time) was excluded within one production technique, households could still substitute time for market goods, or vice versa, by applying a combination of different production techniques.

In the day-to-day reality of household production, substitution is observed quite often. For example: (a) convenience food is substituted for food preparation time; (b) the services of day-care centers are substituted for a mother's care; (c) do-it-yourself production is substituted for the services of a craftsman. Some households choose a time-intensive form of production, while others choose a market-good-intensive household production method. Besides market goods and labour, households use the services of the durable goods that they own, and personal physical and/or psychic energy to produce final household commodities. The durables play the same role as capital in the production functions of firms. In the short run, the amount of durables that can be used for household production is assumed to be fixed. Labour and market goods are the variable input factors. The output consists of final consumption commodities.

In applied work, a list is often made of the activities that are labelled 'productive' activities and others that are labelled 'leisure' activities. However, one may find some of the productive activities to be rather pleasant. If we enjoy such activities, should not they be considered as leisure activities? For example, playing with children is considered to be 'child care', but for many parents it will be a leisure activity as well. If an activity serves a mixture of goals, or when two activities are done at the same time, it is called 'joint production'. Another example of joint production in the household is when a housewife is cleaning the house, keeping an eye on the children and listening to the radio at the same time. It is hard to determine how many hours are devoted to cleaning, how many to child care and how many to listening to the radio. We mentioned this problem earlier in the section about data collection in Chapter 1.

In Chapter 2 we discussed a simple form of Gronau's (1980) household production model, in which no joint production and no separate contributions of the partners are considered. Here, we shall first introduce an extension in which the separate contribution of the partners to household utility is analysed. Then we shall discuss Graham and Green's (1984) model, in which a form of joint production is introduced and which describes household production by husband and wife simultaneously.

A household production model

In analogy of Gronau's model of Section 2.5 is a household consumption model in which both partners participate in household production and market labour is introduced. The household has one joint utility function, which the partners intend to maximize. This model emphasizes that the interactions between the partners' choices is important.

$$\text{maximize} \quad U(z, l_f, l_m) \tag{6.1}$$

$$z = z_f + z_m$$
$$z_i = Z_i(h_i, x_i) \qquad i = f, m$$
$$h_i + l_i + t_i = T \qquad i = f, m$$
$$x = x_f + x_m$$
$$x = y_0 + w_f t_f + w_m t_m,$$

where

U = household utility function
x = expenditure on market goods
z_m, z_f = home-produced products by m and f
Z_m, Z_f = household production functions of m and f

h_f, h_m = household labour time of f and m
t_f, t_m = paid labour time of f and m
l_f, l_m = leisure time of f and m
w_f, w_m = fixed wage rates of f and m
y_0 = unearned household income.

In most models it is assumed that the household production functions are monotonic, strictly quasi-concave and differentiable, so that a utility maximum can be derived. The production functions of m and f are different if they show different efficiency. The household's full income $Y = y_0 + w_f T + w_m T$ is spent on market goods, leisure and household labour time.

Exercise 6.1
Show that in the optimum

$$\frac{\partial z_m / \partial h_m}{\partial z_f / \partial h_f} = \frac{w_m}{w_f} \tag{6.2}$$

assuming that there is an interior solution.

The result of Exercise 6.1 tells us that the ratio between marginal household productivities equals the ratio of the labour market productivities; the latter are expressed by the wage rates. Since it is assumed that the household production functions have positive decreasing marginal products and that they are not necessarily identical, the division of household labour and paid labour is optimal when the partner who is more efficient in household production than the other spends more time on household production, and the one whose market wage rate is higher performs more paid labour. Consequently, even if $w_m = w_f$, and m works more efficiently in the household than does f, then $m's$ marginal product when spending h_m^* hours in the household (see Figure 6.2) equals $f's$ marginal product when spending h_f^* hours ($h_m^* > h_f^*$), so m will spend more hours in the household.

Since this is a static model, the long-run consequences of this optimal choice stay out of sight. By working in a household, one learns and becomes more and more experienced in household production: the productivity per hour increases. By working in the labour market, the productivity of paid labour increases, which will normally lead to an increase in wages (see Chapter 11). Assuming that husband and wife have equal market wage rates at the time of marriage and that they decide to specialize because of differences in household productivity (one on paid labour and the other on household production), then an asymmetric development of their market wage rates and of their productivity at home will result. Because of differences in experience, their market wage rates will be quite unequal after some years. In general,

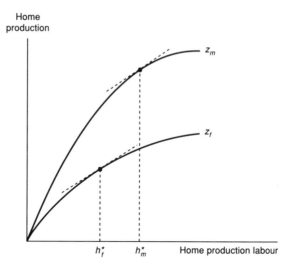

Figure 6.2   *Unequal efficiency of household production of two partners*

market productivity increases faster than does household productivity. Rational consumers would, of course, take this development into account when making a decision about the distribution of labour in their household. After a divorce, a non-working partner usually faces more financial problems than does a working partner. In our economies there are often barriers of (re)entering the labour market and low re-entry wages, as illustrated by the figures in Table 11.3 on page 190. These problems seem to be more serious than the problems of the working partner, who faces a loss of household production.

The empirical implementation of the model in Equation (6.1) requires that the household production functions and the utility function be specified. It would be hard to identify the parameters of this model because usually so little is observed within a household. If we knew who produced what and how, this problem could be solved. Instead of looking for an application of Equation (6.1) we introduce in the next section a model in which there is one joint household production function for both partners. Identification problems will, however, also arise in Graham and Green's model, but for other reasons.

Graham and Green's household production model

Graham and Green introduce a model in which household utility is determined by the level of consumption, and the level of 'effective' leisure of husband and wife. Consumption consists of market goods and of home-produced goods, as in Gronau's model. However, if the consumer enjoys direct utility from this activity, part of the time spent on home production can in fact be considered as leisure time. These hours, plus pure leisure time, together form what is called 'effective' leisure. The other part of the time spent on home production is called 'effective' home production time input. So home production allows for a form of joint production.

The model is:

maximize $U(x_M + z, c_m L_m, c_f L_f)$ (6.3)

s.t. $z = Z(x_z, (c_m)^a h_m, (c_f)^b h_f)$

$\qquad x_z + x_M = y_0 + w_m t_m^w + w_f t_f^w$

$\qquad t_i^w + h_i + l_i = T \qquad i = m, f$

$\qquad L_i = l_i + g_i(h_i) \qquad i = m, f,$

where L_i = effective leisure time, $i = m, f$
$\qquad\;\;\, c_i$ = measure for productivity (human capital), $i = m, f$
$\qquad\;\;\, x_z$ = market goods used as input in household production
$\qquad\;\;\, x_M$ = market goods for direct use
$\qquad\;\;\, g(.)$ = function explained below.

The amount of household production time that is considered as a perfect substitute for leisure is given by the functions: $g_m(h_m)$ and $g_f(h_f)$. These functions are assumed to be twice differentiable, concave and initially increasing:

$$0 \leq g'(h) \leq 1$$
$$g''(h) < 0$$
$$\lim_{h \to 0} g'(h) = 1 \qquad\qquad\qquad\qquad\qquad (6.4)$$
$$\lim_{h \to \infty} g'(h) = 0.$$

This means that negative effects of home production on utility are excluded, but the last hours contribute less than the first hours. The functional form chosen by Graham and Green is:

$$g_i(h_i) = h_i - \frac{1}{T^{\delta_i}} \cdot \frac{h_i^{1+\delta i}}{1 + \delta_i} \qquad i = m, f. \qquad (6.5)$$

This form allows for the possibilities of no jointness:

$\delta_i = 0$, then $g_i(h_i) = 0$, and effective leisure $L_i = l_i$,

as well as perfect jointness:

$\delta_i \to \infty$, then $g_i(h_i) \to h_i$, and $L_i \to l_i + h_i$.

When discussing the results of Gronau's model it has been mentioned already that human capital can be more labour-market orientated or more home-production orientated. The effect of human capital is captured in the factors c_m and c_f. It is assumed that these affect labour market productivity as well as home productivity. These effect on productivity in a paid job is reflected by the wage rates:

$$w_i = rc_i, \qquad i = m, f.$$

The effect of human capital on home production is reflected by:

$$(c_m)^a \text{ and } (c_f)^b,$$

where a and b are positive parameters, that can be less than, equal to, or greater than 1, depending on whether the individual is less productive, equally productive or more productive at home than in market work.

For the home production function, a Cobb–Douglas form is chosen:

$$z = \alpha(c_m^a h_m)^{\gamma_m} (c_f^b h_f)^{\gamma_f} x_z^\beta. \tag{6.6}$$

After deriving the first-order conditions (assuming that none of the non-negativity constraints is binding), the parameters of the model are estimated. Note that no special functional form of the utility function is needed to find these first order conditions.

Exercise 6.2

(a) Derive the first-order conditions for the Graham–Green model (Equation (6.3)), for interior solutions.

(b) Derive the Kuhn–Tucker conditions for the Graham–Green model.

(c) Use the results of (a) and (b) to show that the functional form of the utility function is only relevant if one of the partners is not participating in the labour force; if t_i are both > 0 the functional form of U is not needed for the household production decisions.

Exercise 6.3

Show that the virtual prices of labour (see Sections 4.4 and 5.3) are equal to $\partial U/\partial l_i - (\partial U/\partial z)w_i$, when i has no paid job ($t_i = 0$).

Graham and Green faced identification problems when estimating the parameters of this model, as we mentioned earlier. Since they needed two more pieces of information to overcome this problem, they considered several special cases (no jointness: $\delta_f = \delta_h = 0$; neutrality: $a = b = 1$; constant returns to scale: $\gamma_f + \gamma_h + \beta = 1$, or equal jointness and equal effect of human capital on household productivity: $\delta_f = \delta_h$ and $a = b$).

In two papers, Kerkhofs (1991, 1994) analyses the identification problems of the Graham–Green model and suggests some slight modifications of the Cobb–Douglas specification. He also considered the case of a non-working partner, $t_i = 0$. However, the estimation results are still not satisfactory. Therefore Kerkhofs suggests using the more flexible quadratic specification of the household production function:

$$z = \beta_m h_m + \beta_f h_f + \tfrac{1}{2}\gamma_{mm}(h_m)^2 + \tfrac{1}{2}\gamma_{ff}(h_f)^2 + \gamma_{mf} h_m h_f. \tag{6.7}$$

The z in Equation (6.7) is the value added in the production process. This option is chosen because the input of market goods x_z, used in the production process, is not observed. The estimated values of jointness parameters δ_m and δ_f are in this model 0.14 and 0.22 respectively, which suggests that the jointness is more important for females than for males.

In all household choice models it is difficult to identify differences in preferences from differences in production technology. In previous models it was assumed that (some) home products and market goods are perfect substitutes, but differences in perceived quality may be reflected in the preference structure. For instance, a mother may subjectively consider her own care for her young children to be better (of a higher quality) than professional child care. This identification problem also complicates the valuation of home production.

6.3 The value of household production

Home production contributes to the welfare of a household and to the welfare of a country. Comparing the welfare levels of households or countries only on the basis of income could give a wrong impression of how wealthy these households or countries are. Now a days most economists will agree with this statement, but a question that remains is how the value of home production should be determined. Since there is no market and no market price for home-produced goods and services, it is not simply a case of Quantity × Price. This kind of problem also exists with the production of the government: there is no market and no market price for public goods. However, the production of the government does appear in the national accounts; it is valued by the money that is paid as salaries to government employees. This method cannot be applied to home production, however, since no salaries are paid. Several methods have been developed to estimate the value of home production, but the outcome can vary considerably with the method used. Some examples are given in Table 6.3. There is no international agreement about the valuation method for home production.

Input and output methods

Here we shall focus on the assessment of a monetary value of household production at the micro level. Two kinds of method are distinguished: input

Table 6.3   Some estimates of the value of household production

Year	Name	Country	Period	Percentage of GNP
1921	Mitchel	USA	1909–29	25–31
1941	Kuznets	USA	1929	26.3
1958	Clark	UK	1956	43 of NNP
1966	Morgan, Siragedin, Baenvaldt	USA	1929–65	38
1970	Bruyn–Hundt	Netherlands	1964	12–39 of NNP
1972	Nordhaus, Tobin	USA	1929–65	46–54
1973	Ec. Council	Japan	1955–70	8.7–11.2
1974	Weinrobe	USA	1960–70	16–34
1978	Murphy	USA	1960–70	34–38
1982	Santti	Finland	1980	42

Source: Bruyn-Hundt (1985).

and output. Both measure the value added of home production. Input methods concentrate on production costs: first household labour time is measured and then a price is attached to each hour. Output methods measure the value added as the difference between the (market) value of the products and the price of the market input, consisting of non-durable goods and (services of) durable goods. We shall follow Homan (1988) in his discussion of these methods.

Homan compares two input methods:

1. The market cost method; and
2. The opportunity cost method and a modified opportunity cost method;

and three output methods:

3. The production function method;
4. The income evaluation approach; and
5. The contingent value method.

We add one more output method to this list, namely a very direct measurement method proposed and applied by Fitzgerald and Wicks (1990):

6. Direct measurement of physical output.

A description of the various methods

The market cost method
The procedure to evaluate production of this kind is based on the market prices of labour input. One has to look for the market equivalent of the

home-produced goods and the wages paid in that sector. The time spent on preparing a meal is valued at the wage rate of a professional cook; the time spent on child care at the wage rate of a professional nursery nurse; the time spent on painting the house at the wage rate of a house painter, and so on.

Value added $= h_m w_{pr} + h_f w_{pr}$,

where, $w_{pr} = $ price paid to the professional market equivalent worker; and h_m and h_f are m's and f's household labour time.

Exercise 6.4
Indicate the weak points of this method (think of the choice of wage rate, the number of hours, and efficiency).

The opportunity cost method
This method uses the individual's own market wage rate to evaluate the hours spent on home production. In the models where the choice between labour market participation and home production is analysed, it is assumed that the value of the first hours spent on home production is higher than an individual's value in the market (represented by his or her wage rate). The income the individual misses by spending time on home production is found by the multiplication of his/her wage rate by these hours.

Value added $= h_m w_m + h_f w_f$,

where w_m and w_f are the net (after tax) wage rates of m and f.
Criticisms of this method have to do with such things as:

(a) Why should the value of home production performed by a well-paid lawyer be worth more than that of an unskilled labourer?
(b) If the number of hours individuals spend on the labour market are rationed, h_i does not represent their optimal choice.
(c) The wage rate of a non-working individual is not known (retired people, full-time housewives): it must be estimated.
(d) Efficiency differences in home production.

A modified opportunity cost method
If non-participation in the labour market is, in fact, an optimal choice, it means that the value of all hours spent on home production, including the last, is greater than the individual's market wage rate. In that case, one tries to discover for what wage rate the individual would be willing to supply at least one hour of labour to the market. This wage rate is called *the reservation wage rate*, w^R (see also Section 10.3 on page 172).

Then the Value of Home Production $= h_m w^*_m + h_f w^*_f$,

where $w^*_i = w_i$ if i has a paid job; and
$w^*_i = w^R_i$ if $w_i < w^R_i$, and i has no paid job, $i = m, f$.

Production function method
In Section 2.5 Gronau's model was introduced in its general form. When putting this model into practice, Gronau started by estimating the logarithm of the marginal product function:

$$f_h = \partial Z/\partial h = w$$
$$\log f_h = \log \partial Z/\partial h = \log w = \alpha_0 + \alpha_1 h + \alpha_2 s, \qquad (6.8)$$

in which s is a vector of variables affecting the value of marginal productivity at home. Total production is derived by integration:

$$\partial Z/\partial h = \exp(\alpha_0 + \alpha_1 h + \alpha_2 s),$$

so that:

$$Z = \int_0^H \partial Z/\partial h =$$

$$[\exp(\alpha_0 + \alpha_2 s)(\exp(\alpha_1 H) - 1)]/\alpha_1.$$

Since market goods and home-produced goods are assumed to be perfect substitutes, home-produced goods have the same 'price' as market goods.

Graham and Green define a Cobb–Douglas household production function which allows for joint production (see section 6.2). After estimating the parameters of the production function and substituting the value of input factors, the output is known. As we know, the Graham–Green estimates are not very convincing: they often have the 'wrong' (theoretically unacceptable) sign. The value of household production in Gronau's, as well as in Graham and Green's model, depends on the choice of the functional form of the production function and on the possibility of finding reliable parameter estimates.

The income evaluation approach
Homan (1988) applied a subjective income evaluation method to the measurement of the value of home production. As utility of income depends on family composition, it may just as well depend on the amount of home production that household members perform. In the neo-classical theory, utility functions are only an ordinal representation of preferences, and utility levels of different households are not comparable. Van Praag (1968) introduced what he calls the 'income evaluation question' (IEQ), and with that he introduced a kind of cardinal utility concept. The method is described in more detail in Chapter 7. If a household is asked what amount of money it would

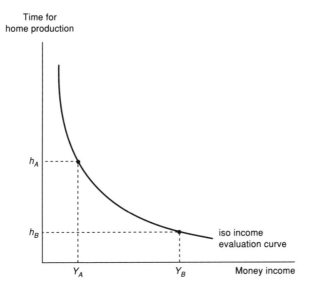

Figure 6.3 Valuation of home production with the income evaluation question

need in order to evaluate its situation as 'good', the answer can be interpreted as the minimum amount to reach the utility level 'good' (the cost or expenditure needed to attain a utility level corresponding to the level 'good'). This minimum amount depends on the household's own income, on the income level of its reference group, on family composition, and on household production. Two families with similar composition and similar income are not equally wealthy if one family has more hours available for home production (and leisure activities) than the other.

The numbers of hours available for home production does, in fact, affect the answers to the income evaluation question. If households that have 10 hours fewer available for home production say that they need more money to reach a 'good' welfare level, this can be used as an estimate for the value of home production. This is illustrated in Figure 6.3: the household is equally well-off in positions *A* and *B*, so the value of $(h_A - h_B)$ hours of home production equals $(Y_B - Y_A)$. We shall return to this method and give more details in Chapters 7 and 12.

The contingent value method
According to Homan (1988), the basic idea behind the contingent evaluation approach to estimation of the monetary value of non-market goods is the construction of a hypothetical market where this good is traded; see also Brookshire and Crocker (1981). After describing the (non-market) good, its qualities and the current available quantity, the interviewer explains to the respondent how the market operates. Then the quantity is changed and the respondent is asked to state his or her 'willingness to pay' to preclude the change, or his/her 'willingness to accept' compensation for the change.

Table 6.4   Mean willingness to pay for household production,
opportunity costs and average number of hours in
household production

	Per week ($)	Per hour ($)
Average number of hours	23.88	
Mean total willingness to pay (total value)	117.31	4.91
Mean net willingness to pay (net value)	101.10	4.23
Mean total opportunity cost	16.21	0.68
Mean opportunity cost at the margin (marginal value)		2.22

Source: Quah (1987).

Quah (1987) introduced the contingent evaluation approach into the research area of the evaluation of home production. Quah introduces a hypothetical auction. First the respondent is asked whether s/he would be willing
to pay, say, $2 if s/he could be released from two hours of home work. A
hired substitute worker would do the work for him or her. If the answer is
'no', the price is lowered, until s/he accepts. If the answer is 'yes', the price
is raised until s/he refuses. In this way the value of the 'last' two hours of
home production is determined (the marginal value). The procedure is then
repeated for another two hours. For these hours a different price may result.
In this way, Quah continues to determine the value of home production.
Some of Quah's results are represented in Table 6.4. The average number
of hours spent on home production is about 24 and the mean willingness to
pay is a little over $4. This is much higher than the mean opportunity costs
($0.68) we could expect, but also higher than the mean opportunity cost at
the margin. We would expect this value to be equal to the willingness to
pay at the margin (which is not in the table).

Direct measurement of physical output
Fitzgerald and Wicks (1990) used a very direct evaluation approach by
measuring household outputs in physical units and attributing market prices
to them. It is not always simple to define meaningful output units of activities, as can be seen from the examples we give in Table 6.5. Fitzgerald and
Wicks distinguish eight groups of activities and define the unit of measurement for each activity. To obtain market prices for these output units, they
chose what firms would charge for an item as close as possible to the household
production output. For example, they priced meals as the average meals
sold by 'family' restaurants and fast food establishments. For the price of
one machine load of laundry, local laundry services were contacted. To calculate the value added of a person's output the quantity produced is simply
multiplied by market price, and the value of any intermediate goods (but
not capital) used in the activity is subtracted.

Table 6.5   Some examples of household production and their unit definition

Activity	Unit definition
1 Cleaning (23 activities)	
Garbage disposal	bag
Vacuuming	room/each time
Bathroom floor mopping	bathroom
2 Child care (4 activities)	
Child feeding	child/each time
Child changing	child/each time
3 Meals (1 activity)	
Meal preparation and cleanup	meal for 1 person
4 Care of clothing (4 activities)	
Washing and drying	machine load
Ironing	article of clothing
5 Repair and maintenance (22 activities)	
Plumbing repair	job
Exterior painting	house
Vehicle tune-up	job
6 Food production (5 activities)	
Fishing harvest	pound
7 Miscellaneous (4 activities)	
Tax preparation	federal/state return
8 Activities for which output is hour	
Child sitting (3 activities)	hour

Source: Fitzgerald and Wicks (1990).

A person's average productivity at an activity can be calculated by dividing his or her production by his/her labour time. Fitzgerald and Wicks made a comparison between household productivity and the productivity of firms. They found that for some activities, households are more productive than firms, but for other activities, firms are more productive. For 50 per cent of cases the difference is not significant.

Discussion

All evaluation methods are based on the imputation of a price, either to the time spent on home production, or to total value of the output of the production processes. In an economy where it is possible to trade labour time against consumption, rational decisions are based on a comparison of gains from supplying time in the labour market set against the losses of sacrificing home production and leisure. This means that when labour market behaviour of individuals is analysed, the value of an hour spent in the labour market is to be compared with the value of an hour spent in the household. The input methods are fairly easy to apply, but the choice of wage rate is quite a problem, and measuring the time spent on household production leaves out the point of joint production.

For welfare comparison we would prefer an objective output method, such as the direct measurement of Fitzgerald and Wicks, or a subjective output method, such as van Praag's income evaluation approach. The use of production functions is theoretically attractive, but the application is far from straightforward.

In the models of Section 6.2, the optimal choice for working time, t, and household labour time, h, provides the optimal choice for leisure, since:

$$t + h + l = T.$$

In the next sections we take a closer look at leisure activities.

6.4   Volunteer labour supply

Volunteer labour is an organized form of labour that is supplied to the community by individuals on a free basis. The volunteer receives no wage or income in kind. Helping a sick neighbour is not considered as volunteer labour (because an individual doing so is not associated with a 'sick neighbour help organization'), but dealing with the administration of a soccer club *is*. According to Hodgkinson and Weitzman (1984) over 80 million adults in the USA volunteered 8.4 billion hours of labour to organizations in 1980, equivalent to over 5 per cent of full-time employment (FTE) in the economy. In the sample analysed by Menchik and Weisbrod (1987), 30 per cent of households supplied some volunteer labour; in Dutch time-use data between 1985 and 1990 it was found that around 13 per cent of the population spends some time as a volunteer (Intomart 1985, 1990). Volunteer labour is especially important for certain industries producing collective-type goods, such as health, education and charity. But also sports clubs, political parties and churches would face great financial (or manpower) problems if their volunteers gave up. The individual who supplies this kind of labour does not receive money nor in-kind benefits, so why do a number of people supply this kind of labour?

Our starting point for the analysis of individual choices has always been rationality. Menchik and Weisbrod hold on to this assumption and distinguish two kinds of models that are used to explain volunteer labour supply: a 'consumption' model and an 'investment' model. The first model treats volunteering (a gift of labour) and charity contributions as normal utility-bearing consumer goods. The second model considers volunteering as a way of obtaining on-the-job experience, which increases the human capital of the volunteer: the earnings of the volunteer could increase in a future paid job. In Chapter 11 we shall analyse investments in human capital and return to this subject.

In the consumption model it is interesting to know whether charity and volunteering are complements or substitutes. Do people with a shortage of time ease their consciences by giving money, or are those who volunteer

Table 6.6   Tobit regression estimates: annual hours of volunteer
work, persons with annual income of $50,000 or less, 1973

Explanatory variables	Coefficient*
Fulinc	0.0150
Fulinc squared	-0.1571×10^{-6}
Nwage	-21.61
Price	-314.4
Female	31.91
Married	37.36
Young children	18.05
Other children	53.93
Age	19.56
Age squared	-0.2282
Large city	74.54
Medium city	78.12
Suburb	38.36
Small city	70.95
Background giving	-1.535
Background religious	-16.18
Background education	57.03
Local government	0.1019
Constant	-497.2

Note: All coefficients other than for young children are statistically significant at
the 0.01 level. Sample size $N = 901$.

Source: Menchik and Weisbrod (1987).

also the ones who spend the most on charity? If the investment motive is
most important, one would expect that the wage rate of the individual has a
negative effect on the voluntary time, because the opportunity costs are higher.
Menchik and Weisbrod estimate a Tobit model, in which the hours of volunteer work are a function of full income, net wage rate and some other
variables that might affect preferences (see Table 6.6).

Menchik and Weisbrod find a positive, but decreasing, income effect (see
Fulinc' and 'Fulinc squared' in Table 6.6), so supply increases with full
income. Full income is defined as the individual's money income if s/he
worked full-time at a market wage rate, rather than volunteered any labour.
It includes unearned income such as property income, and imputed rental
income from owner-occupied homes. Besides full income, the net wage rate
is introduced as the opportunity cost or 'own price' of volunteer labour.
Supply decreases with the net wage rate (Nwage), which shows a negative
coefficient. The variable 'Price' is the price of giving money. Variation in
price is induced by the tax system. Giving one dollar will cost the donor
only 70 cents if the marginal tax rate is 30 per cent, and if charity is deductible. If the tax rate varies over states and varies with income level,
there is price variation for charity. The coefficient of 'Price' is negative,
implying that contributions of money and time are complements, rather than

substitutes. Furthermore, women supply more than men, married people more than unmarried, and those with children at home more than those without children.

6.5   Household leisure and leisure activities

The working hours that go with full-time jobs depend on the number of hours worked per week and the number of days off. While these vary widely over countries, the average number of hours a year of a full-time job decreased considerably in the whole Western world during the first half of the twentieth century. The length of the average working week decreased and the number of holidays increased. In Western Europe this trend continued in the second half of the century, while in the USA it stabilized at approximately the 1940 level. Coleman and Pencavel (1993a, 1993b) analysed the working hours of male and female workers in the USA between 1940 and 1988. For white male workers they found an average decrease of the working week from 44.1 hours in 1940 to 42.2 in 1988, and for black male workers from 44.5 hours in 1940 to 39.6 in 1988. For whites with little schooling, the working week decreased by more than the average 1.9 hours. For blacks with little schooling by more than the average 4.9 hours. For those with a higher education it increased rather than decreased. The annual number of weeks that white and black men work increased between 1940 and 1988 from 45 to 46.6, and from 43.1 to 44.5 respectively, so there was little change in the average annual number of hours worked: from 2018 to 2012 hours.

For US white and black female workers, similar trends are observed: the average number of hours per week decreased gradually from 40.6 in 1940 to 35.9 in 1980 for white workers, and from 42.2 to 36.5 for black workers. At the time of writing, 60 per cent of the female labour force consists of married women, and in 1940 this was a little over 20 per cent, so there has been a significant change in the participation rate of married women. The average number of weeks work for female workers has increased from 42 to 44.5. Their annual averages decreased from 1763 to 1632 hours for white women, and from 1838 to 1649 hours for black women. According to Schor (1991), a full time US manufacturing employee works, on average at the time of writing, 320 hours more than his/her counterpart in Germany or France.

Household production became more efficient because of the availability of consumer durables and convenience goods, so output can remain constant using less time. Both developments – more efficient home production and shorter working weeks, might have resulted in an easy and relaxed lifestyle, but people still seem to be busy all the time. One reason is that total household production did not remain constant: it increased. For example, as washing clothes is now so easy, more laundry is done now than 100 years ago. Linder (1970) noted in his book, *The Harried Leisure Class*, that household incomes have grown faster than non-labour time. So people can buy more 'things', but to consume, use and maintain these goods one needs more time. Since wages have gone up, services have become relatively expensive compared to industrial products, so the substitution effect causes people to buy relatively more material goods than services.

Some industrial products and some services make household production less-time intensive, others create the desire for extra or new activities. Households can use their extra income to improve the quality of their home production, but not all activities are equally capable of absorbing extra market goods. A way out for the individual is to try to apply forms of joint production for household and leisure activities, of which Linder gives a splendid example:

After dinner, he may find himself drinking Brazilian coffee, smoking a Dutch cigar, nipping a French cognac, reading The New York Times, listening to a Brandenburg Concerto and entertaining his Swedish wife – all at the same time, with varying degrees of success. (Linder, 1970)

Joint production is not included in the Becker models, in which only one commodity at a time was produced, but in the Graham and Green model an attempt was made to include forms of joint production. The problems that go with such models are not only identification problems, but also problems of data collection. Respondents are usually asked for their main activity during a certain period of time (say, 15 minutes) and not for *all* their activities (see Chapter 1). The measurement of joint production is still exceptional.

For most households, leisure time is concentrated in the evenings, the weekends and on holidays. The definition of leisure provided by Juster *et al.* (1983) was refined by Firestone and Shelton (1994) to differentiate between two types of leisure activity: non-domestic and domestic leisure. For non-domestic leisure, people have to leave their homes – for instance, to go and play tennis, to have dinner with friends, to watch a soccer game, to visit a bar and so on. Non-domestic leisure requires some planning and an initial decision to undertake the activity. Once the decision and appointment are made, the leisure activity becomes some kind of a commitment, like work and household production. Domestic leisure is often the remainder of the day, when work and housework are finished. Domestic leisure activities are often carried out as free time comes available, with little advance planning and in conjunction with other activities, and they are often compatible with housework and child care responsibilities. Juster and Stafford (1991) give an international comparison of time allocation averages of men and women in six countries; see Table 6.7.

Kooreman and Kapteyn (1987) estimate a time-allocation model for husbands and wives using data from one-earner and two-earner families. In their model, utility depends on total household consumption and the time spent on various activities by both partners (not simply one broad category of 'leisure'). They find that the total leisure of the husband decreases with

Table 6.7 Average time use (hours per week)

Activity	Men						Women					
	US 1981	Japan 1985	USSR 1985 (Pskov)	Finland 1979	Hungary 1977	Sweden 1984	US 1981	Japan 1985	USSR 1985 (Pskov)	Finland 1979	Hungary 1977	Sweden 1984
Total work	57.8	55.5	65.7	57.8	63.7	57.9	54.4	55.6	66.3	61.1	68.9	55.5
Market work	44.0	52.0	53.8	44.0	50.8	39.8	23.9	24.6	39.3	32.5	35.1	23.7
Commuting	3.5	4.5	5.2	3.0	4.0	3.8	2.0	1.2	3.4	2.5	2.6	2.1
Housework	13.8	3.5	11.9	13.8	12.9	18.1	30.5	31.0	27.0	28.6	33.8	31.8
Personal care	68.2	72.4	67.8	72.5	74.0	70.9	71.6	72.1	69.8	72.7	73.6	73.8
Sleep	57.9	60.0	56.9	60.2	59.4	55.3	59.9	57.0	58.2	60.9	60.4	56.9
Leisure	41.8	40.3	34.6	38.1	30.4	39.0	41.9	40.3	32.0	33.6	25.3	38.5
Adult education	0.6	1.2	1.0	0.9	1.9	1.0	0.4	2.2	2.6	1.2	1.3	1.0
Social interaction	14.9	8.0	7.8	12.1	7.1	9.6	17.6	7.0	9.6	10.2	4.6	11.2
Active leisure	5.6	5.3	4.1	4.3	2.4	7.2	4.2	3.6	3.0	2.7	1.8	8.4
Passive leisure	20.8	25.5	21.7	20.8	19.0	21.2	19.8	27.5	16.8	19.5	17.6	17.9
TV	12.7	17.3	14.5	9.7	10.2	13.4	11.5	21.4	11.2	7.7	9.2	10.8
Total	168.0	168.0	168.0	168.0	168.0	168.0	168.0	168.0	168.0	168.0	168.0	168.0

Source: Juster and Stafford (1991).

age until he reaches 50; after that, total leisure increases. For both one-earner and two-earner households it turns out that the husband's education has a small positive effect on the time spent by both partners in listening to the radio, watching television, reading books and so on (domestic leisure), but no significant effect on the time spent on 'entertainment and social activities' or on 'organizational activities, hobbies and sports'. The wife's education has a slightly negative effect on the time spent on 'radio' and so on for both husband and wife, and a positive effect on her time spent on 'organizations' etc. The wife's income share has a negative effect on the time the husband spends on 'entertainment', but no significant effect on her own time for 'entertainment'. No significant effects of the presence of children, or the age of husband and wife, on leisure activities were found. The presence of children did, of course, affect time spent on child care.

In the models of time allocation by Firestone *et al.* and Kooreman *et al.*, the interaction between partners in a household limited optimal choices of numbers of hours. The effect of the employment status on time allocation of men and women is analysed, but there is no place for the possibility that synchronizing leisure activities of partners may increase the utility for both partners. The utility of going to the theatre with a partner may be higher than the utility of going independently of each other. The same may hold for holidays. As soon as the leisure hours of partners do not keep pace with each other its utility value may decrease. The timing of activities may be one of the extra problems (restrictions) for households with multiple obligations, or irregular working hours.

Besides leisure during working weeks, holidays contribute considerably to household leisure. Again, the differences between US and European workers are considerable. If individual choices are reflected in the results of the negotiations between employers and the employees' unions, it seems that, unlike the US worker, European workers value holidays more highly than extra income. In Table 6.8 the holidays of employees (during which they receive their normal wages) in some European countries are listed. The holidays of US workers vary more than those of their European colleagues, with length determined more on an individual basis; and they are usually shorter.

In the neo-classical model, leisure appeared in the utility function as a variable on its own: $u = U(q_1, \ldots, q_N, l)$. However, leisure activities, like home production, require time and market goods as input: $z_l = f(q_M, l)$. The market goods for leisure activities have become an important industry (for example, TV sets, CD players, boats, football stadiums, camping sites, skis, etc.) since the amount of non-working time on both a weekly and a yearly basis, as well as income, have increased considerably during the twentieth century. Leisure is not equivalent to 'doing nothing'; it has become part of our agenda, just like paid labour and home production. The microeconomic analysis of leisure behaviour is not yet well developed, especially not for households, in which synchronization problems can play an important role.

Part of what most people will call leisure, should in fact be considered as time spent on investments in human capital. A human being can only supply

Table 6.8   Length of vacation in European countries

Country	By law	By agreement
Austria	5 weeks	Conform law
Belgium	4 weeks	5 weeks
Denmark		5 weeks
Spain	30 days	4.5 to 5 weeks
Finland	5 weeks	5 to 6 weeks
France	5 weeks	5 to 6 weeks
Great Britain		4 to 6 weeks
Greece	4 weeks	Conform law
Republic of Ireland	3 weeks	4 weeks
Iceland	4 weeks, 4 days	Conform law
Italy		4 to 6 weeks
Luxembourg	5 weeks	25 to 30 days
Norway	4 weeks	Conform law
The Netherlands	4 weeks	4 to 5 weeks
Portugal	30 days	4.5 to 5 weeks
Sweden	5 weeks	5 to 8 weeks
Switzerland	4 weeks	4 to 5 weeks

Source: European Trade Union Institute (1988–9).

labour in the market or at home if s/he can dispose of a certain amount of energy and knowledge. Health, knowledge and experience are the main components of human capital, and especially for health, we need time to sleep and to relax. Sleeping, which might have been thought of as the ultimate form of leisure, should be considered as an essential form of (replacement) investment in human capital, certainly for some hours every day. Biddle and Hamermesh (1990) emphasize that it is wrong to view sleeping hours as a predetermined deduction from the 24 hours of the day. At least part of the sleep time is a reserve on which people can draw when economic circumstances make other uses of time more attractive. If sleep affects productivity, the wage rate also depends on sleep, and not only on the time spent on education and training.

In this section we showed that leisure, which is a choice variable in the neo-classical utility function, is not just a 'left-over'. Leisure activities should be treated like home production. The main difference between the two is that for home production the final product is important: something is created (a meal, for instance), but for leisure activities this is not the case. There is usually no material final product; only the hours spent on the activity add to our utility, but hours gain value by the input of market goods.

6.6   Summary

In this chapter we analysed the choices made by households concerning their time spent on household production, volunteer labour and leisure in relation the time spent on paid labour. It is generally accepted that household production has value, but it is not easy to determine this value because the household products are usually not observed. Even if they are observed their price is not known, because they are not sold in a market. Therefore, several methods have been proposed to evaluate household production. Another form of productive activity without a market price is volunteer labour. While the products of household production are used by the household itself, the products of volunteer labour are for the benefits of others. The rational consumer may consider volunteer labour as a form of investment in (his or her own) human capital, or as a form of charity that has a positive effect on his or her utility level. Volunteer labour illustrates the fact that households should not be assumed to act completely independently of what is happening in the rest of society. Finally, we looked at leisure activities. Leisure activities also require market goods to increase their value for the individual. The choice between labour, household production and leisure show quite different patterns in Europe and the USA.

CHAPTER 7

Household Expenditures and Children

7.1 Introduction

In the previous chapters considerable attention has been paid to household activities related to earning income. This is one explanation for the scant attention paid until now to the role of children in households. Although some children contribute to household income, their contribution is usually small in quantitative terms.

However, things are different as soon as we look at expenditure. The presence or absence of children strongly influences not only expenditure patterns but also patterns of time use in households. They play a distinct role in other sectors of the economy as well. Children are an important target group in many areas of government policy: education is the largest expenditure item in the government budget in many countries. Child allowances, fellowships and child protection are other examples of government policy directly affecting children. Many firms direct their product and marketing activities towards children, with toys, clothing and food items being obvious examples.

As with other issues, economists look at behaviour with respect to children in terms of broadly defined costs and benefits. In this case most costs and benefits are in terms of intangibles. Love, companionship, entertainment, pride and social status are on the benefit side; time for child care, money spent on children, and anxiety are on the cost side.

Much of the literature on economic aspects of children has tried to provide estimates of the costs of children. In an attempt to avoid much of the confusion that has characterized this literature, we make an explicit distinction between the following three questions[1] in this chapter:

1. How do children affect the expenditure patterns of a household?
2. How do children affect parents' time allocation?
3. How much do parents spend on their children?
4. How much income does a family with children need (in a sense to be defined), compared to a childless family?

The four questions will be addressed in subsequent sections. Throughout this chapter we look at behaviour of households with a given number of children. The issue of the decision to have children will receive attention in Chapter 8.

7.2 How do children affect expenditures?

In a household consisting of more than one person the budget must be shared. Since the activities of parents and children are different, the presence of children will change the allocation of the budget over the various expenditure categories. Young children use toys and drink milk, but they do not drink alcoholic beverages. There exists an extensive literature on how, in terms of functional form, children should be incorporated in demand equations, to asses the effect of their presence on household expenditure. Two simple possibilities are *demographic translation* and *demographic scaling*.

Demographic translation

If $g_i(y, p)$ are the original demand equations (without demographic effects), then the demographically translated demand equations have the form:

$$g_i^*(y, p, z) = d_i + g_i((y - \sum_k p_k d_k), p), \ i = 1, \ldots, n, \tag{7.1}$$

where d_i is a translation parameter depending on the demographic variable z. Thus translation has two effects. On the one hand, the income-independent quantity of good i is increased by d_i, while on the other the income-dependent quantity changes, since the budget for the income-dependent part is decreased by $\sum_k p_k d_k$. In terms of cost functions, demographic translation replaces the original cost function $c(u, p)$ by:

$$c^*(u, p) = c(u, p) + \sum_{k=1}^{n} p_i d_i. \tag{7.2}$$

Demographic scaling

The demographically scaled demand equations have the form:

$$g_i^*(y, p, z) = d_i \cdot g_i(y, (p_1 d_1, \ldots, p_n d_n)). \tag{7.3}$$

Thus scaling has two effects as well. Assume $d_i > 1$. On the one hand, there is a demand increase caused by the multiplication by d_i; on the other, we have (most probably) a decrease, since replacing p_i by $p_i d_i$ decreases demand. Scaling replaces the original cost function $c(u, p)$ by:

$$c^*(u, p) = c(u; p_1 d_1, \ldots, p_n d_n). \tag{7.4}$$

Exercise 7.1

Assume that the original demand system satisfies adding-up, that is, $\Sigma_k p_k x_k = y$, where y is income and x_k the quantity of good k.
(a) Show that the demographically translated demand system and the demographically scaled demand system satisfy adding-up.
(b) Show that Equation (7.2) implies Equation (7.1) and that Equation (7.4) implies Equation (7.3).

Exercise 7.2

Consider the case of the linear expenditure system:

$$x_i = \gamma_i + \frac{\beta_i}{p_i}(y - \sum_k p_k \gamma_k). \qquad (7.5)$$

(a) Show that demographic translation replaces γ_i by $\gamma_i^* = \gamma_i + d_i$.
(b) Show that demographic scaling replaces γ_i by $\gamma_i^* = \gamma_i d_i$.
(c) Assume that $d_i = \delta_{0i} + \delta_{1i} K$. K is a dummy variable for the presence of children below six years old. Show that translation and scaling are identical in this example.

There obviously exist more flexible ways to incorporate demographic variables in a demand system. In the LES example, one might make the β_is dependent on demographics.

Some empirical results

The methods of demographic scaling and translation have been applied in several studies. In some studies the translation or scaling parameter d_i is estimated for every expenditure category, i, but in most studies only one parameter, d, is estimated. This means that it is assumed that the demographic variables affect the expenditures on all categories in the same way. This d parameter is a function of demographic variables, such as the number of people belonging to a household, and their sexes and ages.

Wunderink (1988) applied the scaling method (in an indirect addi-log model), for households with two parents, using the following specification:

$$d = 1 + \alpha_1 K_1 + \alpha_2 K_2,$$

where, K_1 = the number of children younger than 12; and
K_2 = the number of children between the ages of 12 and 18.
The estimated values of α_1 and α_2 are $\alpha_1 = 0.13$ and $\alpha_2 = 0.48$ respectively. The older children have a greater affect on the scaling function than do the younger ones. Although the values of α_1 and α_2 depend on the specification of the utility function and the scaling function, they are typical for most research results in this field.

Table 7.1 Estimated budget shares of food, clothing and miscellaneous expenditure in families with different total budgets and family sizes

Expenditure ($/week)	Food Children			Clothing Children			Miscellaneous Children		
	1	2	3	1	2	3	1	2	3
Qes Model									
225	0.61	.65	.69	.14	.12	.09	.25	.23	.22
325	0.53	.57	.60	.17	.16	.15	.30	.27	.25
425	0.47	.50	.54	.18	.18	.17	.35	.32	.29
525	0.42	.45	.49	.17	.18	.18	.41	.37	.33
625	0.38	.41	.44	.16	.17	.17	.46	.42	.39
725	0.33	.37	.40	.15	.16	.16	.52	.47	.44
Les Model									
225	0.62	.68	.73	.14	.13	.13	.24	.19	.14
325	0.52	.56	.60	.16	.16	.15	.32	.28	.25
425	0.47	.50	.53	.17	.17	.17	.36	.33	.30
525	0.44	.46	.48	.18	.18	.18	.38	.36	.34
625	0.41	.43	.45	.19	.18	.18	.40	.39	.37
725	0.40	.41	.43	.19	.19	.19	.41	.40	.38

Source: Pollak and Wales (1978).

Pollak and Wales (1978) estimated the average budget shares 'food', 'clothing' and 'miscellaneous' for families with one, two and three children with different total budgets, using the Linear Expenditure System in one study and the Quadratic Expenditure System in another. The results, given in Table 7.1, show that the predictions are somewhat different for the two models, but the general trends are the same:

(1) The expenditure pattern is different at different budget levels.
(2) The lower the budget, the higher the food expenditure share (Engel's law).
(3) The more children, the higher the food budget share.
(4) An increase in the number of children seems to have a similar effect on the budget allocation as an income decrease.

7.3 How do children affect time allocation?

The presence of children in a household not only affects the expenditure in a household, it also affects the time allocation of the parents. In Tables 7.2 and 7.3 we repeat some numbers from Tables 6.1 and 6.2 on the average time allocation per week of the parents in households with children. It is clear that children affect the time allocation of the mother differently from the time allocation of the father.

Many women stop working or take a part-time job when they have young children, men usually do not. Tables 7.2 and 7.3 show that, on average,

Table 7.2   *Average time allocation of men in families with different compositions, The Netherlands, 1985 (hours per week)*

	Male & female	Parents & 1 child	Parents & 2 children	Parents & 3 or more children
Household labour	22.0	21.3	20.0	20.3
Paid labour	21.4	32.6	38.1	39.7
Volunteer labour	2.1	2.2	2.4	2.9
Leisure	66.1	57.1	52.9	50.7
Sleeping	56.4	54.8	54.6	54.4

Source: Grift, Siegers and Suy (1989).

Table 7.3 *Average time allocation of women in families with different compositions, The Netherlands, 1985 (hours per week)*

	Male & female	Parents & 1 child	Parents & 2 children	Parents & 3 or more children
Household labour	36.6	49.9	52.4	56.1
Paid labour	14.1	6.0	5.9	5.1
Volunteer labour	1.8	1.7	2.5	2.7
Leisure	57.5	53.7	51.2	49.4
Sleeping	58.0	56.7	56.0	54.7

Source: Grift, Siegers and Suy (1989).

men's market labour time increases and female's market labour time decreases with the number of children. Mothers spend more time than fathers on household labour.

Many couples wish to have children. Contraceptives can be used if couples do not wish to have children. The number of children that couples would like to have could be considered as a choice variable and so it should appear in the household utility function. A distinction is usually made between the number of children and the 'quality' (Becker, 1981; and Nerlove *et al.*, 1987), for example:

$$u = U(z, n, Q), \tag{7.6}$$

where: n = number of children; Q = quality per child; z = household commodities.

It is assumed that every additional child is appreciated by the parents, and has a positive effect on their utility (when q and z are constant). Moreover, it is assumed that $\partial U/\partial q > 0$ and, of course, also $\partial U/\partial z > 0$. Quality originates from child care, and for child care the parents need time and market goods. That is why the presence of children affects not only the household expenditure pattern, but also household time allocation. Child care (quality) can be considered as one of the final products that results from home production. An extended version of the utility function is found in the model:

$$\text{Maximize } U(z_1, \dots, z_N, n, Q), \tag{7.7}$$

$$s.t. \quad z_i = Z_i(x_i, h_i^m, h_i^f) \qquad i = 1, \dots, N$$
$$Qn = Z_c(x_c, h_c^m, h_c^f)$$
$$T = t_w^m + h_c^m + \Sigma h_i^m$$
$$T = t_w^f + h_c^f + \Sigma h_i^f$$
$$y_0 + t_w^m w^m + t_w^f w^f = \Sigma p_i x_i + p_c x_c,$$

where the subscript c is used to indicate child care, and z_i are the other home-produced commodities.

The model shows that alternative ways of child care could lead to the same quality: substitution between time of the parents, h_c, and market goods, x_c (including professional child care), in the child care function is not excluded. This model also allows for substitution between the number of children and quality. The question is whether these assumptions are realistic. Do parents consider professional child care as a perfect substitute for their own care, and to what extent is substitution possible between 'number' and 'quality'?

A simplified form of this model is estimated by Michalopoulos *et al.* (1992). The number of children is given (in Chapter 8 we shall look at some dynamic aspects of household formation, such as the timing of births). In this model, child care is considered as the mother's task only, while the actions of the other household members are exogenous to the decisions that the mother makes. A further simplifying assumption is that during the time that the mother works, free child care is available. This may not seem very realistic, but in the end every working mother has the (unattractive) option of leaving her children alone, resulting in a very low quality of free child care. Michalopoulos *et al.* choose a Stone–Geary (LES) utility function:

$$\text{Max. } \beta_1 \log(x - x_0) + \beta_2 \log(t_{w0} - t_w) + \beta_3 \log(Q - Q_0)$$
$$\text{with } \Sigma \beta_i = 1 \tag{7.8}$$

$$s.t. \quad px + (1 - D) \pi_p Q_p t_w = wt_w + y_0$$
$$TQ = t_w\{(1 - D)Q_p + DQ_f\} + (T - t_w)Q_h$$
$$t_w > = 0,$$

where:

Q = average quality of child care; Q_p = quality of purchased care;
Q_f = quality of free care; Q_h = quality of care provided by the mother;
π_p = price of purchased care per unit of quality;
y_0 = effective non-labour income (including earnings of partner);
D = 1 if free care is chosen; D = 0 if care is purchased.
x_0, Q_0 and t_{w0} are subsistence levels of consumption, child care quality and maximum hours of market time, respectively.

In the first restriction (the budget restriction) it shows that total income is spent on consumption goods and possibly on purchased child care. If $D = 1$ the mother chooses free child care; if $D = 0$ she buys professional childcare during the t_w hours that she works. The second equation indicates how the average child-care quality Q is determined: during the t_w hours that the mother works there is purchased or free child care (depending on the value of the dummy, D) with corresponding qualities Q_p and Q_f, respectively. During the rest of the time, $(T - t_w)$ hours, the care is provided by the mother, with corresponding quality Q_h. So the average quality of child care is a weighted average of the quality offered by the mother herself, while she is at home, and the quality that is offered during the time that she works.

In this model the mother has three possibilities: (i) work and purchase child care; (ii) work and use the available free care; or (iii) not work and take care of the children herself. Here we shall consider only option (i).

Exercise 7.3

(a) Show that the first order conditions of the optimization are:

$$\frac{\beta_1(w - \pi_p Q_p)}{px - px_0} = \frac{\beta_2}{t_{w0} - t_w} + \frac{\beta_3(Q_h - Q_p)}{T(Q - Q_0)}$$

$$\frac{\beta_1 \pi_p}{px - px_0} = \frac{\beta_3}{T(Q - Q_0)}$$

$$px + \pi_p Q_p t_w = wt_w + y_0.$$

(b) Derive the three demand equations for the interior solution (working mothers $t_w > 0$) and show that they are equal to:

$$x = x_0 + \beta_1 I^*/p. \tag{7.9}$$

$$t_w = t_{w0} - \beta_2 I^*/w^*, \tag{7.10}$$

$$Q = Q_0 + \beta_3 I^*/\pi_p T, \tag{7.11}$$

where

$$I^* = y_0 + w^* t_{w0} - px_0 + \pi_p T(Q_h - Q_0),$$

so I^* is full-income, adjusted for the subsistence levels: x_0, Q_0 and t_{w0} and

$$w^* = w - \pi_p Q_h,$$

so w^* is effective (or shadow) wage after deducting the implicit price of child care.

(c) Show that the optimal professional child care quality is:

$$Q_p = Q_h - \frac{1}{t_w} T(Q_h - Q_0) + \frac{\beta_3 I^*}{t_w \pi_p}. \qquad (7.12)$$

The expenditures on market goods px, and on child care, $\pi_p t_w Q_p$ during the hours that the mother works, can be derived, together with the mother's earnings wt_w.

To estimate this model, a subsample of working mothers who buy professional child care is used. This sample does not, of course, represent all mothers. It is probably a selective subsample, representing mothers with a rather high market wage rate. Therefore some corrections have been made for selectivity bias (see Heckman (1979) and Maddala (1983)). The parameter estimates are shown in Table 7.4.

Table 7.4   Structural estimates of Stone–Geary model with professional and mother's child care

	Married mothers (Sample size = 618)	Single mothers (sample size = 228)
β_1	0.977	0.853
β_2	0.004	0.052[1]
β_3	0.019	0.095
Q_h	$1.68	$1.86
$T(Q_h - Q_0)$	$524.16	$755.22
t_{w0}	643	771
px_0	$-4872.70[1]	$1614.48

Notes: [1] Not significant at 10% level, All other estimates are significant at 1% level.

Source: Michalopoulos, Robins and Garfinkel (1992).

The β-estimates (the shares of full income for consumption, leisure and child care) of married mothers and single mothers, are different. The estimated values of the minimum consumption levels (px_0) are negative, but not significantly different from zero for married mothers, and positive but very low for single mothers. The value of home quality child care (Q_h) is slightly higher for single mothers, although the difference between a mothers' care and the minimum acceptable quality (Q_0) is larger for single mothers.

In the long run, the quality provided to children can be considered as an investment in human capital. The loss of human capital that could result from a withdrawal from the labour market by one of the parents (usually the mother) because he or she wants to spend time on the care of their children, may well be offset be the increase of human capital of the children. In Chapter 11 we shall return to the subject of human capital.

7.4   How much do parents spend on their children?

However interesting the effect of children on expenditure may be, it does not tell us how much parents spend on their children. Suppose that we observed total expenditure for transportation, T, and that T could be described by the equation $T = \alpha_0 + \alpha_1$. (income) $+ \alpha_2$. (presence of a child). Thus a child increases household transportation expenditure by an amount α_2. It is probable, however, that the transportation expenditure for a child is larger than α_2, but that this is allied to smaller transportation expenditure for adults. The expenditure question plays a role in the determination of child support payments by a non-custodial parent in the case of divorce.

The most straightforward way to solve the expenditure question would be to record who gets what in households. The solution is conceptually simple but, as we have already seen in Chapter 3, there are many practical difficulties, not at least because of the problem of public goods such as housing.

An indirect answer uses the concept of *adult goods*, as in Chapter 3. Note, however, that in Chapter 3 we were interested in whether there were *differences* in the allocation of resources to boys and girls, not in identifying the *level* of expenditure. If we wish to infer the level of expenditure on children, further assumptions are required. Consider two households, one with a child and one without, both with an income of $1000. Suppose that the childless household spends $50 on alcohol, whereas the household with a child spends $40. The latter household is likely to have lower expenditure for other adult goods (for example, clothing and transportation) as well. If we assume, for example, that the ratio between expenditure on alcohol and total expenditure for adults is the same in both households, the household with a child spends $800 on adults, so the expenditure remaining for children equals $200. This type of approach is discussed and implemented in Lazear and Michael (1988). Some of their results are shown in Table 7.5.

The method clearly rests on strong assumptions. In fact, it requires that the utility function takes the form:

$$u(x_A, x_C, z) = F(\psi(x_A), x_C, z), \tag{7.13}$$

where x_A and x_C are expenditure on adults and children, respectively, and with $\psi(\cdot)$ being a homothetic subutility function. Homotheticity implies that the ratio between expenditure on alcohol and total expenditure for adults is independent of income. The implicit assumption is that childless couples have preferences represented by the homothetic utility function $\psi(\cdot)$, which is most unlikely (recall that homotheticity implies that all income elasticities are unity).

Table 7.5 Estimated lifetime expenditure on children to age 18 and on adults, by selected household characteristics*

	Mean characteristics of households with children**					
Income and T($)	First year($)	First yr adult ($)	18 year ($)	18 yr adult ($)	18 yr child adult	φ
	(1)	(2)	(3)	(4)	(5)	(6)
Whites						
$5 000	1 621	3 379	16 231	28 877	0.562	0.423
10 000	3 130	6 870	31 548	58 668	0.538	0.401
15 000	4 520	10 480	45 904	89 419	0.513	0.380
20 000	5 786	14 214	59 254	121 177	0.489	0.359
30 000	7 917	22 083	82 728	187 919	0.440	0.316
40 000	9 465	30 535	101 522	259 340	0.391	0.273
50 000	10 362	39 638	115 124	335 955	0.343	0.230
Blacks						
5 000	1 431	3 569	14 692	30 416	0.483	0.353
10 000	2 737	7 263	28 367	61 849	0.459	0.332
15 000	3 910	11 090	40 973	94 351	0.434	0.311
20 000	4 943	15 057	52 455	127 977	0.410	0.289
30 000	6 558	23 442	71 802	198 845	0.361	0.247
40 000	7 512	32 488	85 878	274 985	0.312	0.204
50 000	7 723	42 277	94 068	357 011	0.263	0.161

Notes: * Discount rate is 10 per cent throughout: South = Rural = Female 0.
** Educ = 12.39; Adult Emp = 0.71; K = 2.19; A = 1.93; own child = 0.98.
Column 1 shows the calculated expenditure on the zero-aged children. Column 2 shows the calculated expenditure on all the adults in the household during that same year. Column 3 shows the discounted value of the estimated expenditure on children over the first 18 years of the children's lives. Column 4 shows the analogous calculation to column 3 for adults, the discounted value of the estimated expenditure on adults over the first 18 years of the children's lives. Column 5 is the ratio of column 3 to column 4, the ratio of total expenditures on children to those on adults during the first 18 years of the children's lives. Column 6 is the calculated ratio of the expenditure per child to the expenditure per adult during the children's first year of life.

Source: Lazear and Michael (1988).

7.5 How much extra income is required for children?

The answer to this question is usually given in terms of *equivalence scales*. An equivalence scale is a number that tells us at which income ratio two households with different household compositions are equally well off. Simple equivalence scales only take into account household size, irrespective of other household characteristics, such as age of the household members. One rather extreme equivalence scale is obtained by assuming that families are equally well off if they have identical *per capita* income. At the other extreme, households are assumed to be equally well off if they have identical income irrespective of their size. In the formula $E = FS^\alpha$, E is the equivalence scale and FS family size. The first extreme occurs when $\alpha = 1$, the second when $\alpha = 0$. The larger the value of α, the smaller are the economies of scale.

The notion of needs (the choice of α) is a relative and a subjective one, and in fact it is strongly related to the issue of defining and measuring poverty, which will be the theme of Chapter 12. Buhmann *et al.* (1988) distinguish two types of scale using experts' general knowledge, and two types developed empirically from analysis of survey data. Experts' scales are developed by social science analysts using a variety of materials. They are either developed for statistical purposes (to distinguish the poor from the non-poor) or social benefit programs. Examples of statistical scales are the OECD scale ($\alpha = 0.73$) and the European Poverty Line scales based on LIS data (varying between 0.70 and 0.84) and Per Capita Consumption ($\alpha = 1$). Scales for social benefit programs are used in several countries, for example, Britain, Canada, Germany, Sweden, Switzerland, the USA and other countries, and range from 0.54 to 0.67.

The scales that are based on data collected from households (usually surveys) use either the revealed consumption patterns (as discussed in Section 7.2), or the answers to income evaluation questions, or minimum income questions. The first group of scales provide αs ranging from 0.23 to 0.57, while the second group consist of subjective scales varying between $\alpha = 0.12$ and $\alpha = 0.36$. These results suggest that these four kinds of scale tend to populate different regions of the $[0,1]$ interval:

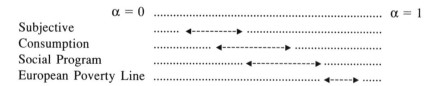

This means that there is little consensus about the 'true' value of α. The problem is that there is no 'true' α-value, as will be explained below.

Non-identifiability of the costs of children from estimated demand systems

Economists typically have phrased the question of the costs of children in terms of how much extra income a household needs to be as well off as a household without children that is otherwise identical. Cramer (1969) and Pollak and Wales (1979) have shown that it is a fundamental impossibility to answer such a question on the basis of utility consistent demand systems alone. The reason for this is that answering the question requires a cardinal utility concept, rather than an ordinal one as in case of a utility-consistent demand system.

We take a closer look at the identifiability problem by means of an example. Consider a household with the following utility function:

$$U(x_1, x_2; K) = \frac{1}{4}\log (x_1 - 100K) + \frac{3}{4}\log (x_2), \qquad (7.14)$$

where, x_1 = expenditures on clothing; x_2 = expenditures on other goods; K = the number of children in the household; and $U(\cdot)$ is the utility level. The household has an income, y. The number of children is given and cannot be chosen by the household. It is not difficult to verify that the utility maximizing expenditures are:

$$\begin{cases} x_1 = \frac{1}{4}y + 75K \\[2mm] x_2 = \frac{3}{4}y - 75K. \end{cases} \qquad (7.15)$$

The utility level as a function of the number of children, and income is found by substituting the expenditure functions in Equation (7.15) into Equation (7.14), yielding:

$$\psi(y, K) = \frac{1}{4}\log\left(\frac{1}{4}y + 75K - 100K\right) + \frac{3}{4}\log\left(\frac{3}{4}y - 75K\right) =$$
$$= \log\left(\frac{1}{4}y - 25K\right) + \frac{3}{4}\log 3. \qquad (7.16)$$

If there is an additional child, the income increase, Δy, necessary to keep utility at the same level is defined by:

$$\psi(y + \Delta y, K + 1) = \psi(y, K). \qquad (7.17)$$

In the case of the utility function in Equation (7.14) the solution is $\Delta y = 100$, independent of the original income level, y, and number of children, K. Now consider the alternative utility function:

$$U^*(x_1, x_2; K) = \frac{1}{4}\log(x_1 - 100K) + \frac{3}{4}\log(x_2) - 50K. \qquad (7.18)$$

The additional term does not have any effect on utility maximizing expenditures. However, if we use U^* rather than U, the additional income required to keep utility at the same level when there is an additional child is implicitly defined by:

$$\log\left(\frac{1}{4}(y + \Delta y) - 25(K + 1)\right) - 50(K + 1) = \log\left(\frac{1}{4}y - 25K\right) - 50K. \qquad (7.19)$$

For $y = 1000$ and $K = 2$, the (numerical) solution is $\Delta y = 327$.

In fact, one can choose a normalization to obtain any positive value for the equivalence scale (Blundell and Lewbel, 1991). The identifiability problem provides an explanation for the large variety in estimated equivalence scales: existing estimates have used different additional identifying assumptions. The solution to the problem is either to invoke additional assumptions or to use additional data.

Using additional assumptions to achieve identification

1. One example of the former approach is Rothbarth's method. Rothbarth (1943) assumed that households with similar levels of some reference (adult) good have similar welfare. As a consequence, the compensated demand for the reference good should be independent of demographic variables. This requires the cost function to be of the form:

$$c(p, z, u) = \phi(p, u) + \tau(p_{-a}, z, u). \tag{7.20}$$

where p_{-a} is the price vector for all goods except the reference good, and z is demographic variables.

For example, we could assume that households are equally well off if they spend an identical amount on adult goods such as men's and women's clothing, alcoholic beverages and newspapers: c_{adult}. Then the coefficients of the following regressions are estimated; first for households without children, then for households with one child, then households with two children and so on:

$$C^0_{total} = \beta_0 + \beta_1 C^0_{adult}$$
$$C^1_{total} = \beta_0 + \beta_1 C^1_{adult}$$
$$C^2_{total} = \beta_0 + \beta_1 C^2_{adult}$$

For these different types of household, different parameter estimates are found. To make an equivalence scale, a certain level of C_{adult} is chosen and substituted in the regressions, which will result in different estimated levels of C^0_{total}, C^1_{total} and C^2_{total}. Households with zero, one or two children, whose total consumption is C^0_{total}, C^1_{total} and C^2_{total} respectively, are assumed to be equally well off. The equivalence scale becomes:

$$1, C^1_{total}/C^0_{total}, C^2_{total}/C^0_{total}, \ldots$$

2. A related example is the Iso-prop method, which goes back to Engel (1883, 1895). This method assumes that households have a similar welfare level if they have a similar budget share for food or some composite of 'necessities'. The figures given in Table 7.1 show estimated budget shares of food and other goods. If the food share in a household with one child is 0.47, the total expenditure level is 425. It is seen that a household with two children must have a higher total expenditure level in order to have a food share of 0.47,

namely an amount between 525 and 425, say 485. A household with 3 children will have an amount around 565. Households without children, which are not given in Table 7.1, would probably spend less than 425, when having a food share of 0.47. The equivalent scale is derived as above. While relatively easy to implement, both approaches are quite arbitrary.

Exercise 7.4
Show that with the cost function shown in Equation (7.18) the compensated demand for the reference good is independent of demographic variables.

Using additional data to achieve identification

1. An example of the use of additional data is van Praag's cardinal utility concept. The concept is based on respondents' subjective evaluation of incomes. People are asked what income they would find 'very good', 'good', 'sufficient', 'insufficient', 'bad', or 'very bad'. The method uses interpersonal comparisons by assuming that two people who have a similar verbal evaluation of an income level have a similar welfare level. Table 7.6 shows some of van Praag's estimation results.

   As expected, family size has a positive effect on the income levels associated with each verbal label. The positive signs of the household's own income on its evaluation of income levels is a reflection of *preference drift*:

Table 7.6 Estimation results for income evaluation regression[1]

Dependent variable	Constant	ln(family size)	ln(income)	R^2
ln(very poor income)	4.98	0.15	0.43	0.50
	(0.21)	(0.02)	(0.02)	
ln(poor income)	4.66	0.13	0.49	0.57
	(0.18)	(0.01)	(0.02)	
ln(insufficient income)	4.23	0.12	0.54	0.62
	(0.16)	(0.01)	(0.02)	
ln(sufficient income)	3.87	0.10	0.60	0.63
	(0.16)	(0.01)	(0.02)	
ln(good income)	3.55	0.08	0.65	0.60
	(0.17)	(0.07)	(0.70)	
ln(very good income)	3.32	0.07	0.70	0.51
	(0.20)	(0.02)	(0.02)	
$N = 2603$				

Note: 1. Standard errors in parentheses.

Source: Van Praag (1985).

the higher a person's actual income, the higher the income that person needs to be satisfied.

A household with family size fs_n will evaluate its own income y_n as 'good' if:

$$\ln y_n = \alpha_0 + \alpha_1 \ln fs_n + \alpha_2 \ln y_n, \tag{7.21}$$

where the αs are the regression coefficients of the ln(good income) regression. In the examples in Table 7.6, these are $\alpha_0 = 3.55$, $\alpha_1 = 0.08$ and $\alpha_2 = 0.65$. Solving y_n from Equation (7.21), we obtain:

$$y_n = e^{\left(\frac{\alpha_0}{1-\alpha_2}\right)} \cdot fs_n^{\left(\frac{\alpha_1}{1-\alpha_2}\right)}. \tag{7.22}$$

Equation (7.21) can be used to calculate an equivalence scale. Normalizing the scale to unity for a two-person family, it is given by:

$$E = \left(\frac{fs}{2}\right)^{\frac{\alpha_1}{1-\alpha_2}} \tag{7.23}$$

For the welfare levels 'good' and 'sufficient', the scales are given in Table 7.7.

Table 7.7   Equivalence scales based on income evaluations

Welfare level	fs = 2	fs = 3	fs = 4	fs = 5	fs = 6
'Good'	1	1.10	1.17	1.23	1.29
'Sufficient'	1	1.11	1.19	1.26	1.32

2. Instead of asking people how they appreciate income levels, (including their own) van Praag has also asked the opinion of households on their total quality of life: see Chapter 12.5. The results of this study show that households with one child are as content as households without children, even if they have a somewhat lower income level. The phenomenon is very pronounced for households in the upper part of income distribution. This may not be very surprising, realizing that parents choose to have children; the number of children is not an exogenous variable. Parents expect utility to increase when having a child. The study also shows that families with two or more children indicate that they need more income to be as well off as a household without children.

7.6   Child allowance systems

Many countries have some system of financial benefits for households with children. This child support can take different forms. One form is direct child allowance, which may or may not depend on income, and which is usually paid to the mother. Other forms are tax exemption or a tax credit. In the first of these two cases, the actual benefit equals the exemption amount times the marginal tax rate. Hence, the higher one's marginal tax rate, the larger the benefit. This is not the case with tax credit, which is a fixed reduction of the amount of tax one has to pay.

Several studies have found significant positive effects of these policies on fertility; Whittington *et al.* (1990) for the USA, Zhang *et al.* (1994) for Canada, and Buttner and Lutz (1990) for the German Democratic Republic. In the discussion on child allowance policies, the emphasis seems to have shifted from alleviating the financial burden of having children to influencing fertility decisions. It is a remarkable fact that some countries attempt to encourage births, whereas others have created financial incentives to achieve the opposite. An example of the first type of country is Canada, where fertility rates have been below replacement level since about 1972, while China, with its one-child policy (see, for example, Ahn (1994)), is an example of the second type of country.

7.7 Summary

In this chapter we analysed the effects of the presence of children on the expenditure and time allocation of the household. Children certainly change the consumption and time pattern of the household, as we saw in Sections 7.2 and 7.3. Young children need the attendance of adults, so when there are young children in a household either a parent, a relative (such as a grandparent) or friend will take care of the children, or the parents will buy professional child care. In economic terms, child care is a matter of time, money and quality. If the parents take care of their children it will affect their labour market behaviour and income; if they buy professional child care it will cost them money. Moreover, parents may perceive the quality of these two types of child care to be different.

These efforts by the parents raise the question of how much extra money a family with children should have to be as well off as a family without children. To answer this question, we first need to answer the question of how we can determine that two families are equally well off. Several authors have answered the latter question in different ways, and they have also found very different equivalence scales, as we saw in Section 7.5.

In most studies the number of children in a household is an exogenous variable, but parents can, to a certain extent, choose the number of children they wish to have. The more children they have, the more time and money is needed to provide a good quality of child care. Some governments use tax and child benefit policies to encourage or discourage potential parents from having children.

Note

1. Part of what follows is based on Browning (1992).

CHAPTER 8

Dynamic Aspects of Household Formation and Dissolution

8.1 Introduction

Over the course of their life-cycle most individuals typically will make several transitions from one type of household to another. Although the range of possible biographies in terms of household membership is virtually unbounded, most people experience transitions out of the parental home; marriage; the birth of one or more children; and the dissolution of the marriage, either because of death or because of divorce.

In the present chapter we study these most frequently occurring transitions from an economic point of view in a dynamic setting. The use of dynamic models opens up the possibility of analyzing not only whether the transition is made at all, but also when these transitions take place. On the other hand, the additional complexity stemming from a dynamic approach demands a price in terms of a simplification of other aspects of the model. Given the present state of the art, static and dynamic approaches should therefore be viewed as complements, with their unification being one of the challenges for future research.

Section 8.2 discusses the transition out of the parental home and into marriage and Section 8.3 examines the timing of births. Section 8.4 discusses parental gender preferences and their possible effects on fertility decisions. Section 8.5 deals with divorce and remarriage. Although these transitions are all obviously interrelated, we shall study them in separate sections, both to keep things manageable and because each transition has its own peculiarities.

The use of duration models

Much of the empirical analysis in this area uses duration models rather than the perhaps more common regression and discrete choice models. Duration models specify for any point in time the *hazard rate* (or failure or departure rate). Roughly speaking, the hazard rate is the probability that a transition out of the initial state (being unmarried, for example) into the new state (being married) is made, conditional on not having made the transition before. Given the nature of a transition, the hazard is the most natural starting point for an analysis. Moreover, duration models allow us, relatively easily, to take care of the peculiarities that often characterize data on durations and transitions, in particular *right-censoring*. An observation is right-censored if we know that a person has *not* made a transition before some given point in time, but we do not know when the transition will be made. In Appendix A, the principles of duration models are outlined.

8.2 Leaving the parental home and marriage

While, for most individuals, making the transition out of the parental home at some point in time is almost certain, there is considerable variation – both across and within cohorts – in the age at which individuals leave their parents. In this section we discuss some of the literature that has attempted to explain these patterns. Leaving the parental home is a transition that has been paid very little attention by economists, and most of the research discussed here stems from the demographic and sociological literature.

The intra- and intercohort variation in the timing of the transition is shown clearly in Figure 8.1. This shows the cumulative percentages (vertical axis) of young adults who have left the parental home at different ages, for a number of subsequent birth cohorts (horizontal axis) in The Netherlands. The numbers along the curves refer to the age of transition. So, for example, from all men from the birth cohort 1910–19, 40 per cent had left the parental home by the age of 25, whereas from all men from the birth cohort 1950–9, more than 70 per cent had left the parental home by the age of 25. The figure clearly shows a lower age of transition from the parental home for younger birth-cohorts. Comparing both genders, we see that females leave the parental home at younger ages than do males, for all birth-cohorts.

In addition to the changes in the transition age, there have been changes in the destination. While the percentage of people who made a transition into living with a partner (usually marriage) is almost 80 per cent for the cohort 1910–19, it is about 60 per cent for people from the birth cohort 1950–59. Similar trends have been observed for other Western countries; see, for example, Goldscheider and Goldscheider (1993). Most researchers attribute the intercohort shift to increased participation in education, in turn caused partly by an increased availability of education fellowships, the increased availability of cheap housing and rent allowance, and a general change in cultural norms. Intracohort differences can be explained by social class and income of the parents, school achievements, and regional differences. Cooney and Hogan (1991) reported similar results in an analysis of the timing of the first marriage of American men. In particular, employment opportunities

144

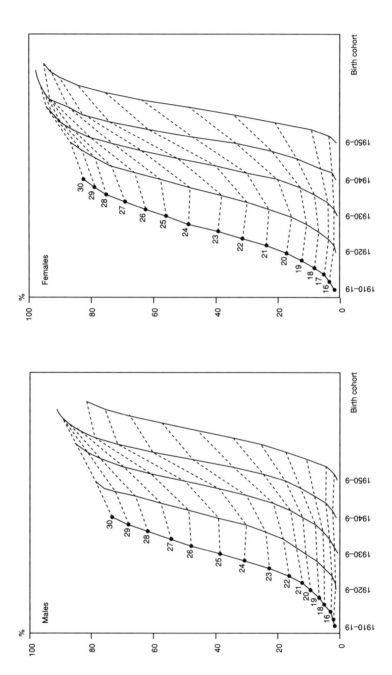

Figure 8.1 *Age of leaving the parental home*

Source: Baanders (1991).

and military service requirements were found to be significant in explaining intercohort differences.

One of the few economic models of leaving the parental home is the paper by McElroy (1985). She estimated a multivariate Probit model describing the joint determination of market work and family status of young men. The specification of the Probit equations was based on a Nash-bargaining model (see Chapter 3), implying that a young man's, as well as his parents' non-wage incomes should enter the system of commodity demand and labour supply equations separately. The sample consisted of 203 observations of families with sons who were between 19 and 24 years of age (in 1971), white, never-married and out of school. Out of the 155 men who lived with their parents, 121 were working, whereas out of the 48 men who lived on their own, 41 were working. The model showed that at sufficiently low of-fered wages a young man lives with his parents and does not work; when the offered wages rise, he works in the market, but remains in his parents' household; finally, if the offered wages are sufficiently high, he works and quits the parental home. McElroy concludes that parents insure their sons against poor market opportunities.

8.3 Timing of births

In the economic literature on fertility, the positive relationship between a woman's wage and her age at the birth of her first child is a stylized fact that has been observed for many countries and time periods; see, for example, O'Neill (1985) for the USA and Heckman, Hotz and Walker (1985) for Sweden with evidence based on aggregate data. Heckman and Walker (1990) and Groot and Pott-Buter (1992), using micro data, found significant nega-tive wage effects on the hazard rate of maternity. Groot and Pott-Buter esti-mated a Mixed Proportional Hazard model of the timing of maternity, using a sample of 484 women who were between 15 and 35 years in January 1980. In April 1985, 44 per cent of these women had made the transition into maternity. The time dependence of the hazard function, which was specified as a quadratic function in time, implied an increase in the hazard of mater-nity up to age 28, and a decrease thereafter. Because of this decrease, the model is 'defective', which means that it has the – in this case desirable – property that the probability of ever having a child is strictly smaller than one. A significant negative effect on the hazard rate was found not only for the wage rate of the wife but also for the wage rate of the husband. The probabilities of having a child at age 40, as predicted by Groot and Pott-Buter's model, for women with different characteristics, are listed in Table 8.1.

A few papers have investigated the relationship between the timings of a first birth and subsequent births. Some of these document the existence of the 'engine of fertility': the phenomenon that the longer a preceding birth interval, the longer the subsequent one. The empirical evidence, however, is far from unequivocal (see Heckman *et al.*, 1985).

Table 8.1 Probability of maternity by age 40

Wages and income at mean values	0.616
Wage wife + 10%	0.556
Wage husband + 10%	0.568
Income + 10%	0.636
Non-working	0.981
Profession	
Industry	0.819
Medical	0.769
Teaching	0.790
Church; regular visits	0.996

Source: Groot and Pott-Buter (1992). For all other variables, mean values (wages and income) or modal values (dummy variables) are used.

A theoretical model of the timing of fertility

In the remainder of this section, we present a theoretical model which provides a simple explanation of the relationship between wage and the timing of maternity. The model, which is very similar to the models studied by Montgomery and Trussell (1986) and Blackburn *et al.* (1993), describes the timing of fertility as the outcome of the maximization of the woman's expected discounted utility flow in a continuous time setting. Some details on the calculation of the expected present value of discounted flows are given in Appendix B (page 218).

Consider a woman who has decided to have a child and faces the problem of the optimal timing of its birth. At time $t = 0$ the woman is working and receives a wage, w. While working, her wage rate grows at rate $s(\geq 0)$ because of accumulated experience (human capital). For example, after a period of length Z of uninterrupted employment, her wage rate at $t = Z$ equals $w.e^{sZ}$. At the time of childbirth, $t = T$, the woman withdraws from the labor market for a period of length τ. At time $T + \tau$ she is able to resume employment with probability $p(0 \leq p \leq 1)$. If she resumes employment, her wage at time $T + \tau$ is equal to the wage she received when she left employment, that is, $w.e^{sT}$. During periods of unemployment the woman receives no income. The woman must choose to have her child some time between $t = 0$ and $t = F < R$, where F represents the end of the fertile period and R the time of retirement. The woman's lifetime utility, U depends on the present value of her lifetime income, Y, and on the duration of motherhood. For tractability, we use a linear utility function, $U(T) = Y(T) - aT$, with $a > 0$. Under these assumptions, utility is given by:

$$U(T) = \int_0^T we^{(s - \delta)t}dt + \int_{T + \tau}^R wpe^{-\delta t} \cdot e^{s(t - \tau)}dt - aT, \qquad (8.1)$$

where δ is the discount rate. The first integral in Equation (8.1) represents the discounted income flow up to T. Between T and $T + \tau$ the woman does not receive an income, so this time interval does not appear in the integrals. The second integral is the discounted income flow between resuming unemployment at $T + \tau$ and the time of retirement, R.

Evaluating the integrals, we obtain:

$$U(T) = \frac{w}{s - \delta}[e^{(s - \delta)T} - 1] + \frac{wp}{s - \delta}e^{-s\tau}[e^{(s - \delta)R} - e^{(s - \delta)(T + \tau)}] - aT. \quad (8.2)$$

The first-order condition for an interior utility extremum is given by:

$$U'(T) = we^{(s - \delta)T}(1 - pe^{-s\tau}) - a = 0, \quad (8.3)$$

which is solved for:

$$\hat{T} = \left(\frac{1}{s - \delta}\right)\ln\left[\frac{a}{w(1 - pe^{-s\tau})}\right]. \quad (8.4)$$

From the second-order condition:

$$U''(\hat{T}) = (s - \delta)\, a < 0, \quad (8.5)$$

it follows that $\hat{T}$ represents a maximum if $\delta > s$. The shape of the function $U(T)$ is depicted in Figure 8.2 for $\delta = 0.10$; $s = 0.01$; $\tau = 10$; $p = 1$; $w = 30\,000$; $a = 10\,000$, $F = 20$ and $R = 45$. In this case, $\hat{T} = 7.11$. So, if we take the age of 20 years to coincide with $t = 0$, the optimal timing of birth is at age 27. As will be clear from Figure 8.2, the optimization problem is solved at either $T = 0$ or at $T = F$ if $\hat{T}$ falls outside the interval $(0, F)$. If $\delta < s$, $\hat{T}$ represents a minimum and the solution will again be at one of the corners $t = 0$ or $t = F$. In our numerical example, the woman would choose to have her child at $t = 0$ if her initial wage falls below $15\,819$.

Let us look again at the optimization problem and its solution in case $\delta > s$. As Equation (8.4) shows, both a strong preference for children (a large value for a) and a low wage decrease the optimal time of a first birth.

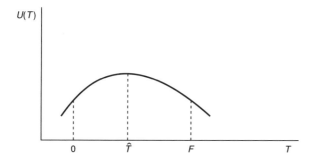

Figure 8.2   Lifetime utility and the timing of birth

The shorter the period of non-participation on the labour market after birth (τ), the earlier childbirth will take place. A low probability of re-employment acts like a long period of non-participation after childbirth. If the woman received some income during her maternal leave, the model would imply a lower optimal time of maternity.

The model is based on a number of restrictive assumptions. For example, the woman has only one child, rearing the child involves no other costs than forgone income, and the utility function is strongly separable in Y and T. The latter assumption may not hold in practice, because having children may generate more utility when income is high than when income is low. Nevertheless, the model provides a simple explanation of the observed positive relationship between wages and the timing of maternity, and it may serve as a starting point for developing more elaborate models.

Exercise 8.1
(a) Derive Equations (8.2), (8.3), (8.4) and (8.5).
(b) How would the solution be affected when $a \leq 0$?
(c) Examine the consequences of using the utility function $U(T) = Y(T) - a(T - \psi)^2$, with $a > 0$ and $\psi > 0$.
(d) Examine the consequences of a very steep income profile, such that $s > \delta$.

Exercise 8.2
A couple maximizes a joint household utility function $U(T) = Y(T) - aT$, where $Y(T)$ is now the sum of the lifetime incomes of both spouses. What does this model predict about who will withdraw from the labour market to take care of a child (you may assume $p_A = p_B$ and $s = 0$).

8.4   Parental gender preferences

Leung (1988), using samples of Chinese and Malaysian women in Malaysia, has estimated some models describing the hazard of having an additional child. His primary purpose was to investigate whether parents have gender preferences, an issue that has attracted some attention in the demographic literature. Earlier work in this field has often used three indicators of sex preference: the *sex ratio at birth*, the *parity progression ratio* and the *duration until the next birth*. The sex ratio at birth is the number of boys divided by the total number of children born in the family. If parents have a preference for boys, then the average sex ratio at birth may not be equal to the probability of a male birth (see Exercise 8.3 below). The second indicator, the parity progression ratio, is defined as the probability that a woman with a given number of children will have an additional child. If parents have a preference for boys, they are more likely to have an additional birth if they have no sons or a small number of sons, other things being equal. In addition, they may have shorter subsequent birth intervals. A problem with this type of analysis is that the data usually include women whose fertility is not yet completed. In particular, younger women are likely to have additional children after the survey has been completed, so their observations are right-censored. Much of the work in this field has ignored this problem and is therefore difficult to interpret. By using hazard analysis, Leung was able to account appropriately for the right-censoring problem. To test for the existence of gender preferences, Leung included the number of boys already in the family as an explanatory variable. Hazard models with a quadratic as well as a Weibull specification of the time dependence were estimated. Allowance was made for unobserved heterogeneity using Heckman and Singer's method (see Appendix A). Leung found evidence of boy preference among the Chinese but not among the Malaysians.

Using similar methods, Dobbelsteen (1996) found evidence that couples in The Netherlands have a preference for a *mixture of sexes*. The results were confirmed by analysing data on decisions to sterilize: couples with both a boy and a girl turned out to have a significantly larger probability of being sterilized than other couples with the same total number of children.

Exercise 8.3
Consider a family that will have N children (N is given). Let the number of boys and the number girls in the family be denoted by B and G, respectively. So $B + G = N$. The probability of a male birth is equal to p at each birth. (The actual value of p is approximately 0.515.) The sex ratio at birth is defined by B/N.

   (a) Show that the expected sex ratio $E(B/N) = p$.

Now suppose that parents have a preference for boys and stop having children as soon as they have one son. Assuming that the number of possible births is unrestricted, this stopping rule implies that $B = 1$ and $G = N - 1$ with certainty. (So N is now a random variable.)

   (b) Show that the expected number of boys $E(B) = 1/p$.
   (c) Show that $E(B/N) > p$.
   (d) (Difficult) Show that $E(B/N) = p.\ln(p)/(p - 1)$. *Hint*: Use a series expansion of $\ln(1 - x)$.

8.5 Divorce and remarriage

In most Western countries, divorce rates have shown a substantial increase since the 1960s, as illustrated in Table 8.2.

Table 8.2   Divorce rates in a number of OECD countries[1]

Country	1960	1965	1970	1975	1980	1985	1990
Belgium	2.0	2.3	2.6	4.4	5.6	7.3	8.7
Denmark	5.9	5.4	7.6	10.6	11.2	12.6	12.8
France	2.9	3.1	3.3	4.5	6.3	8.4	n.a.
Germany	3.5	3.9	5.1	6.7	6.1	8.6	8.1
The Netherlands	2.2	2.2	3.3	6.0	7.5	9.9	8.1
UK	2.0	3.1	4.7	9.6	12.0	13.4	n.a.

Notes: 1. Number of divorces per 1000 existing marriages; n.a. = not available.

Source: Eurostat (1992).

A few dynamic models of divorce have been proposed in the literature based on the economic theory of optimal search. According to this theory, an individual will marry as soon as the expected discounted utility of a marriage exceeds the expected discounted utility of staying single. The marriage will end in divorce as soon as one of the partners expects a utility improvement outside the marriage (taking into account the monetary and non-monetary costs of a divorce), either as a single person or in a new marriage. Such a situation may arise if the present marriage appears to have an unexpected low quality. This simple theory has implications in terms of the effect of a number of variables on the duration of the marriage and the probability of divorce. One example is the age at marriage. Since younger people will generally be less informed about themselves and potential partners, the risk of a low-quality marriage is greater. This makes it more likely for a marriage to end in a divorce when the age at marriage is low. Another prediction is that the presence of children is likely to decrease the divorce probability. Children represent a marriage-specific investment, and their presence is likely to increase the costs of divorce.

Ott (1991a) has studied the divorce probability of first marriages using data from the German Social Economic Panel. A mixed Weibull-model was estimated, using responses of 2244 women who married for the first time in 1950 or later. At the time of data collection (1985) 248 of the first marriages had ended in divorce. Ott's results included significant positive effects on the divorce hazard of the woman's education level, early marriage (before the woman's 21st birthday), the absence of children, and being born after 1950. These results are thus broadly consistent with the theory sketched above. The data did not allow inclusion of characteristics of the husband.

We conclude this section by presenting some results for a quite different transition – remarriage after the death of a spouse – and for an entirely different epoch. The results are taken from a historical analysis by van Poppel (1992) of marriage, marital dissolution and remarriage in two Dutch municipalities in the period 1815–1930. By extracting data from municipal records of population and marriage, van Poppel obtained large samples of individual life histories. Here we present his estimation results for Proportional Hazard

Table 8.3   Relative hazard of remarriage after death of a spouse

Municipality	Gouda	1.00
	Breda	0.68*
Sex	Female	1.00
	Male	3.30*
No. of children when spouse died	0	1.00
	1	0.58*
	3–4	0.47*
	5+	0.36*
Age at death of spouse	≤34	3.99*
	35–49	2.99*
	50–59	1.00
	≥60	0.14*
Age of youngest child	0–2	1.00
	2–4	0.90
	4–12	0.81*
	≥12	0.69*
Oldest child ≤12	Yes	0.78*
	No	1.00
Social group	Upper class	0.75
	Middle class	0.92
	Intellectuals and civil servants	0.90
	Farmers	0.92
	Skilled labourers	1.00
	Unskilled labourers	0.93
	'Lumpen proletariat'	1.04
	No profession	1.25*

Note: *Significant at the 1% level.

Source: van Poppel (1992).

models of remarriage after death of a spouse (see Table 8.3). The results were obtained using Cox's method of partial likelihood maximization (see Appendix A). Given that all explanatory variables are dummies, the estimates are easily expressed by calculating the hazard rate of a particular individual relative to some reference group. For example, consider the effect of the dummy variable SEX, which is 1 for males and 0 for females. Then the hazard rate of remarriage for men relative to the hazard rate of remarriage for women (the reference group) is given by:

$$\frac{\exp\ (\beta_{SEX} + x_0\beta_0).\ \psi\ (t)}{\exp\ (x_0\beta_0).\ \psi\ (t)} = \exp\ (\beta_{SEX}), \tag{8.6}$$

where $x_0\beta_0$ represents the effect of all other explanatory variables. It is interesting to note that the presence of children seems to impede remarriage, especially if they are of school age.

As we have noted earlier, the transitions considered in this chapter are interrelated in various ways. A simultaneous dynamic analysis would be desirable from a conceptual point of view. One of the very few examples of a simultaneous analysis of hazards is the paper by Lillard (1993) on marriage duration and fertility timing.

8.6 Summary

Households are dynamic entities. They are formed, change in size and nature, and cease to exist at some point in time. Most individuals experience several transitions from one type of household to another, which are in part the results of their own decisions. Economic variables appear to play a role in most cases. One example we encountered is that a higher wage rate reduces a woman's probability of maternity. Another example is that a higher wage rate increases a young man's probability of leaving the parental home. Of course, this is not to say that these transitions are primarily governed by economic motivations, but merely that they play a role, among many other factors.

CHAPTER 9

Dynamic Aspects of Household Consumption

9.1 Introduction

In most of the previous chapters we have studied aspects of household behaviour using static models, that is, models without a time dimension. Static models are a natural starting point to study behaviour and they appeal to the general notion in (economic) research that one should first analyse the simplest possible cases. But almost any economic decision a household makes has time-related aspects. Present decisions are affected by decisions in the past, and future decisions are affected by current ones.

In the present chapter we modify and extend our models of household consumption to make them a more realistic description of reality. Section 9.2 discusses the basics of a life-cycle model. The literature on this topic has recently expanded rapidly, and several reviews carried out in the 1990s, notably those by Deaton (1992) and Browning and Lusardi (1996), are available. Our discussion will be elementary, and readers interested in further reading are referred to these reviews and the literature cited there.

An essential characteristic of dynamic decision-making is the trade-off between benefits or costs received or paid today, and benefits or costs received or paid tomorrow. The way in which households make these trade-offs is summarized by the concept of the subjective rate of time preference. Section 9.3 investigates its characteristics more closely and we discuss a number of contributions from the economic–psychological literature. Section 9.4 looks at the purchase of durables, that is, household appliances, which – in terms of the New Home Economics theory of Section 2.5 – determines household production technology. In particular, we pay attention to the interrelationship between purchase, use and replacement. Section 9.5 presents some data on the assets, debts and net wealth of households; while Section 9.6 discusses problematic debts. Section 9.7 summarizes and concludes the chapter.

9.2 Basics of the life-cycle model

We introduce the life-cycle model by considering the case of a two-period life-cycle. The consumer has to decide how much of his or her wealth to consume in the first period (C_1), and how much in the second (C_2). The consumer's initial level of wealth, that is, the wealth level at $t = 0$, is W_0, and wealth earns an interest at rate r. The exogenous income is μ_i, and the price level p_i in period i, $i = 1, 2$. At the end of the first period, at $t = 1$, the consumer's wealth equals:

$$W_1 = (1 + r)W_0 + \mu_1 - p_1C_1. \tag{9.1}$$

At the end of the second period, at $t = 2$, it is given by:

$$\begin{aligned} W_2 &= W_1(1 + r) + \mu_2 - p_2C_2 \\ &= W_0(1 + r)^2 + (\mu_1 - p_1C_1)(1 + r) + (\mu_2 - p_2C_2). \end{aligned} \tag{9.2}$$

Assume the consumer's lifetime utility is given by:

$$V(C_1, C_2) = U(C_1) + \left(\frac{1}{1 + \delta}\right)U(C_2). \tag{9.3}$$

This lifetime utility function is *intertemporally separable*, that is, it is a separable function in the consumption in both periods. δ denotes the individual's subjective rate of time preference. If an individual is infinitely myopic $(\delta = \infty)$, consumption in the second period does not generate any utility and total wealth will be consumed completely in the first period. The intratemporal utility function $U(.)$ is assumed to be increasing and concave, that is, $U'(.) > 0$ and $U''(.) < 0$. Note that concavity implies the following equivalence: $U'(x_1) < U'(x_2) \Leftrightarrow x_1 > x_2$.

In the absence of a bequest motive, the consumer will choose his or her consumption path such that $W_2 = 0$. In that case, Equation (9.2) can be written as:

$$\frac{p_1C_1}{(1 + r)} + \frac{p_2C_2}{(1 + r)^2} = W_0 + \frac{\mu_1}{(1 + r)} + \frac{\mu_2}{(1 + r)^2}. \tag{9.4}$$

Equation (9.4) is called the *intertemporal budget constraint*. Maximization of Equation (9.3) subject to Equation (9.4) yields the first order conditions:

$$U'(C_1) + \frac{\lambda p_1}{(1 + r)} = 0 \tag{9.5}$$

and

$$\left(\frac{1}{1 + \delta}\right) U'(C_2) + \frac{\lambda p_2}{(1 + r)^2} = 0,$$

where λ is the Lagrange multiplier corresponding to the wealth constraint. If we eliminate λ from Equation (9.5), we find that the optimal consumption path should satisfy:

$$U'(C_1) = \frac{p_1}{p_2} \cdot \frac{1 + r}{1 + \delta} \cdot U'(C_2). \tag{9.6}$$

If prices are constant ($p_1 = p_2$), Equation (9.6) implies

$$\begin{aligned}
\delta > r &\Leftrightarrow U'(C_1) < U'(C_2) \Leftrightarrow C_1 > C_2 \\
\delta = r &\Leftrightarrow U'(C_1) = U'(C_2) \Leftrightarrow C_1 = C_2 \\
\delta < r &\Leftrightarrow U'(C_1) > U'(C_2) \Leftrightarrow C_1 < C_2,
\end{aligned} \tag{9.7}$$

because of the concavity of $U(.)$. Thus the model predicts that a consumer whose subjective rate of time preference equals the market rate of interest will equalize consumption in both periods. This central prediction of the life-cycle model implies that there is no direct relationship between income in a particular period and consumption in that period. It also implies that wealth increases during periods where income is relatively high, and decreases during periods with low income (such as at the end of the life-cycle). Note, however, that it is based on a number of assumptions. An important assumption is the complete absence of *liquidity constraints*, which is not likely to hold in practice for most households. The more binding the borrowing restriction a household is faced with, the closer consumption will follow the income path.

Uncertainty

Of course, the model may be elaborated in various directions, depending on the particular aspect of life-cycle behaviour we are interested in. Suppose, for example, that we would like to use this type of model to describe behaviour at the end of the life-cycle. The individual may anticipate the possibility that s/he will not live during the second period. To formalize this notion, let q be the individual's (subjective) probability of still being alive during the second period. Assuming that the individual maximizes expected lifetime utility, the first order condition becomes:

$$U'(C_1) = \frac{p_1}{p_2} \cdot \frac{q(1 + r)}{1 + \delta} \cdot U'(C_2) \tag{9.8}$$

Equation (9.7) shows that the possibility of dying at $t = 1$ has the same effect as an increase in δ or a decrease in r. As a consequence, we expect consumption to decrease at the end of the life-cycle, all other things being equal.

Consider the extension of Equation (9.3) to L periods:

$$V(C_1, \ldots, C_L) = \sum_{t=1}^{L} (1 + \delta)^{-t+1} U(C_t). \tag{9.9}$$

Equation (9.2) for wealth accumulation now becomes:

$$W_t = W_0(1 + r)^t - \sum_{\tau=1}^{t} (p_\tau C_\tau - \mu_\tau)(1 + r)^{(t-\tau)}. \tag{9.10}$$

With the terminal condition $W_L = 0$, this implies:

$$W_0 = \sum_{\tau=1}^{L} (1 + r)^{-\tau} (p_\tau C_\tau - \mu_\tau). \tag{9.11}$$

We now assume that current income and the current price of consumption are known at time t, but future prices and income are uncertain. In the sequel we suppress p_t and interpret μ_t as real income. The consumer now maximizes not Equation (9.8), but rather its expected value with respect to all future prices, subject to Equation (9.10). Since new information, namely the realization of p_t, becomes available each period, the consumer will solve the optimization problem during each period. It can be shown that the optimal consumption path satisfies:

$$E_t U'(C_{t+1}) = \frac{1 + \delta}{1 + r} U'(C_t). \tag{9.12}$$

Equation (9.12) is the famous Euler equation, and it plays a key role in the analysis of intertemporal choice problems. Hall (1978) gives the following derivation. At time t the consumer chooses C_t so as to maximize:

$$(1 + \delta)^{-t}U(C_t) + E_t \sum_{\tau=t+1}^{L} (1 + \delta)^{-\tau}U(C_\tau), \tag{9.13}$$

subject to

$$\sum_{\tau=t}^{L} (1 + r)^{\tau-t}(C_t - \mu_t) = W_t. \tag{9.14}$$

The optimal sequential strategy has the form $C_t = g_t(\mu_t, \mu_{t-1}, \ldots, \mu_0, W_0)$. Consider a variation from this strategy: $C_t = g_t(\mu_t, \mu_{t-1}, \ldots, \mu_0, W_0) + x$; $C_{t+1} = g_{t+1}(\mu_{t+1}, \mu_t, \ldots, \mu_0, W_0) - (1 + r)x$. Note that the new consumption strategy also satisfies the budget constraint. Now consider maximizing:

$$(1 + \delta)^{-t}u(g_t + x) + E_t[(1 + \delta)^{-t-1}u(g_{t+1} - (1 + r)x)$$

$$+ \sum_{\tau=t+2}^{L} (1 + \delta)^{-\tau}u(g_\tau)], \tag{9.15}$$

with respect to x. The first order condition is:

$$(1 + \delta)^{-t}u'(g_t + x) - E_t[(1 + \delta)^{-t-1}(1 + r)u'(g_{t+1} - (1 + r)x) = 0, \quad (9.16)$$

which is equivalent to Equation (9.12).

The Euler equation has a number of important implications for empirical work. For the simple life-cycle model considered here, the most important ones are the following (see Hall (1978)):

- In period t, all variables other than C_t are irrelevant for predicting C_{t+1}.
- Marginal utility satisfies the regression equation:
  $U'(C_{t+1}) = \alpha U'(C_t) + \epsilon_t$, with $\alpha = (1 + \delta)/(1 + r)$ and $E\epsilon_t = 0$.
- If $\delta = r$, the marginal utility of consumption is a random walk:
  $U'(C_{t+1}) = U'(C_t) + \epsilon_t$.

Exercise 9.1
Consider the utility function:

$$U(C_t) = -\frac{1}{2}(\bar{C} - C_t)^2 \qquad (9.17)$$

(a) What do Equation (9.13) and the Euler equation imply for the pattern of consumption over time?

In Chapter 10 we shall extend the life-cycle model by including leisure as an argument in the intratemporal utility function, and by considering multi-person households. Another extension is the incorporation of liquidity constraints. As noted before, most households will not be able to borrow (large) proportions of life-cycle income with only future earnings as collateral. These liquidity constraints set lower bounds to W_t. These bounds are possibly inversely related to (current) earnings, since the amount of credit a credit association is willing to lend is often positively related to current income. We shall not discuss this issue further here. The interested reader is referred to Alessie *et al.* (1989) and Zeldes (1989) for examples of empirical studies on liquidity constraints.

9.3   The subjective rate of time preference

The subjective rate of time preference (SRTP) (equivalently the subjective discount rate, or rate of impatience) is a central concept in intertemporal choice models. It summarizes conveniently how the consumer values paying or receiving one dollar tomorrow instead of today, and this is what the consumer is likely to do in choice situations where costs and benefits accrue in different time periods.

Although the presence of the SRTP in intertemporal choice models is almost universal, it is treated quite differently in the various branches of microeconomic modeling. For example, in the job search literature, the annual SRTP is usually assumed to be constant for all individuals in the sample, and typically fixed at 5 or 10 per cent. Several authors have reported that an attempt to estimate the SRTP failed because of numerical problems (see, for example, Narendranathan and Nickell (1985) and van den Berg (1990)), or generated implausible results (Alessie *et al.* (1989). At the other extreme, authors have attempted to estimate individual discount rates and investigated the relationship with socioeconomic characteristics.

Before discussing some of this literature, it is useful to make explicit a number of assumptions that are made when using the concept of a subjective discount rate. First of all, the concept is strongly connected with the assumption of intertemporally separable preferences. In a model with a nonseparable preference structure, such as Browning's (1991), it is far from obvious how a subjective rate of time preference could be defined in a meaningful way. Second, it is assumed most of the time that the SRTP of an individual is the same for each period, that it is the same for costs as for benefits, and that it does not depend on the size of the amounts involved. On the basis of students' responses to hypothetical questions, Thaler (1981) found evidence that neither of these assumptions hold: discount rates for small amounts were higher than for large amounts, discount rates for benefits were higher than for costs, and discount rates (per unit of time) declined when the length of the total period of time involved increased.

A number of authors have found significant relationships between discount rates and ethnic and socioeconomic characteristics of individuals. Fuchs (1982), who analysed discount rates inferred from responses to hypothetical questions, found a negative relationship between discount rate and education, and lower discount rates for Jewish people than for others. Lawrance's (1991) discount rates were based on Euler equations estimated on data from the Panel Study of Income Dynamics (PSID). Controlling for age and family composition, she found that non-white families without a college education with incomes in the lowest fifth percentile have discount rates that are about seven percentage points higher than those of white, college-educated families with incomes in the ninety-fifth percentile. One explanation for these results is that high discount rates may reduce investment in education, leading to a lower (permanent) income. The results of both Fuchs and Lawrance indicate that discount rates may have cultural components, a view that is supported in the sociological and psychological literature. The congruence of the results of Fuchs and those of Lawrance is remarkable, given that they were obtained using very different methods and sources of information.

9.4   Durables

Consumer's decisions with respect to durable consumption goods are of an inherently dynamic nature. By definition, a durable provides services during

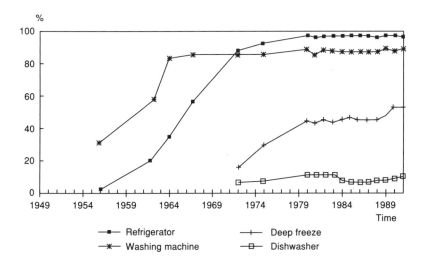

Figure 9.1   Penetration rates for some consumer durables, The Netherlands, 1956–90

more than one period, and in combination with the relatively high investments associated with their purchase, decisions with respect to durables imposes stronger ties between present, current and future decisions than in the case of non-durables. Another distinguishing aspect is that decisions are not only confined to purchase, but also comprise replacement, scrappage and repair.

Figure 9.1 shows, for a number of consumer durables, how the penetration in households has evolved over a thirty-year period. The curves in Figure 9.1 have the typical sigmoid shape which is often encountered in the analysis of growth processes. A convenient mathematical representation is the logistic growth curve:

$$P(t) = \frac{1}{1 + \exp(\alpha_0 + \alpha_1 t)}, \qquad \alpha_1 < 0, \qquad (9.18)$$

where $P(t)$ is the proportion of households that owns the durable at time t. Equation (9.18) satisfies the differential equation:

$$\frac{\partial P(t)}{\partial t} = - \alpha_1 P(t).[1 - P(t)]. \qquad (9.19)$$

Thus growth is proportional to the percentage of households that already owns durables as well as to the percentage that are not yet owners. The first of these two components might be interpreted roughly as a reference group effect (see also Section 4.5), whereas the second reflects the room that is left for further growth. The absolute value of the parameter α_1 measures the speed of growth.

A household production approach

Household demand for consumer durables is another example where the household production theory provides a useful framework for analysis. Households have demands for services such as heating, lighting, refrigeration, and cleaning of textiles and dishes. These services can be produced with the time of household members, energy, water and durable appliances as inputs. In general, the household may choose among different technologies. For example, the dishes may be done by hand, which requires a relatively large amount of time and low investment, or they may be done using a dishwasher, which requires less time, but a higher investment. The household's behaviour may, again, be thought of as resulting from maximizing a utility function subject to restrictions with respect to the available time, income and technologies.

In many cases, the appliances available on the market offer substantial possibilities for trade-offs between purchase and operating costs. Examples are central heating boilers. The consumer has the option between relatively expensive types with high fuel efficiency, and less expensive types which use more fuel per unit of heating. Figure 9.2 provides a simplified representation of the household's choice behaviour in this case. The utility function has two arguments, heating and other goods.

Line I represents the technology with high efficiency. It is steeper than line II, that is per unit of forgone other goods, it generates more heating than technology II. On the other hand, technology I is associated with higher fixed costs than technology II, so that intersection Point A of line I with the horizontal axis is closer to the origin than the intersection Point B of line II. The difference between A and B may be interpreted as the annualized difference in purchase costs of the two technologies.

If a household's demand for heating was completely insensitive to income and prices, it would choose technology II if the demand for heating way smaller than h^*, and technology I otherwise. In that case, the household's behaviour would be based exclusively on the comparison of the net present value of the expenditures associated with both technologies.

To describe behaviour in an explicit dynamic setting, we use the following notation, in which L and H refer to the low-efficiency and high-efficiency version of the durable, respectively.

τ_i : energy use per time period (in kilowatt hours, for example) of type i, $i = L, H$;

R_i : the purchasing price of type i, $i = L, H$;

T : lifetime of both types;

p : price per unit of energy.

If electricity is paid at the end of each period, the total of discounted purchasing and operating costs of type i is given by:

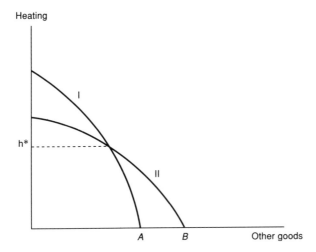

Figure 9.2 Technology choice

$$C_i(\delta) = R_i + \sum_{t=1}^{T} \frac{p\tau_i}{(1 + \delta)^t} \tag{9.20}$$

$$= R_i + p\tau_i \left(\frac{1 - (1 + \delta)^{-T}}{\delta} \right),$$

with δ being the subjective discount rate. The *implicit subjective discount rate* is defined as the value of δ that solves the equation $C_L(\delta) = C_H(\delta)$. Using Equation (9.20), this can be written as:

$$\frac{\delta}{1 - (1 + \delta)^{-T}} = \frac{p(\tau_L - \tau_H)}{R_H - R_L}. \tag{9.21}$$

Exercise 9.2
Show that Equation (9.21) has a unique positive solution if $\tau_L > \tau_H$ and $R_H > R_L$.

Exercise 9.3
Consider the purchasing and operating costs of type i over an infinite horizon, assuming that at $t = kT$, $k = 1, 2, \ldots$, the durable is replaced by an identical one. Derive the expression for the discounted purchase and operating costs, and investigate how the comparison of $C_L(\delta)$ and $C_H(\delta)$ is affected.

Exercise 9.4
Gately (1980) has calculated the implicit discount rate for a high-efficiency and low-efficiency version of Sears refrigerators, with $T = 10$

(lifetime in years), $p(\tau_L - \tau_H) = 15.6$ US\$ (annual difference in operating costs at an electricity price of 3.8 cents per kilowatt hour (national average)) and $R_H - R_L = 34$ US\$ (difference in purchase costs). Verify that the annual implicit discount rate is 45 per cent. Comment on the result.

One of the assumptions we made is that the lifetime of the durable is fixed. This assumption is obviously not satisfied in practice. Product information often mentions the expected lifetime 'on average' or makes some other statement in probability terms. To investigate the effects of a violation of the fixed lifetime assumption, suppose that the lifetime t is a random variable with expectation T. For simplicity, assume in addition that the hazard rate is constant over time, so that t follows the geometric distribution $f(t) = (1 - T^{-1})^{t-1}.T^{-1}$, $t = 1, 2,\dots$. Then the expected discounted purchase and operating costs of type i are given by:

$$C_i(\delta) = \frac{R_i}{1 - (\delta T + 1)^{-1}} + \frac{p\tau_i}{\delta};$$

(9.22)

and the implicit discount rate now follows from

$$\delta + \frac{1}{T} = \frac{p(\tau_L - \tau_H)}{R_H - R_L}.$$

(9.23)

Exercise 9.5
Derive Equations (9.22) and (9.23). Show by comparing the left-hand sides of Equations (9.21) and (9.23) that, for $T > 1$, the δ that solves Equation (9.23) is always smaller than the δ that solves Equation (9.21).

From the statement in Exercise 9.5 it follows that ignoring the randomness of the lifetime of the durable results in an upward bias in the implicit discount rate. In fact, it can be shown that this is the case for any distribution with $Et = T$ (see Kooreman, 1995). The intuitive explanation is that the possible benefit of a late failure does not offset the possible loss incurred at an early failure, because 'late' is discounted more heavily than is 'early'.

Definition

Consider a consumer with utility function $u(.)$. Let x denote a random variable.

- The consumer is said to be *risk neutral* if and only if $E(u(x)) = u(E(x))$. This condition implies that $u(.)$ is linear.

- The consumer is said to be *risk averse* if and only if $E(u(x)) < u(E(x))$. This condition implies that $u(.)$ is concave.
- The consumer is said to be *risk loving* if and only if $E(u(x)) > u(E(x))$. This condition implies that $u(.)$ is convex.

In the analysis above, our behavioural assumption was that the consumer minimizes expected costs. So risk neutrality was assumed implicitly.

The choice set a consumer is facing when purchasing a durable consumption good has both discrete and continuous dimensions. For example, a household without a car that considers buying one has to decide about the preferred mode of transportation (use a car, or use public transportation). If it decides to buy a car, decisions have to be made concerning make, size, type of fuel, type of transmission and so on. Of course, these discrete decisions are closely related to the continuous aspect of the choice, notably the amount of money to be spent on the car and the number of kilometers it is to be driven. While it is conceivable that these decisions are made simultaneously, researchers often distinguish several stages of the decision process. While analytical convenience is, admittedly, an important reason to do so, there is also empirical evidence that households' decision processes are sequential. We mention one example from a somewhat different context. In Dutch data on households that were seriously searching for a new home, 95 per cent of the searchers had already decided whether to search for a rented dwelling or an owned one (Woning Behoefte Onderzoek [Housing Needs Survey], CBS 1992).

In the remainder of this chapter we shall consider a stylized decision process of car ownership in which the discrete aspect is a binary choice. We use the following notation:

y = household income;
f = fixed costs of a car;
p = price per driven kilometre;
R = expenditures on other goods (including public transportation);
K = number of kilometres driven.

The corresponding household budget set is shown in Figure 9.3. It consists of two parts. The first is the triangle which corresponds to the case of car ownership. The second part is Point N on the vertical axis, which corresponds to the case of not owning a car; the number of kilometers driven is zero and income, y, is completely available for other goods. Note that the budget set is non-convex because of the existence of fixed costs of car ownership. As a consequence, finding the optimal choice requires two steps. First, the tangency point of the indifference curves and the solid line has to be determined; this point gives the optimal number of kilometers conditional on owning a car. Second, this indifference curve has to be compared to the indifference curve that passes through Point N. Figures 9.4(a) and 9.4(b) show two different outcomes. The household in Figure 9.4(a) prefers not to own a car, since the indifference curve that passes through Point N

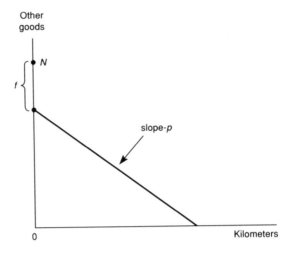

Figure 9.3   Budget set and car ownership

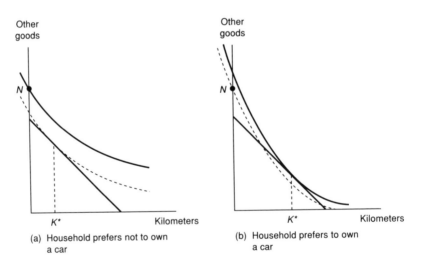

Figure 9.4   Household preferences, car ownership

represents a higher utility level than the indifference curve corresponding to K^*. In Figure 9.4(b), the household prefers to own a car, and will drive K^* kilometers. Note that the model addresses ownership and usage simultaneously.

Exercise 9.6

In a particular country, only one type of car is for sale. The fixed costs are 300 copecks per month, the variable costs are 5 copecks per kilometre. The preferences of a utility-maximizing household with respect to car use and other goods are given by:

$$U = 5.526 + 0.7\log(R) + 0.3\log(K + 10) \qquad (9.24)$$

The monthly household income is 1250 copecks.

(a) Determine algebraically whether the household prefers to own a car, and if so, how many kilometres will be driven.

(b) Calculate the income where the household is indifferent whether it owns a car or not.

(c) Draw the Engel curve of car use.

An empirical study on investments in durables

Brechling and Smith (1992) have performed an interesting empirical analysis of the decision by households to invest in energy-saving measures. The range of measures included loft insulation, wall insulation, double glazing, draught-proofing and hot water tank insulation. In many cases, these measures have not been undertaken by households, although they would be effective according to a mere comparison of expected discounted costs and benefits. The authors present a number of explanations for the incomplete take-up of apparently beneficial energy-saving investments. First, other costs than the monetary amounts that appear in expressions such as Equation (9.21) may play a role in the investment decision. Examples are inconvenience resulting from the installation of the measure and the costs of acquiring all relevant information. There may also exist 'hidden' benefits (of course, working in the opposite direction): for example, a reduction in outside noise in the case of double glazing. Another example is the case where a consumer attaches a positive value to energy conservation *per se*. Second, there may exist credit market failures, that is, households that would be willing to invest in insulation, but would need credit to do so, may be unable to borrow. Other explanations are related to the fact that the benefits and costs of energy-saving investments may accrue to different individuals. This may occur in rented dwellings where the tenant is responsible for paying the energy bills but the landlord is responsible for maintenance and capital investments. Finally, households may not behave optimally, and use inappropriate decisions rules, because the decision problem is too complicated. Brechling and Smith's empirical results – largely based on Logit models explaining the possession of the energy-saving measures – show a strong effect of tenure type on the investment decision, indicating the importance of who benefits

Table 9.1   Consumer credit in The Netherlands (billions Dfl)

	1970	1975	1980	1985	1990	1992
Debit balance (on January 1)	n.a.	n.a.	12.5	11.0	14.7	17.3
Credit granted	1.0	3.2	8.1	5.9	8.5	10.3
Personal loans	0.9	2.4	4.6	3.0	4.3	3.7
Continuous credit	0.1	0.8	3.5	2.9	4.2	6.6

Note: n.a. : not available.

Source: Statistical Handbook (various volumes), Central Bureau of Statistics, The Netherlands.

from energy-saving investments. Evidence of a role of credit constraints was not found.

9.5   Household assets, debts, and net wealth

As shown in Table 9.1, the role of consumer credit (exclusive of mortgages) in household economic affairs has increased rapidly since the 1970s. The annual amount of granted credit increased almost tenfold between 1970 and 1991, corresponding to an annual growth of more than 11 per cent. The popularity of so-called continuous credit increased tremendously, with its share growing from only 10 per cent of total credit granted in 1970 to more than 50 per cent after the mid-1980s.

Both demand- and supply-side factors have been responsible for the increased take-up of credit. The banking sector diversified the forms of credit supply, and improved methods to assess the solvency of credit applicants. From the demand side, demographic developments have played a role. A large proportion of households were in a stage of the life-cycle during which the take-up of credit is likely to occur more frequently than in other stages. The take-up of consumer credit appears to be sensitive to economic conditions and business-cycle fluctuations. As shown in Table 9.1, the credit take-up dipped in the early 1980s, a period that was characterized by high real interest rates, high unemployment and virtually no real wage growth.

Ritzema and Homan (1991) have studied, within a cross-section framework, the take-up of credit for financing the purchase of a car. In a sample of 608 households owning at least one car, 22 per cent had taken up credit to finance the car, with an average credit amount of Dfl. 9900 (approximately US$ 6600 in 1995). Ritzema and Homan also studied the relationship between a large number of characteristics of the household on the one hand and the probability of credit take-up and the amount of credit on the other. The effect of life-cycle stages was generally in accordance with theoretical expectations, although the support was weak in terms of statistical significance.

Mortgages

In terms of monetary amounts, by far the most important credit form used by households is the mortgage. In 1992 the total amount of credit granted to private households through mortgages was more than twice as large as the amount of consumer credit. In most cases, the taking out of a mortgage coincides with the purchase of a house. In Ritzema and Homan's sample, 90 per cent of house owners had taken out a mortgage when the house was purchased. The average initial mortgage amount was Dfl. 93 000. Good job prospects, high education and an early stage in the life-cycle were found to be positively related to the probability of taking out a mortgage.

Ritzema and Homan used their sample to estimate the net balance of household wealth. Debts were defined as the sum of mortgages and other loans; and assets as the sum of objective estimates of the value of the house, car and other property. Annualized wealth embodied in pension claims or a life insurance were not taken into account. For the average household, the total assets amounted to Dfl. 125 000, and net wealth to Dfl. 85 000. For house owners, the corresponding numbers were Dfl. 259 000 and Dfl. 179 000; 7 per cent of the households had negative net wealth.

9.6 Problematic debts

Much of the research on household debts and savings in The Netherlands was initiated in the early 1980s, when a recession led to a sharp increase in the number of households with problematic debts. The percentage of households with financial problems that have been reported in various studies vary from approximately 1 per cent in cases with a strict definition (financial affairs have been reorganized after the involvement of a social security agency), to more than 10 per cent in cases with a wide definition (household states it experiences financial problems regularly).

To find explanations for the existence of problematic debts, we might first look at the characteristics of households with an above-average occurrence of financial problems. Ritzema and Homan estimated a Logit with the existence of financial problems as the dependent variable. They used a large number of explanatory variables including economic characteristics (income, labour-market status, life-cycle stage variables) as well as socio-psychological variables (attitude towards debts, subjective measures of time preference, religious affiliation). A selection of their estimation results is reported in Table 9.2.

Perhaps the most remarkable result is that the probability of financial problems does not appear to be related to income and labour-market status. Table 9.2 also shows that financial problems are associated with a high rate of time preference. For these households, financial problems may be not completely unanticipated and a mere consequence of myopic behaviour. In other cases, households may have been confronted with large unexpected expenditure

Table 9.2   Occurrence of financial problems (selected logit estimation results)[1]

Explanatory variables	Coefficient	St. error
Economic variables		
Logarithm of net monthly income	0.01	0.07
Logarithm of monthly fixed expenditures	0.18	0.11
Unemployed; receives social security benefit	0.41	0.30
Interest rate on first loan	0.08	0.03
Interest rate on second loan	0.14	0.12
Socio–psychological variables		
Parents used to have debts	0.58	0.29
Respondent prefers to save	−1.17	0.58
Respondent prefers to borrow	0.11	0.88
Subjective measure of time preference	0.32	0.10

Notes: 1. The total number of explanatory variables was 46. The number of observations was 800 households; 91 reported financial problems. All coefficients on life–cycle stage variables (not reported here) were insignificant.

Source: Ritzema and Homan (1991).

(for example, because of the failure of durable goods). Financial problems are also associated with high interest rates on the household's loans. Note, however, that high interest rates can be both a cause and a consequence of financial problems.

9.7   Summary

Taking into account dynamic aspects of household behaviour enriches as well as complicates the analysis of household behaviour. It becomes necessary to make a distinction between consumption and investment; between flows and stocks. Increased complexity is one explanation for the fact that most dynamic models assume that preferences are intertemporally separable. This assumption also allows the introduction of the concept of the subjective rate of time preference, which conveniently summarizes how a consumer values the delay of costs and benefits.

As the future is inherently uncertain, a realistic dynamic model should take uncertainty into account explicitly. In Section 9.4 we saw an example of the role it might play. Uncertainty with regard to the lifetime of a consumer durable changed consumer behaviour, even in the case of risk neutrality.

CHAPTER 10

Dynamic Aspects of Household Labour Supply

10.1 Introduction

In Chapter 5 we analysed household labour supply, taking the simplest static neo-lassical model as a starting point. It appeared to be well-suited to extension in various directions. These extensions allowed us to study some important aspects of household labour supply, such as the effects of taxes and social security benefits and the effects of constraints imposed by the demand side of the labour market. Nevertheless, the static nature of the model remains restrictive, as many aspects of household labour supply are of an inherently dynamic nature. For example, a proper analysis of unemployment while ignoring its dynamic aspects is difficult to imagine. Unemployment which lasts for only a few weeks poses a different problem from long-term unemployment, and it also calls for different policies. While Chapter 5 primarily analysed within-period labour supply behaviour (for example, whether to work or not, and if so, how much), the present chapter primarily analyses the timing of events related to labour supply.

The chapter is structured as follows. In Section 10.2 we briefly review some models of life-cycle labour supply. Section 10.3 presents a model of job search. It describes the behaviour of an employed individual who gets job offers and has to decide whether to accept an offer or to reject it and continue searching. We also discuss the similar though more complicated problem when two individuals within a household are looking for jobs simultaneously. Section 10.4 describes the decision about when to retire and the interrelationship of the retirement decisions of husband and wife.

10.2   Life-cycle labour supply models

The model presented in this section is closely related to the two-period consumption model described in Section 9.2. The main difference is that the utility function is now defined over both consumption and hours of work:

$$V(c_1, h_1, c_2, h_2) = U(c_1, h_1) + \left(\frac{1}{1 + \delta}\right) U(c_2, h_2),\tag{10.1}$$

with c_i denoting consumption in period i, and h_i the number of hours worked in period i ($i = 1, 2$). Wealth at the end of the first period now includes labour income. As a result, the analogue of Equation (9.4) in Section 9.2 is:

$$\frac{p_1 c_1}{(1 + r)} + \frac{p_2 c_2}{(1 + r)^2} = W_0 + \frac{\mu_1 + w_1 h_1}{(1 + r)} + \frac{\mu_2 + w_2 h_2}{(1 + r)^2}.\tag{10.2}$$

Now consider the Lagrangean function corresponding to the maximization of Equation (10.1) subject to Equation (10.2). The first order derivatives with respect to c_1 and h_1 imply:

$$\partial U/\partial c_1 = \lambda \cdot \frac{p_1}{1 + r}\tag{10.3a}$$

$$\partial U/\partial h_1 = \lambda \cdot \frac{w_1}{1 + r}.\tag{10.3b}$$

The important characteristic of Equation (10.3) is that both $\partial U/\partial c_1$ and $\partial U/\partial h_1$ depend on p_1 and w_1, but not on p_2 and w_2. This is a direct result of the time-separability assumption. Solving Equations (10.3a) and (10.3b) with respect to c_1 and h_1 yields the so-called Frish-demand functions:

$$h_1 = f_1 (\lambda, w_1, p_1)\tag{10.4}$$

$$c_1 = f_2 (\lambda, w_1, p_1),$$

While h_1 and c_1 depend directly on current prices and wages, the dependency on wages and prices from other periods is transmitted only through λ. Although λ is unobserved, it can be 'differenced away' if panel data are available. However, this requires not only the availability of repeated observations, it also restricts the range of possible parametric forms of Equation (10.4); see, for example, Browning *et al.* (1985).

   In the more general case of a lifetime of L periods, and a household utility function defined over hours of work (or leisure) of two spouses, the household maximizes:

$$V_t = \sum_{s=t}^{L} \left(\frac{1}{1+\delta}\right)^{s-t} U(l_{ms}, l_{fs}, c_s). \tag{10.5}$$

In this formulation, l_{is} is non-market time of partner i ($i = m, f$) and c_s is household commodity consumption in period s.

Since the overall utility function is time-separable, the idea of two-stage budgeting is applicable; see Chapter 2. In the first stage the household decides how much of total life-cycle wealth will be allocated in period t, y_t, say, and at the second stage l_{mt}, l_{ft} and c_t are chosen conditional on y_t. It is important to note the second-stage decision is based on (full) expenditures $y_t = w_{mt}l_{mt} + w_{ft}l_{ft} + c_t$, not on (full) income $Y_t = w_{mt}T + w_{ft}T + \mu_t$ (with μ_t being unearned income and T being the total time budget per spouse). The two are equivalent if μ_t is redefined as the sum of unearned income and net dissavings in period t (the latter being defined as $c_t - w_{mt}h_{mt} - w_{ft}h_{ft} - \mu_t$).

To summarize, the static labour supply model as described in Chapter 4 is *life-cycle consistent*, given that the lifetime utility function is time separable, and provided that the measure of unearned income includes net dissavings.

10.3 Job search

The basic model

Consider an individual who is unemployed at time 0 and who is looking for a job. Jobs are characterized by wages only. While searching, the individual is receiving an income flow, b, which we will refer to as the unemployment benefit (although it may also refer to other sources of income). A job offer is a realization of the random variable, w, which has probability density function $f(w)$. The job offers arrive randomly according to a Poisson process with parameter λ; in this case the waiting time between job offers follows an exponential distribution with parameter λ.[1] If a job is accepted, the individual receives the wage, w, for ever. If it is rejected, the individual continues to receive an income flow, b. Future incomes are discounted continuously at rate δ.

Note that the model contains two elements of uncertainty. First, although the job searcher knows the arrival rate of job offers, he does not know exactly when an offer will arrive. Second, he knows the distribution from which wage offers are drawn, but he does not know in advance which wage will be offered.

The behavioural assumption is that the individual maximizes the expected present discounted value of all future income flows. Denote the maximum of this expected value by V ('the value of optimal search'), and let t be the point in time at which the individual receives a job offer, w.

The present discounted value of the income flow between 0 and t is:

$$\int_0^t be^{-\delta s}ds = \frac{b}{\delta}(1 - e^{-\delta t}),$$ (10.6)

(see Appendix B). If the job searcher accepts the offer at time t, the present discounted value of the income flow after t is:

$$\int_t^\infty w \cdot e^{-\delta s}ds = \frac{w}{\delta} \cdot e^{-\delta t}.$$ (10.7)

If the offer is rejected and optimal search is resumed, the present discounted value of optimal search is $V.e^{-\delta t}$. (Recall that V is a stock variable.) Thus the total value of optimal search satisfies the equation:

$$V = E_t\left[\frac{b}{\delta}(1 - e^{-\delta t}) + e^{-\delta t}E_w\max\left(\frac{w}{\delta}, V\right)\right].$$ (10.8)

Note that Equation (10.8) is a recursive equation in V; in the dynamic programming literature, this type of equation is known as a Bellman equation.

Using the fact that $Ee^{-\delta t} = \lambda(\lambda + \delta)$ (see Appendix B), Equation (10.8) can be written as:

$$V = \frac{b}{\lambda + \delta} + \frac{\lambda}{\lambda + \delta}E_w\left[\max\left(\frac{w}{\delta}, V\right)\right].$$ (10.9)

Equation (10.9) shows that an optimal strategy implies that the job should be accepted if $w > \delta V \equiv \xi$ and rejected if $w < \xi$; ξ is referred to as the *reservation wage*.

To obtain a formulation in terms of ξ, note that $E_w\max(w/\delta, V) = V + E_w\max(w/\delta - V, 0) = V + (1/\delta)E_w\max(w - V\delta, 0)$. Replacing V by ξ/δ in Equation (10.9), we obtain, after rewriting:

$$\xi = b + \frac{\lambda}{\delta}E_w\max(w - \xi, 0).$$ (10.10)

The hazard rate at time t implied by the model is equal to the probability that the individual receives an offer between t and $t + dt$, times the probability that the offer is acceptable:

$$\theta(t)\, dt = \lambda P(w > \xi)\, dt = \lambda(1 - F(\xi))\, dt.$$ (10.11)

Since all parameters in the model are independent of t, the hazard is independent of t as well. As a consequence, the duration of search follows an exponential distribution with expectation $[\lambda P(w > \xi)]^{-1}$. In this case, the model is called *stationary*. Below we shall discuss an example of non-stationarity.

Equation (10.10), which is implicit in ξ, can be solved analytically only for very simple forms of the wage offer distribution $f(w)$. An example is the case where wages are drawn from the uniform distribution:

$$f(w) = \frac{1}{A} \cdot I \ (0 \leq w \leq A), \qquad (10.12)$$

with $A >> \xi$ and where $I(z) = 1$ if z is true and $I(z) = 0$ otherwise. The solution for ξ is then given by:

$$\xi = A + \frac{\delta A}{\lambda} \left(1 - \sqrt{(1 + \frac{2\lambda}{\delta} (1 - \frac{b}{A})}\right), \qquad (10.13)$$

which associated hazard:

$$\theta = \lambda P(w > \xi) = \lambda \ (1 - \frac{\xi}{A}) =$$
$$\qquad (10.14)$$
$$\sqrt{\delta^2 + 2\lambda\delta \ (1 - \frac{b}{A})} - \delta;$$

see Exercise 10.2 on page 177. The hazard of accepting a job increases when the unemployment benefit, b, becomes smaller, when the mean of the offered wages $(A/2)$ becomes larger, and when the arrival rate of job offers, λ, increases. If the individual becomes more myopic, that is, if δ increases, then any job that has a wage larger than b is acceptable, so that the hazard approaches to $\lambda P(w > b) = (1 - b/A)$.

Satisficing

We have seen that the optimal strategy for a job seeker is to accept a job as soon as the offered wage exceeds some unique reservation value. This type of strategy is sometimes referred to as satisficing: an individual will not wait until the highest possible wage is being offered but stop searching as soon as a wage is offered that can be considered satisfactory. Satisficing and maximizing are not conflicting paradigms, as has sometimes been suggested. As the job search model shows, they can be reconciled quite easily.

Some elasticities

For policy purposes, two interesting numbers are the elasticities of the hazard rate with respect to b and with respect to λ. It can be shown that these are equal to:

$$\frac{\partial \log \theta}{\partial \log b} = - \frac{f(\xi)}{F(\xi)} \cdot \frac{b}{1 + \theta/\delta}$$

and

$$\frac{\partial \log \theta}{\partial \log \lambda} = 1 - \frac{f(\xi)}{F(\xi)} \cdot \frac{\xi - b}{1 + \theta/\delta} \,, \tag{10.15}$$

respectively; see Lancaster and Chesher (1983) for a derivation. Note that

$$\frac{\partial \log E(t)}{\partial \log z} = \frac{z}{E(t)} \cdot \frac{\partial E(t)}{\partial \theta} \cdot \frac{\partial \theta}{\partial z} =$$

$$z\theta \left(-\frac{1}{\theta^2} \right) \frac{\partial \theta}{\partial z} = -\frac{\partial \log \theta}{\partial \log z} \,, \tag{10.16}$$

with $z = b$ or $z = \lambda$. Thus the elasticity of the expected duration of search equals minus the elasticity of the hazard.

While the elasticity of the expected duration of search with respect to the unemployment benefit must be positive, it is not possible to sign a priori the elasticity with respect to the arrival rate of job offers. A change in the offer arrival rate has two opposite effects. On the one hand, there is a negative effect on the expected duration because of the increased expected number of occasions on which the unemployed person is able to accept an offer. On the other hand, there is a positive effect because the increased number of opportunities makes the searcher more selective and therefore raises the reservation wage. Although is seems plausible that the more offers one receives the sooner an offer will be accepted, this is not necessarily so (see also van den Berg, 1994).

Some empirical studies

The pioneering articles by Lancaster (1979) and Lancaster and Nickell (1980) have been followed by a large number of empirical studies, based on data from various countries and time periods. Most of the papers estimate reduced-form models; that is, models which directly specify the hazard rate as a function of explanatory variables without a direct link with an underlying search model. Estimation of structural models, in which the structural parameters such as the job offer arrival rate and the wage distribution are estimated directly, is less common. Structural models generally require a tighter set of assumptions than reduced-form models, in particular with respect to the form of the wage-offer distribution. Moreover, estimation is more complicated, partly because it is usually required to solve the reservation wage numerically, for each individual, at each evaluation of the likelihood function. On the other hand, structural models potentially provide more insight, since they allow us to disentangle the roles of the various components in the search process.

The estimates for the elasticity of unemployment duration with respect to

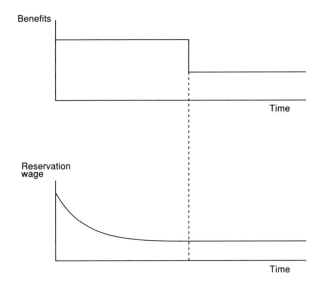

Figure 10.1   Reservation wage when benefits decrease over time

the level of unemployment benefits varied between 0.5 and 1.0 in studies that used data from the 1970s. Studies based on more recent data generally found somewhat lower estimates. An interesting study, both from a theoretical and empirical point of view, is the paper by van den Berg (1990). His model explicitly accounts for the fact that the benefit level during unemployment decreases over time. The unemployed individual in his data set receives approximately 70 per cent of the previous wage during the first two years of unemployment. Thereafter, the individual obtains public assistance benefits, which are often substantially lower. As a consequence, the model is non-stationary, and the reservation wage decreases over time; see Figure 10.1

The elasticity of expected unemployment duration with respect to the benefit level during the first two years was found by van den Berg to be approximately 0.1, whereas the elasticity with respect to the benefit level after two years was approximately 0.5. This implies that reducing benefits after two years would be much more effective in shortening the duration of unemployment, than reducing initial benefits. Note that the model assumes that individuals fully anticipate the future decrease in unemployment benefits.

Simultaneous search by husband and wife

The models we have presented were based on a number of simplifying assumptions. In addition to the relaxation of the stationarity assumption, authors have considered extensions of the model in various other directions, such as the inclusion of job characteristics other than the wage, search costs, and the distinction between different destinations (employed, out of the labour force) when leaving unemployment.

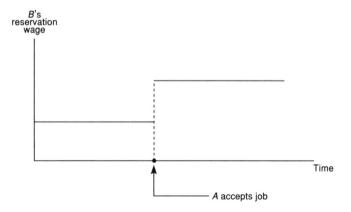

Figure 10.2   B's reservation wage as a function of time

Here we discuss how the model might be extended to describe simultaneous job search by husband and wife in a household. Such a situation is not uncommon, given the increased prevalence of double-career households. If both spouses are looking for jobs, the interdependency of their optimal strategies will be crucially dependent upon the form of the utility function. If it is the couple's mere objective to maximize their joint income $(y_m + y_f)$, it is not difficult to verify that their strategies will be independent. It is likely, however, that the utility function is not separable into y_m and y_f. Suppose, for example, that high wages are associated with less leisure, and that spouses attach a positive value to the sum of the time they have available for non-market work (for example, to taking care of children). Then the marginal utility of the wage of spouse A is a decreasing function of the wage of spouse B, and vice versa. The reservation wage of spouse B, will generally change as soon as spouse A accepts a job, with wage w_A, say, and the new value of B's reservation wage will depend on w_A. Suppose, for example, that A was lucky enough to get a wage which was substantially larger than his reservation wage. Then the decrease in the marginal utility of B's wage will be large and her reservation wage is likely to increase substantially; see Figure 10.2.

As a consequence, as long as both spouses are looking for jobs, the reservation wage of each spouse will depend not only on the distribution and arrival rate of his or her own job offers, but also on those of his/her spouse. The formalization of a simultaneous search is conceptually straightforward, but the formulas become quite complex, even for the simplest specifications. As yet it has not been used in empirical work.

Exercise 10.1

Let y denote the current income flow of a job seeker. Assume that s/he wishes to maximize the expected discounted value of $U(y)$ rather than of y, with $U(y)$ being an increasing function of y. Show that the reservation wage satisfies:

$$U(\xi) = U(b) + \frac{\lambda}{\delta} E_w \max \{U(w) - U(\xi), 0\}. \qquad (10.17)$$

Exercise 10.2

Assume that wages are distributed according to Equation (10.12)

(a) Show that:

$$E_w \max(w - \xi, 0) = \frac{1}{2} \frac{\xi^2}{A} - \xi + \frac{A}{2}. \qquad (10.18)$$

(b) Show, using Equation (10.11), that the reservation wage satisfies:

$$\xi = b + \frac{\lambda}{\delta} \left(\frac{1}{2} \frac{\xi^2}{A} + \frac{A}{2} - \xi \right). \qquad (10.19)$$

(c) Show that one of the two solutions of Equation (10.19) is not admissible as it implies $\xi > A$ and $\theta < 0$.

(d) Show that:

$$\lim_{\delta \to \infty} \sqrt{\delta^2 + 2\lambda\delta \left(1 - \frac{b}{A}\right)} - \delta = 1 - b/A. \qquad (10.20)$$

Exercise 10.3

Consider the case where an individual anticipates receiving the wage w only until time z; z is a random variable which follows an exponential distribution with parameter $\tau > 0$.

(a) Assume that at time z the individual again receives a benefit b and resumes optimal search. Show that the reservation wage satisfies:

$$\xi = b + \frac{\lambda}{\delta + \tau} E_w \max(w - \xi, 0). \qquad (10.21)$$

(b) Assume that after time z the individual remains unemployed for ever while receiving no income at all. Show that the reservation wage satisfies:

$$\xi = b \left(\frac{\delta + \tau}{\delta} \right) + \frac{\lambda}{\delta} E_w \max(w - \xi, 0). \qquad (10.22)$$

Interpret the result.

10.4   Retirement

Retirement is obviously an important dynamic aspect of labor supply. Recently, it has received considerable attention from labour economists, especially in the USA. Much of this work is based on the comprehensive Retirement History Survey (RHS) and focuses on the effects on the date of retirement of the financial incentives of the social security system.

Figure 10.3 plots non-parametric retirement hazard rates for men calculated from panel data in the RHS. The non-parametric retirement hazard rate at age 62, for example, is defined as the ratio between the number of individuals who retire when they are 62, by the number reaching 62 without having previously retired.

The hazard rates show clear peaks at the ages of 62 and 65. The first peak coincides with the youngest age at which one can receive benefits from the social security system. Note that, in theory, there would be no such peak if individuals were able to borrow against future social security benefits. Between the ages of 62 and 65, benefits increase by 7 per cent per year of work, whereas after age 65, benefits increase by only 1 per cent per year. This provides one explanation for the second peak at the age of 65. The 65-year peak is also related to the absence of well-developed health insurance markets for large groups of retirees younger than 65. The distribution of health expenditure is long-tailed (that is, there is a non-negligible probability of having to make very high expenditure for health care), which makes it too risky for these people to retire before the age of 65; see Rust and Phelan (1993). Finally, retirement at the age of 65 is mandatory in many jobs.

Simultaneous retirement decisions of husband and wife

Most research on retirement has focused on the individual. The analysis of retirement decisions in dual career household, however, is much more complex. For example, if one spouse retires, household income decreases, which may provide an incentive for the other spouse to remain in work. On the other hand, spouses may want to retire together if their non-market times are complements. Given that the percentage of married couples with both spouses working has increased rapidly since the 1960s in many countries, as we saw in earlier chapters, analysing joint retirement decisions becomes more relevant.

An interesting empirical study of retirement decisions when both partners are working is the paper by Hiedemann (1993). The interdependence of the partners' decisions and the possibility that they have different preferences was recognized explicitly by using the Stackelberg model, with male leadership described (see Chapter 3) as a theoretical framework. Hiedemann opted for this solution concept because survey responses indicated that the wife makes her retirement decision conditional on the husband's behaviour, and after the husband has made his decision. The assumption seems plausible for the RHS cohorts analysed in the paper (the primary respondents were born between 1905 and 1911).

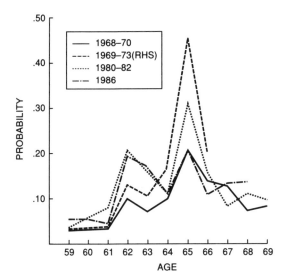

Source: Hurd (1990).

Figure 10.3 Retirement hazard rates

Hiedemann found that the older the husband is relative to the wife, the more likely the wife is to retire early. This finding indicates that husband and wives tend to retire simultaneously. In addition, she found weak evidence that husbands regard the non-market time of both spouses as substitutes, whereas wives regard them as complements.

10.5 Summary

Job-search and retirement are two important aspects of labour supply that are hard to analyse and comprehend using static models alone. The job-search model described here builds on the basic premise of the neo-classical model – utility (or income) maximization – but accounts for the uncertainty that characterizes the individual's environment. We have also seen that the duration of unemployment is sensitive not only to the level but also to the timing of unemployment benefits.

The discussion of retirement decisions showed that institutional settings (such as the impossibility of borrowing against future social security benefits, and a limited accessibility to health insurance) are important determinants of retirement behaviour.

Note

1. For a discussion of Poisson and exponential relationships, see, for example, Mood *et al.* (1974), sections 2.4 and 4.2; or Lancaster (1990), section 5.2.

Investment in Human Capital

11.1 Introduction

Human capital consists of all those qualities of a person, such as knowledge, health, skills and experience, that affect his or her possibilities of earning current and future money income, psychological income, and income in kind. Human capital is a stock variable that characterizes some important aspects of a person. The flow variables corresponding to this stock variable are investment (which increases the stock) and depreciation (which decreases the stock).

The founders of the human capital theory, Mincer (1958), Schultz (1960) and Becker (1962), concentrated their attention on the effects of education and training. However, the health or physical condition of individuals is also a component of their human capital. In the beginning (during the 1960s) this aspect was paid less attention than education, mainly because of measurement problems and the fact that health was often considered to be an exogenous variable.

Since the pioneering work of Mincer and the others, a large body of research, both theoretical and empirical, has emerged. Most research concentrates on investment in education and its effect on future income. After formal education in school, investment in human capital continues in the form of on-the-job training and the building-up of experience. However, individuals also spend time and money on investments that will not necessarily increase their earning capacity. When they learn how to swim, how to play the guitar, or how to prepare a delicious meal, this will generally not affect their future money income, but it may have great influence on their future utility level.

Human capital is built up during several periods, and returns are expected for the current and future periods. Therefore, models for human capital formation are necessarily dynamic. The simplest models are two-period models: investments are concentrated in the first period, and the returns in the second. The more complicated models distinguish several life-cycle periods, or consider time as a continuous variable. The models are used to study the optimal choice of time and money expenditures on education.

Some important results of the research in this field are that there is evidence that: (i) the rate of return on investments in formal education is high compared to returns on other investments, even if this is not subsidized; (ii) individuals do indeed base their schooling decisions on expected returns; and (iii) a form of self-selection takes place, showing that those with greater ability and a higher probability of success are more inclined to invest than individuals who are less talented or ambitious.

In most analyses, the time and money that individuals spend on education and schooling are considered as investments, but these activities could have a consumption aspect as well. People may enjoy studying because it satisfies their curiosity and because it is a form of self-realization that gives them self-esteem. So, even if expected financial returns are low, individuals may still be inclined to spend part of their time and money budget on education.

Health is another component of human capital. Although it could be considered partly as an exogenous variable, it certainly also has an endogenous part that can be influenced by investments. Also, the direct utility of health is clear, although most of us may only realize this when we become ill.

In Section 11.2 we shall concentrate on investments in formal education, and in Section 11.3 on on-the-job training. Aspects of interrupted work careers are discussed in Section 11.4. Not only the individual and his or her parents invest in schooling, so does the government. We shall pay attention to public and private expenditure on education in Section 11.5. In Section 11.6 investments in health are discussed.

11.2   Formal education

In this section we shall discuss two-period models of the demand for formal education. The number of years that people spend in school depends on the demand and supply of education. In most countries, elementary education is free or almost free, but the duration and quality of this education varies over countries. In Table 11.1 some averages of schooling durations are mentioned for different regions of the world. The average period of schooling is shortest in Africa and longest in high-income countries. The pattern is similar for the annual public expenditure per child.

After completing their elementary schooling individuals can choose either to continue their education, or to stop and start working. This is the point where most models about human capital formation start.

The central point in all human capital models is the relationship between earning capacity per hour, w, and someone's stock of human capital, HC. In particular the relationship between wage rate and schooling is studied in most applied work. Let us assume that after leaving obligatory education at the beginning of Period 1, a person's stock of human capital is at a level HC_1 and his or her earning capacity is w_1 per hour. By investing t_s hours in

Table 11.1   Years of school enrolment and annual public expenditure
per school–aged child, 1960s and 1970s

Region (number of countries observed)	Expected enrolment per child (years)	Annual public expenditure per child (1970$)
World (47)	8.9	2 878
Africa (13)	5.7	455
Latin America (8)	8.0	801
East and Southeast Asia (6)	9.4	913
West and South Asia (5)	7.3	1 234
High–income countries (15)	12.0	6 854

Source: Schultz (1993).

schooling in Period 1, this person's stock of human capital increases. The fruitfulness of the investment may depend on the person's abilities, A; A is assumed to be an exogenous variable. Therefore, the increase in human capital is $\Delta HC(t_s, A)$. At the beginning of the second period the stock of human capital would be:

$$HC_2 = HC_1 + \Delta HC(t_s, A)$$

if there were no depreciation of human capital. However, human capital deteriorates, (for example because people forget things, or because new technologies reduce the value of old skills. Even to keep skills and knowledge at a constant level (replacement) investment is necessary. Therefore:

$$HC_2 = (1 - \delta)HC_1 + \Delta HC(t_s, A),$$

where δ is the depreciation rate of human capital ($0 < \delta < 1$). As a result, the wage rate in Period 2 (w_2) is determined by HC_1, the investment effort $\Delta HCT(t_s, A)$ and δ:

$$w_2(HC_2) = w_2(t_s, HC_1, \delta, A).$$

If HC_1, δ and A are exogenous, w_2 can only be affected by t_s, the time spent on education.

Consider a person who wishes to maximize utility over two periods. Assuming that utility depends only on consumption in these two periods and that earnings can be influenced by schooling, the consumer has to decide how much to invest in schooling. The costs of this investment consists of direct costs related to t_s (fees, books): $p_s t_s$, plus the opportunity costs of the time involved in schooling: $w_1 t_s$. The costs are concentrated in the first period and the expected gains in the second. Since the consumer's horizon does not go beyond the second period, investments in the second period do not make sense: there is no third period in which to collect the gains.

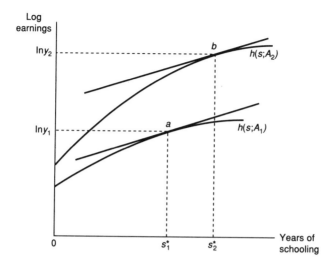

Figure 11.1 The relationship between wage rate and years of schooling, for persons with different abilities

The relationship between w_2 and schooling time, t_s, and abilities, A:

$$w_2 = h(t_s, A),$$

is characterized by the assumptions:

$$\frac{\partial w_2}{\partial t_s} > 0, \; \frac{\partial^2 w_2}{\partial t_s^2} < 0, \; \frac{\partial w_2}{\partial A} > 0, \tag{11.1}$$

as illustrated in Figure 11.1 (Willis, 1986).

It is further assumed that the consumer can borrow money, B, to finance consumption and the costs of investment in the first period at an interest rate, r; the loan has to be paid back in the second period. In both periods a total of T hours are available for work and schooling. The model becomes:

Maximize $U(x_1, x_2)$ $\qquad$ (11.2)

$$s.t. \; p_1 x_1 + p_s t_s = Y_{01} + w_1 t_w + B$$
$$p_2 x_2 + B(1 + r) = Y_{02} + w_2 T$$
$$t_w + t_s = T$$
$$0 \leq t_s \leq T$$
$$w_2 = h(t_s, A),$$

where

x_i = consumption in period i, i = 1, 2
p_i = price of consumption in period i, i = 1, 2
Y_{0i} = unearned income in period i, i = 1, 2

t_s = time spent on schooling in period 1
t_w = labour time, period 1
p_s = price of schooling (per hour)
w_i = wage rate in period i, $i = 1, 2$.

The wage rate w_1 is predetermined, but w_2 depends on t_s and A, with properties mentioned in Equation (11.1). It is assumed that there is no uncertainty with respect to the relationship between earnings in the second period and investment made. The consumer's choice variables are x_1, x_2 and t_s (or $t_w = T - t_s$).

The restrictions of the model in Equation (11.2) can be combined into one intertemporal budget restriction, by eliminating B (see Section 9.2):

$$Y_{01} + w_1 T + \frac{Y_{02} + Tw_2 (t_s)}{1 + r} = p_1 x_1 + (p_s + w_1) t_s + \frac{p_2 x_2}{1 + r}. \quad (11.3)$$

According to Equation (11.3), the total discounted value of full income equals the total discounted costs of consumption and schooling. Recall that the costs of schooling consist of direct costs ($p_s t_s$) and opportunity costs ($w_1 t_s$).

Exercise 11.1
Show that the first-order conditions for an interior maximum of U, in the case of part-time demand for education, ($0 < t_s < T$), imply that:

$$\frac{\partial w_2}{\partial t_s} \frac{T}{(1 + r)} = w_1 + p_s$$

$$\frac{\partial U}{\partial x_1} \bigg/ \frac{\partial U}{\partial x_2} = \frac{p_1(1 + r)}{p_2}. \quad (11.14)$$

The full price of an extra hour spent on education in the first period is $p_s + w_1$, and the income gain in the second period as a result of such an extra hour is $T \, \partial w_2 / \partial t_s$ (without discounting). The rate of return on marginal investments in education is found by solving i from:

$$\frac{\partial w_2}{\partial t_s} \frac{T}{(1 + i)} = w_1 + p_s. \quad (11.5)$$

This means that in the optimum this rate of return equals the market interest rate, r.

In Figure 11.2 it is shown what the net discounted wealth function of schooling could look like. Net discounted wealth is found by adding net income of Period 1 and net discounted income of Period 2. Utility is maximized in two stages: first maximize net discounted wealth, then choose the

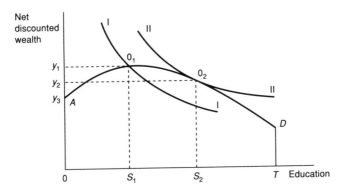

Source: Kodde (1985).

Figure 11.2 Net discounted wealth and the optimal schooling choice in an integrated human capital/consumption model

optimal allocation of consumption over the two periods. Maximum net wealth (level y_1 in Figure 11.2) is found at education level s_1.

Exercise 11.2
Show that maximum utility is achieved by first choosing t_s, such that total discounted net wealth is at a maximum, and then allocating consumption in an optimal way over the two periods.

Exercise 11.3
Show that if the optimum is a corner solution with $t_s = T$, the rate of return on the Tth hour invested in human capital is greater than or equal to the market interest rate. Show that if the optimum implies that $t_s = 0$, the rate of return for the first hour is already less than the market interest rate.

Exercise 11.4
Show that it is only possible to apply the two-stage procedure in the human capital model in Equation (11.2) because leisure and household production time in both periods are assumed to be fixed. Check what happens to Equation (11.2) if leisure appears in the utility function of the model.

In Equation (11.2) education is purely a form of investment. The model concentrates on the monetary aspects of education. Traditionally, however, education has been treated as a form of consumption. In the static neo-classical models it was just one of the budget categories, and the optimal amount spent on education depended on preferences, income and prices.

Equation (11.2) totally ignores the consumption aspect of education. The consumption and human capital models are integrated in Equation (11.6) by an extension of the utility function of Equation (11.2):

Maximize $U(x_1, t_s, x_2)$ (11.6)

$$s.t. \ p_1 x_1 + (p_s + w_1) \ t_s + \frac{p_2 x_2}{1 + r} = Y_{01} + w_1 T + \frac{Y_{02} + w_2 T}{1 + r}$$

$$w_2 = h \ (t_s, A)$$

$$0 \le t_s \le T.$$

Since the marginal utility of time spent on education is positive, it can be exchanged for net wealth, keeping the utility level constant. It means that a person may spend more time and money on education than necessary for maximizing total net wealth, just because s/he likes studying. In Figure 11.2, two indifference curves are drawn. The one representing the highest utility level passes through Point O_2. In O_2 the level of schooling is higher and net wealth is lower than in O_1. Point O_1 is no longer optimal.

In the optimum O_2 the marginal rate of substitution equals the ratio between net costs of education and the price of consumption goods:

$$\frac{\frac{\partial U}{\partial t_s}}{\frac{\partial U}{\partial x_1}} = \frac{w_1 + p_s - \frac{\partial w_2}{\partial t_s} \frac{T}{1 + r}}{p_1} .$$ (11.7)

These net costs of education equal the full marginal costs, $w_1 + p_s$, minus the marginal discounted benefits.

Empirical results for the pure investment model, the pure consumption model and the integrated model are listed in Table 11.2. The results represent the decision of individuals to continue, or not to continue, formal education after finishing their high-school education. The estimated parameters of the Logit regression relate to the probability of choosing post-secondary education, not to the optimal number of hours. In the pure human capital model this probability is related to future earnings, net forgone earnings and two ability indicators: 'ability score mathematics' and 'ability score languages'. These are added to see whether a form of self-selection makes the more able students choose extra education, as Rosen (1977) suggested. The probability that these students are able to complete post-secondary education is greater. The ability variables do indeed have a significant effect on the probability for further education.

In the pure consumption model, family income and taste variables (the background of the parents) are introduced, but future earnings are excluded from the analysis. On the basis of this model we conclude that the consumption aspect of education should not be neglected. Family income has a significant influence. The background of the mother is more pronounced than

Table 11.2 Logit parameter estimates of the demand for post-secondary education

	Human capital model	Consumption model	Integrated model
Log (net forgone earnings)	−0.73**	−0.12	−0.73*
Log (net future earnings)	1.55**		1.24**
Ability score mathematics	0.42**		0.43**
Ability score languages	0.31*		0.26**
Log (family income)		1.21**	1.01**
Education father low		−0.01	−0.05
Education father high		0.06	−0.03
Education mother low		−0.44*	−0.33
Education mother high		0.38	0.38
Constant	−8.86**	−6.61**	−13.98**

Notes: ** = significant 5% level.
* = significant 10% level.

Source: Kodde (1985).

that of the father, although most coefficients are not significant.

The fact that family income has a significant effect on the decision to continue education could also be caused by the *liquidity constraint* that some students face when trying to borrow money. In the model it is assumed that everybody can borrow as much money as they think is optimal, but in real life uncertainty about future earnings exists for both the individual and the bank. Banks may refuse the provide a loan, on the basis of an uncertain future income, thus making it impossible for a student to continue his or her education. However, the student's family may be willing to take more risk than is the bank. Therefore, family income is not only an indicator for the consumption aspect of education, but it could also be an indication for the presence of liquidity constraints. Students with a high ability score may face fewer restrictions from the supply side, since the banks will also interpret this score as an indicator for the risk of failure. Those with low risk may get a loan and continue to study; those with a high risk of failure may not get the loan.

11.3 On-the-job training

So far we have assumed that human capital is only affected by schooling and that it remains constant, or even deteriorates, after the schooling period ends. However, when individuals work, human capital continues to form. Work experience and on-the-job training are also very important forms of human capital formation. This is reflected by the age–earnings profiles of most workers. These profiles start off at different levels and at different ages, depending on the years of schooling of each individual and their job

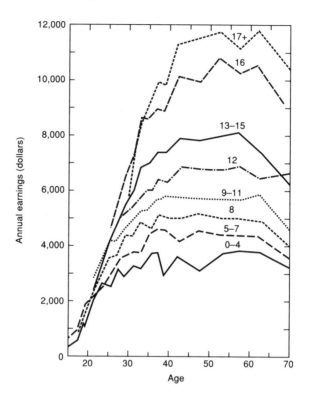

Source: Mincer (1974).

Figure 11.3   Some age–earnings profiles

characteristics, but they all look alike: they have a positive slope in the
beginning and a negative or zero slope during the last period of the working
career of the individual. This is illustrated in Figure 11.3. The shape of the
curves explains the popularity of the well-known quadratic earnings function:

$$\log Y = \beta_0 + \beta_1 t_s + \beta_2 t_w + \beta_3 t_w^2, \tag{11.8}$$

where Y = annual earnings; t_s = years of formal education; and t_w = years
of paid labour. When $t_w = 0$, the starting point of the profile is found at
level $\beta_0 + \beta_1 t_s$. Mincer (1974) provides a theoretical basis for the quadratic
training part of Equation (11.8). Here we shall only provide an intuitive
explanation of the quadratic shape. Assume that the earning capacity of the
individual at the start of the post-school period is at a certain level. In each
period during the working career the individual has to allocate his or her
earning capacity to earnings and investments in training. It is assumed that
the investment ratio will decrease gradually during the working career. At
the beginning of the working career, investments will cause human capital
and the corresponding earning capacity to increase. Annual income rises,

even though part of the earning capacity, are spent on investments. Later in the working career the investments will not be enough to compensate for the depreciation of human capital. Broadly, this explains that:

$$\log Y = \beta_0 + \beta_1 t_s + \beta_2 t_w + \beta_3 t_w^2. \tag{11.9}$$

11.4   Interrupted careers

The earning profiles of women are often interrupted. During the period that they have young children, some women withdraw from the labour market, and others work fewer hours. The earning profiles of households show jumps because of the changing composition of the household over time and the changing labour market position of its members. In the models we have introduced so far in this chapter, this behaviour could not be optimal, because in these models either life-time wealth or life-time utility based on consumption is maximized. However, in earlier chapters we emphasized that utility depends not only on consumption. Children, for example, play an important role in households, as we saw in Chapters 7 and 8. In dynamic household choice models, family composition cannot be considered as an exogenous variable. The number of children in the household reveals the parents' preferences and the expected utility of having children (and less net wealth) is apparently greater than the utility of having maximum net life-time wealth and no children.

During the interruption to the working careers of women (or men), investments that could increase the earning capacity of the mother stop. There is no more on-the-job training and human capital depreciates. This is illustrated in Figure 11.4. At the same time, new human capital is created (children). Parents educate their children and when these children enter school they already seem to have different levels of human capital stocks. In terms of the models of Chapter 7, we would say there are 'quality' differences in child care. Since the foundation of child development is laid down during the first years, normally the loss of human capital of a parent is (more than) outweighed by the growth of human capital of the children raised. The consequences of child neglect can be very serious; see, for example, Wolfe (1987).

The decrease in earning capacity of women who return to the labour market after an interruption was first studied by Mincer and Ofek (1982). Their results are shown in Table 11.3. The drop in the wage rates increases with the length of the period of interruption.

Weiss and Gronau (1981) indicate that interruptions do not merely result in the loss of current earnings and a lower level of earnings after re-entering the labour market. They also affect the investment in human capital of women when these interruptions are anticipated. For example, many companies are not willing to invest as much in the careers of their female employees as in those of male employees, because they expect the women to stop work,

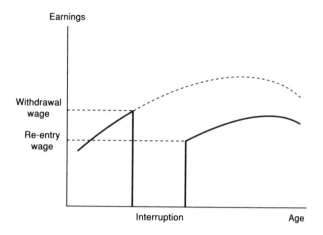

Figure 11.4   Earnings profile of an interrupted career

Table 11.3   Withdrawal and re-entry wage rates, by length of interruption period

| | Years of non–participation | | | |
	0	1–2	3–4	5–6
Withdrawal hourly wage rate ($)*	2.27	1.92	1.70	1.73
Reentry hourly wage rate ($)**	2.35	1.75	1.46	1.27
Number of observations	931	128	141	104

Notes: * Wages are in constant 1976 prices.
** $2.27 and $2.35 are average hourly wage rates for continuous workers in 1971 and 1972, respectively.

Source: Mincer and Ofek (1982).

or reduce working hours, when they have children. This phenomenon might explain some of the wage differences between men and women.

11.5   Private and public expenditures on schooling

The models we have studied so far all had to do with private investments and private returns. However, society also invests in individuals. In Table 11.1 we showed some average amounts that are spent in different countries. The social returns are the increase in productivity of the labour force. But higher productivity usually means higher wages, so the individual benefits from the investment by society. Only the difference between productivity and wage is a social return. Despite measurement difficulties, the difference between social and private returns is an important criterion for allocating public resources among competing programs to maximize social welfare.

Table 11.4 *Public and private expenditure on education as a percentage of GDP, 1988*

	Public	Private	Public and private
Japan	3.8	1.2	4.9
Spain	3.9	1.1	5.0
Germany	4.3	1.9	6.2
Portugal	4.7	0.2	4.9
United Kingdom	4.7	–	–
Italy	4.8	–	–
Australia	4.8	–	–
United States	5.0	0.7	5.7
France	5.1	0.7	5.7
Switzerland	5.1	–	–
Austria	5.6	–	–
Sweden	5.7	–	5.7
Republic of Ireland	5.8	0.4	6.2
Luxembourg	6.0	–	–
Belgium	6.1	–	–
The Netherlands	6.3	0.3	6.6
Canada	6.4	0.8	7.2
Norway	6.6	–	–
Finland	6.8	–	6.8
Denmark	6.8	0.1	6.9
Average OECD	4.8	0.9	5.7

Source: OECD (1992).

Assuming that the individual invests to maximize his private life-time wealth, society should only invest where social returns exceed private returns, if governments act only on economic grounds. In Table 11.4 we show some OECD figures on public and private expenditure on education. Public expenditure, on average, amounts to 4.8 per cent of the GDP, and private to only 0.9 per cent. It should be noticed that in this table only the private 'out-of-pocket' expenses are included; (private) opportunity costs are neglected.

Within countries it is important to know which households benefit most from government expenditure on education. Low income-groups or high-income groups? In Western Europe, governments spend money on elementary, high school and university education. All income groups benefit from the expenditure on elementary and high school education, but it is different for university education. If we consider university students as still being members of the households of their parents, it is found that high-income classes benefit most. However, if we consider students as being independent of their parents' households, they form an extremely low-income group during the time they are studying, and these low-income groups benefit most from government expenditure on university education. However, in contrast, their life-time earnings are above average.

Human capital is not only important for the earning capacity of individuals and it is not formed only by schooling and training. Another important component of human capital is health. In the next paragraph we shall pay attention to this health factor. Human capital is also important for the non-earning activities of individuals: household production and leisure, or recreational activities. Human capital may affect the output of all these different kinds of activity, not just labour market activities.

11.6   Investments in health

In the models that have been introduced so far, health has been an exogenous variable that could cause heterogeneity in choices. Most of the time it was not given explicit attention. The question is whether health, or morbidity, is indeed an exogenous variable, or whether it can be affected by consumer choices and consequently should be considered as endogenous. In some cases an individual can avoid falling ill by having medical check-ups. If s/he nevertheless falls ill, s/he can try to get healthy again by calling the doctor, taking medicines or even undergoing hospitalization and surgery. Individuals and society spend a lot of money on medical care, fitness and so on. To a certain extent health can be considered as endogenous, although our expenditure cannot prevent us all dying ultimately.

The first problem that arises in economic models is how health should or could be measured. On a macro level, historical figures about mortality rates have frequently been used. Anthropometric indicators of health, such as birth weight, height for age, body-mass index (defined as weight divided by height squared) and skin-fold thickness are used (Schultz, 1993). They are justified as readily measured proxies of people's health status by the fact that they show a strong correlation with age-specific mortality rates (Fogel, 1990). But mortality may not be the best indicator for the health of people: morbidity figures should be added to make the picture more complete.

Factors that affect the health situation of individuals are in the first place the quantity and quality of the food and medical care available to them, and second, the dangers that threaten them, for instance in their work, from traffic, or their environment. Investments by society or individuals to improve nutrition and medical care and to reduce threats of health from other factors are likely to improve the health situation. The returns on such investments are even harder to measure than the returns on the investment in education, but the productive benefits can be estimated by including health characteristics of the worker in the Mincer's wage function Equation (11.8).

Health and education are not independent of one other. The education of the parents not only influences their own health, longevity and welfare, but also that of their children and perhaps other family members. Moreover, if earnings are used partly to improve health or nutrition, then these factors may also have an impact on wage rates. Because of these mutual effects, estimating the size of the effects requires the use of a simultaneous equation system.

Rosenzweig and Schultz (1983) developed a health production model. The model consists of a utility function representing preferences – see Equation (11.10); a health production function (Equation (11.11)); and a budget constraint (Equation (11.12)). The authors distinguish between goods that do not affect health (x_i, $i = 1, \ldots, n$) and goods that *do* affect health (y_j, $j = n + 1, \ldots, m$). Child health, H, and the consumption of goods, x and y, jointly determine household utility:

$$u = U(x_1, \ldots, x_n, y_{n+1}, \ldots, y_m, H). \tag{11.10}$$

The production of child health, H, depends on family specific endowments, μ, that are known, but not controlled by the household, such as genetic and environmental factors, on health inputs (z_k, $k = m, \ldots, N$) that do not generate utility directly, and y_j that do affect utility:

$$H = \Gamma(y_j, z_k, \mu). \tag{11.11}$$

The budget constraint:

$$Y = \sum_i p_i x_i + \sum_j p_j y_j + \sum_k p_k z_k, \tag{11.12}$$

where Y is income.

Maximizing Equation (11.10) subject to Equations (11.11) and (11.12) leads to the demand functions:

$$x_i = f_i(Y, \mu, p)$$
$$y_j = f_j(Y, \mu, p)$$

and

$$z_k = f_k(Y, \mu, p), \tag{11.13}$$

so that the reduced form of the health production function can be derived by substituting Equation (11.13) in Equation (11.11):

$$H = g(Y, \mu, p). \tag{11.14}$$

However, what we are interested in is the relationship in Equation (11.11): $H = \Gamma(y_j, z_k, \mu)$: the relationship between health inputs and health. It is not usually possible to identify the structural parameter estimates from the reduced form estimates (see Chapter 2), because of a lack of information on specific health inputs and health production technology. The problem is similar to the one we faced in the household production models, where it was also hard to distinguish differences in preferences from differences in technology. In most research, so-called hybrid equations are estimated:

$$H = h(y_s, p_i, Y, \mu) \quad i = 1, \ldots, s - 1, s + 1, \ldots, M,$$

where $y_s =$ is one specific input item, and p_i, Y and μ are determinants of the other inputs.

Rosenzweig and Schultz emphasize that if there are exogenous variations in endowment health (for example, biological) that are known to the individuals involved, but not known to the researcher, the observed correlation between input behaviour and health cannot be used to derive causal conclusions. The estimates of health technology must be obtained from a behavioural model in which inputs affecting health are themselves choice variables. However, so far it has not been possible to disentangle the roles of preferences and technology. It is the same kind of identification problem that we faced in the household production models in Chapter 6.

Rozenzweig and Schultz estimate two types of household health production function (Cobb–Douglas and Translog), in which the dependent variable is the 'log(birth weight)', and the explanatory variables are variables such as 'age of the mother', 'smoking mother, yes or no' and so on. Although some of the variables do have a significant influence on birth weight, such as 'smoking' (negative), only a very small proportion of the variability in birth weights is explained by the models. More interesting to show here are perhaps the estimates of the effects of household characteristics on the variables that appear in this health production function. These are represented in Table 11.5. In the last column of the table are the effects on birth weights. The variable 'doctor delay' measures the number of months of elapsed pregnancy before the mother visited a medical doctor. The age of the mother when giving birth ('age mother'), appears in the relationship, as in the models describing the timing of births that we introduced in Chapter 8. However, in this health model it is not necessarily the mother's first child. Most of the coefficients are not significant and also the R^2 is low, only 0.03.

Strauss *et al.* (1993) investigated the patterns and determinants of adult health in developing countries. As a measure of health they used self-reported general health condition and a variety of measures of problems in physical functioning (such as, 'when walking up a hill'), see Figure 11.5. Strauss *et al.* found differences in physical functioning of men and women in Jamaica. They formulated and estimated a reduced-form model and focused on the effects of education. In general, the effect of education on health is strongly positive, but the effects diminish (or even disappear) at older ages.

11.7 Summary

Human capital is a stock variable which affects the individual's functioning in all his or her activities. It can be considered as a stock of knowledge, skills and experience, physical and psychological health. In this chapter it is assumed that human capital is an endogenous variable that can be affected by investments. Traditionally, economic theory concentrated on the earning

Table 11.5   Estimates of log–linear input and birth characteristic demand equations

	Log (Doctor delay)	Log (Smoking)	Log (Number of the birth)	Log (Age mother)	Log (Birth Weight)
Mother's education:					
High school incomplete	−0.09*	0.20*	−0.19*	−0.08*	−0.01
High school complete	−0.22*	−0.06	−0.30*	−0.00	0.00
College incomplete	−0.26*	−0.09	−0.38*	0.01	0.01
College incomplete	−0.26*	−0.15*	−0.45*	0.08*	0.01
Father's education:					
High school incomplete	−0.01	0.19*	−0.27*	−0.11*	−0.01
High school complete	−0.01*	0.04	−0.36*	−0.11*	−0.01
College incomplete	−0.12*	−0.04	−0.39*	−0.12*	−0.00
College complete	−0.15*	−0.04	−0.26*	−0.05*	−0.01
Log husband's life–cycle income	−0.08*	0.07*	0.06*	0.01*	0.01*
1967	−0.08*	0.15*	0.02	0.01	0.01
1968	−0.07*	0.08*	−0.02	−0.00	0.01
Black	0.14*	−0.30*	0.25*	0.00	−0.07*
Exogenous area characteristics:					
Metropolitan residence	−0.05*	0.09*	−0.03	−0.01	−0.02*
SMSA size (10^9)	−0.02	27.2*	1.03	3.10*	−0.17
Health expenditures	0.01	0.30	−0.47	−0.24	0.16
Health department family planning	−0.23*	4228	−2414*	−586	−143
Cigarette price (x 100)	0.19	−7.56	8.93*	0.41	1.07
Cigarette price squared (x 10^4)	−0.69	12.10	−13.6*	0.34	−1.43
Milk price (x 10^3)	−0.13	10.92	0.06	0.40	−1.74
Hospital family planning	385.9	22280*	−3942	83.3	−1822
Population per doctor (x 10^5)	0.30	−2.74	1.81	0.12	0.14
Obstetrician–genaecologists per cap.	604	246	98.4	302*	−98.3
Manufacturing jobs (x 10^3)	−0.17	−0.06	−0.48*	0.05	−0.04
Service jobs (x 10^3)	−0.35	−1.55	−1.54*	−.68*	−0.36
Government jobs (x 10^3)	−0.43	−1.3	−1.15*	0.05	−0.11
General unemployment (x 10^3)	1.88	5.66	−1.58	−.07	0.25
Female unemployment	0.02	−6.71*	1.40	−0.26	0.63
Hospital beds per capita	5.02	14.38	11.7	9.86*	2.47
Sales tax on cigarettes (x 100)	−0.01	−4.60	−1.30	0.68	−0.84
Intercept 1.89*	1.25	−0.38	3.09*	3.09*	7.88*
R^2	0.12	0.03	0.11	0.11	0.03

Note: * = significant 5% level.

Source: Rosenzweig and Schultz (1983).

capacity of individuals and the influence of schooling and training on this capacity. For economic modelling this means that the wage rate in dynamic models must be considered as an endogenous variable, and that choices can be made with respect to optimal investments in schooling and training. Schooling also affects an individual's utility in a direct way; it can be considered as a consumption category. When someone stops working, earning capacity diminishes because of loss of experience and knowledge. An example is the case when women temporarily leave the labour market to take care of their (young) children.

However, human capital is not only earning capacity. Knowing how to make music, how to ski or how to cook are also forms of human capital. These forms affect the quality of either leisure activities or household production, including child care.

196

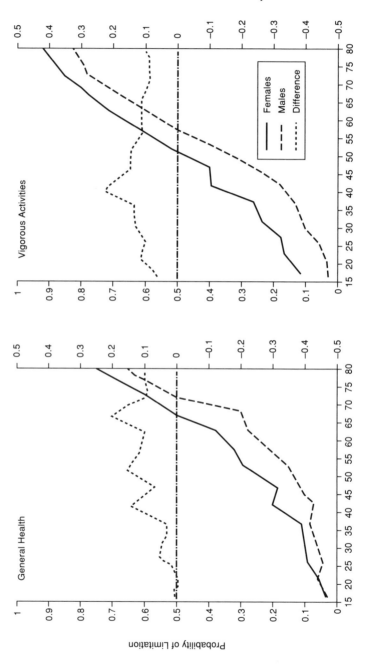

Female and Male Difference in Probability

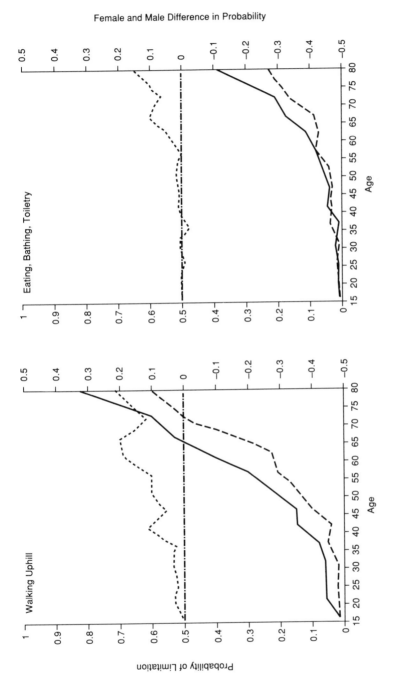

Source: Strauss *et al.* (1993).

Figure 11.5   Female and male differences in probability of health limitations

The health component of human capital is hard to measure, as is the stock of knowledge and skills. In some studies, children's birth weights are used as a proxy for the health of newborn babies; in others, subjective measures of the physical functioning of individuals. On a macro level, mortality and morbidity rates are used, but on a micro level research concentrates on the effects of individual and public choices on the health situation of individuals. The importance of health for an individual's well-being is twofold. Health not only affects well-being in a direct way, but also in an indirect way, as it affects the individual's earning capacity.

CHAPTER 12

Poverty and the Distribution of Income, Welfare and Happiness

12.1 Introduction

The extent of poverty and the distribution of income are important characteristics of the state of a society. Banishment of poverty and an 'equitable' income distribution are acclaimed policy purposes worldwide. The two concepts 'poverty' and 'income distribution' are closely related. Although poverty refers to a particular state of well-being, which has many more dimensions other than income, poverty research usually focuses on the income aspect of well-being. One reason is that redistribution of incomes, by means of income taxation and income transfers, is the primary instrument for policies aimed at relieving poverty.

The close relationship between poverty and income distribution is also borne out by the way poverty is often defined. For example, a widely used poverty measure is the percentage of individuals having an income of less than 50 per cent of the society's median income. Here it is clearly an income inequality measure that serves as a poverty definition. Note, incidently, that according to this measure, poverty is ineradicable unless all incomes are completely equalized.

In this chapter we discuss the question of how to define and measure income inequality and poverty. We shall see that in many instances there are no unambiguous answers. Poverty definitions have subjective elements, which is one explanation for the existence of a large number of them. We also discuss some statistical problems encountered when analysing income data.

Achieving a particular distribution of income does not seem to be a goal in itself, rather it is an instrument to redistribute well-being in a society. We conclude the chapter by looking at the distribution that should ultimately be the more interesting one: the distribution of well-being.

199

12.2 Measuring inequality

Consider a society with N individuals having income $x_1 \leq \ldots \leq x_N$. Let $v = f(x_1, \ldots, x_N)$ be an income inequality measure. (Although we are looking primarily at income inequality, the analysis is obviously applicable to the distribution of other attributes as well.)

There are several conditions one might like the measure to satisfy. A trivial one is that it is zero when all incomes are equal. Second, it seems desirable that it decreases when a (small) amount of income is transferred from one person to a poorer person. This property is known as the Pigou–Dalton principle. Third, it should, remain unchanged when income are expressed in different units, that is, the measure should be homogenous of degree zero. In formulae, these three conditions are expressed as:

(a) $f(\bar{x}, \ldots, \bar{x}) = 0;$ (12.1)

(b) $dv = \dfrac{\partial f}{\partial x_i}(dx_i) + \dfrac{\partial f}{\partial x_j}(-dx_i) < 0,$

or

$\partial f / \partial x_i < \partial f / \partial x_j$ for $x_i < x_j;$ (12.2)

(c) $f(x_1, \ldots, x_N) = f(\alpha x_1, \ldots, \alpha x_N),\ \alpha > 0.$ (12.3)

Exercise 12.1
Two simple income inequality measures are the variance of incomes and the variance of log-incomes. Check for each measure whether the conditions (a), (b) and (c) are satisfied.

Yet another condition that might be imposed on an inequality measure is that it is *additively decomposable*. Consider G groups in society with $\bar{x}_g$ being average income in group g, $g = 1, \ldots, G$ (each income belonging to exactly one group). An inequality measure is additively decomposable when total inequality can be expressed as a weighted sum of the inequality measure applied to each group separately ('within groups inequality'), and a 'between groups inequality' term. An example is the Theil index, defined by:

$$T = \sum_{i=1}^{N} \frac{x_i}{N\bar{x}} \log\left(\frac{x_i}{\bar{x}}\right).$$ (12.4)

See Exercise 12.2.

Exercise 12.2
The Theil index for inequality within Group g is:

$$T_g = \sum_{i \in g} \frac{x_i}{N_g \bar{x}_g} \log \left(\frac{x_i}{\bar{x}_g} \right). \tag{12.5}$$

For the inequality between the groups it is:

$$T_b = \sum_{g=1}^{G} \frac{N_g \bar{x}_g}{N \bar{x}} \log \left(\frac{\bar{x}_g}{\bar{x}} \right). \tag{12.6}$$

Show that:

$$T = T_b + \sum_{g=1}^{G} s_g T_g, \tag{12.7}$$

with

$$s_g = \frac{N_g \bar{x}_g}{N \bar{x}}, \tag{12.8}$$

the share of total income in Group g.

A popular method to represent income inequality is the Gini coefficient. The Gini coefficient is related to the Lorenz curve, a graphical representation of a distribution and its inequality. Consider the part of a population having an income less than a certain given level, x. The Lorenz curve plots the relationship between such a fraction of the population (say, p) on the one hand and their income expressed as a fraction of total income in the population ($q(p)$) on the other. Figure 12.1 shows two examples.

If every individual has the same income, a fraction p of the population will own a fraction p of total income, that is, $q(p) = p$. Thus the 45° line in Figure 12.1 corresponds to complete income equality. Therefore, the area between the 45° line and the Lorenz curve serves as a measure of income inequality. This area, expressed as a fraction of the complete area below the diagonal, is the Gini coefficient.

By definition, the N points of the Lorenz curve are given by:

$$q(p) = \sum_{i=1}^{pN} x_i \bigg/ \sum_{i=1}^{N} x_i, \tag{12.9}$$

for $p = 1/N, 2/N, \ldots, 1$.

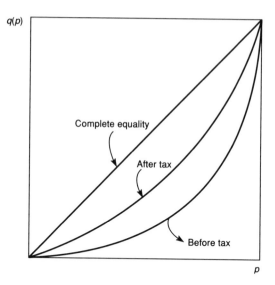

Figure 12.1 Lorenz curves

Exercise 12.3
The Gini coefficient appears in various incarnations. One of them is in terms of the absolute differences between all income pairs: expressed as a fraction of mean income. In formula:

$$G = \frac{\sum\limits_{i=1}^{N} \sum\limits_{j=1}^{N} |x_i - x_j|}{2\bar{x}N(N-1)}.$$ (12.10)

Show that this is equivalent to the earlier area definition of the Gini coefficient. Hint: Use $\Sigma_i \Sigma_j |x_i - x_j| = 2\Sigma_i \Sigma_{j<i}(x_i - x_j)$.

If we assume that the income distribution function has a particular functional form $F(.)$, the Lorenz curve can be written as (12.11) for $0 \le p \le 1$. The Gini-coefficient is then given by (12.12). See Exercise 12.4.

$$q(p) = \int_0^p F^{-1}(z) \, . \, dz \Big/ \int_0^1 F^{-1}(z) \, . \, dz$$ (12.11)

$$G = 1 - 2 \int_0^1 q(p) \, dp.$$ (12.12)

Exercise 12.4

Assume that incomes follow a distribution function $F(.)$ with density function $f(.)$; $p = F(x)$ is the fraction of the population having an income of less than x.

(a) Show that the fraction of total income owned by this fraction of the population is:

$$q = \int_0^x sf(s) \cdot ds \Big/ \int_0^\infty sf(s) \cdot ds. \qquad (12.13)$$

(b) Derive Equation (12.11) using Equation (12.13) and $p = F(x)$.
(c) Show that all Lorenz curves are convex.

Exercise 12.5

Consider two income distributions: one is exponential with parameter $1/\mu$; the other is uniform on $[0, 2\mu]$. Thus both distributions have expectation μ.

(a) Calculate and compare the variances of the two distributions.
(b) Show that the formulae for the Lorenz curves are $q(p) = p + (1 - p) \log (1 - p)$ for the exponential distribution, and $q(p) = p^2$ for the uniform distribution, $0 \le p \le 1$. (Note that both are independent of μ!) Draw the two curves in a single diagram.
(c) Calculate and compare the Gini coefficients for both distributions.

We conclude the section with a measure proposed by Atkinson (1970). Atkinson emphasized that a choice of a particular inequality measure involves some normative judgement. In fact, an inequality measure $f(x_1, \ldots, x_N)$ may be viewed as a social welfare function. Consider the case where social welfare is defined as the sum of the utility functions of all individuals in society, and assume that all individuals have the same utility function. It is not difficullt to show that in such a case social welfare is optimal if all incomes are equal. The social welfare loss caused by inequality, expressed as the ratio between social welfare at the existing income distribution, and social welfare with equally-distributed incomes, is the inequality measure proposed by Dalton (1920). Because Dalton's measure is not invariant to linear transformations of the utility function, Atkinson proposed a transformation of the measure in terms of income rather than utility. This is illustrated in Figure 12.2.

The actual income distribution in the two-person society in Figure 12.2 is represented by Point P. The 'budget line' through P and D is the set of all possible income distributions given the society's level of total income, and Point D corresponds to the case of an equal income distribution. The 'social indifference curve' $SW(y)$ through P and B represents the level of social welfare at the actual income distribution. Point B denotes the income level

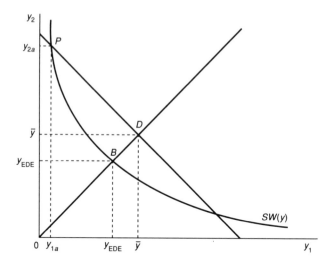

Figure 12.2   Atkinson inequality measure in a two-person society

that would yield the same level of social welfare when incomes were equally distributed. Atkinson's measure, the ratio BD/OD, measures the social welfare loss as a result of unequal income distribution.

The income level of Point B is called the *equally distributed equivalent* level of income (y_{EDE}). In an N-person society it is implicitly defined by:

$$\sum_{i=1}^{N} U(y_{EDE}) = \sum_{i=1}^{N} U(y_i), \tag{12.14}$$

so that:

$$y_{EDE} = U^{-1}\left[\frac{1}{N} \sum_{i=1}^{N} U(y_i)\right]. \tag{12.15}$$

Atkinson's measure is now given by:

$$A = 1 - \frac{y_{EDE}}{\bar{y}}. \tag{12.16}$$

Problems in the measurement of incomes

While income is clearly a key variable in the economics of household behaviour, it is often also a problematical one, from a conceptual as well as a statistical point of view. When collecting and analysing data on income one will have to decide, for example, which income components are to be included; whether to take the household or the individual as the unit of analysis; and whether equivalence scales should be used to correct for differences in needs. Once these choices have been made, the measured incomes will

Table 12.1   Comparison of two income measures

Income bracket (1)	Average income (2)	N_b (3)
< 17 500	17 201	564
17 500–20 000	25 085	355
20 000–24 000	28 690	521
24 000–28 000	32 128	632
28 000–34 000	38 305	635
34 000–43 000	45 412	686
> 43 000	65 006	698

Notes: Column (2) gives the average income of all households in the corresponding income bracket according to the detailed measurement of income.
N_b shows the number of respondents in the income bracket.
Socio–economic Panel (October 1986).

Source: Tummers (1994).

always be subject to measurement errors. Moreover, in many surveys, incomes are recorded only bracketwise, mainly because respondents are often either unable or unwilling to provide a precise income measure.

Suppose that all incomes in a society were equal. If incomes are measured with error, one would still observe some inequality. This suggests that measurement errors generally lead to an overestimation of income inequality. Van Praag *et al.* (1983) have shown that this is, in fact, the case for most inequality measures (provided that some mild assumptions with respect to the properties of the errors are satisfied). Bracketwise classification of incomes generally leads to an underestimation of income inequality because the income variation within classes is neglected.

Table 12.1 shows an example of problems with the income variable in empirical work. The table is taken from Tummers (1994). In the survey Tummers used by income was measured twice. At the beginning of the questionnaire respondents were asked to indicate in which of seven income brackets net household income falls. At the end of the questionnaire, respondents were asked to provide detailed information on a large number of different components of the household's net income, such as earned income, fringe benefits, family allowance, spouse's income and so on. The aggregate of these components is likely to provide a much more reliable income measure. As we see from comparison of the two columns in Table 12.1, the second measure yielded much higher income values than the first.

What we learn from Table 12.1 is that income data may be quite sensitive to the way in which they are collected. Note that without further assumptions regarding the parametric form of income distribution we cannot even calculate the mean or the median income from the data in the first column of Table 12.1. That is to say that for these data the mean and the median are not identified because the data contain insufficient information. We only

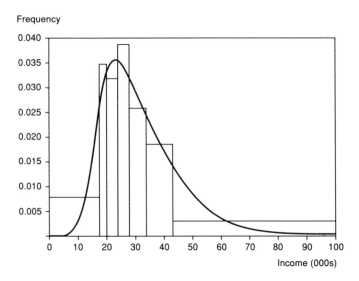

Figure 12.3 Lognormal fit to bracketwise income data

know for sure, using the data from the third column, that the median must be somewhere between Dfl. 24 000 and Dfl. 28 000.

The classification of incomes is one motive for assuming parametric functional forms for income distribution. A particularly popular choice is the lognormal distribution function. In this case the log of income follows a normal distribution. Let $\Phi(.)$ and $\Phi^{-1}(.)$ denote the cumulative standard normal distribution function and its inverse, respectively. It can be shown that the Gini coefficient is $2\Phi(\sigma/\sqrt{2}) - 1$, with σ being the standard deviation of the log of incomes, while the Lorenz curve can be written as $q = \Phi(\Phi^{-1}(p) - \sigma)$. Figure 12.3 shows the lognormal distribution fitted to the data from the first column in Table 12.1, with the parameters being estimated by means of maximum likelihood. Although a two-parameter distribution can hardly be expected to provide a good approximation to the actual distribution, and formal statistical tests almost unequivocally reject the functional form assumption, the procedure is popular because of its convenience and elegance.

Table 12.2 shows some figures on income distribution in a number of countries. Note, that the quintile information provides us with five points of a country's Lorenz curve. In terms of Gini coefficients, the largest inequality occurs in the USA and the smallest in Sweden, for both gross and net family income.

In most OECD countries there has been a trend towards increasing inequality in both incomes and wealth since the early 1980s, after a gradual reduction in inequality in preceding decades. The U-turn in income inequality does not necessarily carry over to the same extent to inequality in welfare. Differences may be caused by changes in household composition and in prices of necessities relative to luxuries, and consumption smoothing (see

Table 12.2 International comparison of income distributions

	Australia (1981–2)	Canada (1981)	Germany (1981)	New Zealand (1981–2)	Norway (1979)	Sweden (1981)	United Kingdom (1979)	United States (1979)
A The distribution of gross family income among quintiles of families (percentage shares of total gross income)								
Lowest quintile	4.6	4.7	5.7	5.7	5.1	6.7	4.9	4.0
Second quintile	9.8	11.1	11.6	11.4	11.4	12.3	10.9	10.1
Third quintile	16.6	17.8	17.6	17.6	18.3	17.2	18.2	16.7
Fourth quintile	24.8	25.3	24.7	24.7	25.4	25.0	25.2	25.1
Highest quintile	44.1	41.2	40.3	40.5	39.7	38.9	40.8	44.2
Gini coefficient	0.40	0.37	0.35	0.35	0.35	0.33	0.36	0.41
B The distribution of equivalent net family income among quintiles of individuals (percentage shares of total equivalent net family income)								
Lowest quintile	7.7	7.6	9.8	8.2	10.2	10.9	9.0	6.4
Second quintile	13.0	13.3	14.3	13.5	14.7	16.0	13.5	12.8
Third quintile	17.5	17.9	18.0	17.6	18.3	19.0	18.0	18.0
Fourth quintile	23.6	23.7	22.8	23.7	22.8	23.0	23.4	24.2
Highest quintile	38.2	37.4	35.2	37.0	34.0	31.1	36.1	38.6
Gini coefficient	0.31	0.30	0.25	0.29	0.24	0.20	0.27	0.32

Notes: The results are derived from the January 1990 version of the (Luxembourg Income Studies) LIS data base, except for Australia and New Zealand.

Source: Saunders *et al.* (1991).

Chapter 9). See, for example, Coulter *et al.* (1994), Cutler and Katz (1992), Wolff (1994) and Slesnick (1994).

12.3 Measuring poverty

Poverty as a social problem seems to be rediscovered by politicians and researchers at regular time intervals. In 1963, the United States' president, Lyndon B. Johnson launched his war against poverty, after Galbraith (1962) and Harrington (1962) had pointed out that the medal of the affluent society had its obverse in terms of the (almost unnoticed) existence of poverty. At about the same time, Abel-Smith and Townsend (1965) drew attention to a similar problem in the United Kingdom. About sixty years earlier, Booth (1892) and Rowntree (1901) had measured and described poverty in London and York, respectively. Sixty years earlier again, Engels (1892) described the 'condition of the working class in England in 1844', and Mayhew (1851), 'London labour and the London poor'. A final step of seventy years further back brings us to Eden (1797), and to Adam Smith (1776) who described 'The state of the poor' in 'An Inquiry into the Nature and Causes of the Wealth of Nations'.

Defining poverty is a necessary first step for measuring poverty as well as for designing policies aimed at alleviating this state. A *poverty line* is an income level at or below which people are defined as being poor. So it dichotomizes society between the poor and the non-poor. Once a poverty line is chosen, one may simply count the number of individuals below the poverty line expressed as a ratio of the total number of individuals (the *head count ratio*). In a more sophisticated approach, individuals may be weighted, with the weight depending on the distance between the poverty line and actual income.

The literature on poverty research shows an almost bewildering variety of possible poverty lines. Most of the definitions fit into one of the following categories:

(i) Poverty is having less than an objectively defined, absolute minimum (*A*).
(ii) Poverty is having less than others in society (*B*).
(iii) Poverty is feeling you do not have enough to get along (*C*).

Hagenaars and de Vos (1988) give the following examples of definitions in each of these categories. (The category a definition belongs to is given in parentheses.)

P1 Basic needs (A)
This method defines a household as poor if its income does not allow the purchase of minimum quantities of 'basic needs', such as food, clothing and housing. Minimum food quantities are sometimes based on nutritional standards.

P2 Food ratio (A)
This poverty definition is based on Engel's law, which states that the ratio of food expenditure to income decreases when income increases. According to this definition, a household is considered as being poor if the budget share of food is larger than some prespecified number; for example, 1/3. The method is closely related to the Iso-prop method described in Chapter 7. Straight application of this method without distinguishing between the nature of food expenditure and food quality does not seem to be useful. For example, many outdoor meals or extensive use of convenience foods may result in a high budget share for food without necessarily implying that the household is poor.

P3 Fixed costs to income ratio (A)
This is a related poverty index that has been used in Dutch social policy. The threshold value to delineate the poor from the non-poor is 0.50. The definition is based on the notion that households cannot control fixed costs. As such, the index is (at best) only useful as a short-term poverty index.

P4 Durables index (B)
According to this definition, a household is considered to be poor if it does not have certain commodities that are common in the society it lives in. Hagenaars and de Vos implemented this method by looking at relative deprivation with respect to four consumer durables: car, TV set, refrigerator and washing machine. A household scores three points on the deprivation index for each durable it does not own, two points for each durable it owns but which would not be replaced in case of a breakdown, one point if it would be replaced by a secondhand model, and zero if it would be replaced by new. The household is defined as being poor if its score exceeds four.

P5 'Just sufficient income' (C)
This definition uses respondents' subjective evaluation of incomes (see also Chapter 7). The respondent is asked which income s/he considers to be 'just sufficient' for his or her household. If the actual income is lower than the income considered to be just sufficient, the household is said to be poor.

P6 Official minimum (C)
If the household's income is lower than or equal to the amount it would receive when on social assistance, the household is defined as being poor.

The list shows that a poverty definition inevitably has arbitrary elements and depends to a large extent on a researcher's (subjective) opinions and evaluations. Using one and the same sample of households, Hagenaars and de Vos calculated the percentage of poor households (that is, head count ratio) according to all definitions. The results are given in Table 12.3.

The main conclusion emerging from Table 12.3 is that the poverty percentages show very large differences across definitions. Thus the number of

Table 12.3 Poverty percentages in social subgroups

Social subgroup	P1	P2	P3	P4	P5	P6
Single, working	7.5	6.6	26.5	42.4	12.1	4.7
One–parent family	32.3	32.6	23.7	21.6	39.9	26.1
Two–earner family	2.0	9.6	15.3	3.7	7.9	0.3
One–earner family	6.9	16.9	22.4	5.4	13.2	1.1
Non–working family	34.7	37.4	24.1	12.1	35.6	20.1
Single, over 65	19.4	12.6	10.3	39.0	36.1	7.6
Nonsingle, over 65	12.7	15.5	8.9	8.5	16.8	6.3
Total	10.9	14.0	17.8	13.6	15.0	5.7

Source: Hagenaars and De Vos (1988).

poor people strongly depends on the poverty definition that has been chosen by the researcher. At the same time, the picture with respect to the groups in society that have relatively large numbers of poor people does not change very much across poverty definitions. As the table shows, one-parent families and non-working families have almost uniformly higher poverty percentages than have other groups. Thus, while it is difficult to claim that a certain percentage in society is poor, it is quite feasible to identify the vulnerable groups with respect to a risk of being poor.

The nature of the economic policy required to alleviate poverty depends on whether relative or absolute definitions are used. Banishing poverty defined in absolute terms primarily requires economic growth, while alleviating relative poverty is primarily a matter of income redistribution.

The social security systems in Western countries often creates a so-called *poverty trap*. Many forms of social assistance are contingent upon a recipient's low income. If the income of a poor household increases, this may result in losing eligibility to (some forms of) social assistance. As a result, increased income does not necessarily imply increased welfare, and in some cases the welfare level may even deteriorate: thus, the household is trapped in poverty.

12.4 Intrahousehold inequality

Suppose one is interested in inequality between individuals, but data are available only on a household level. One would expect that total inequality will be underestimated, since intrahousehold inequality is neglected, and this is, in fact, true for all inequality measures discussed in Section 12.2. Haddad and Kanbur (1990) found an underestimation by 30 per cent and more in an analysis of inequality in calorie intake on the basis of a Philippine data set.

The effect of a neglect of intrahousehold inequality on the incidence of poverty is, in general, ambiguous. The intuition is that on the one hand all members of a household can be counted as poor, whereas only some of them in fact are; on the other hand, all members of a household can be counted as non-poor, whereas in fact some of them *are* poor. Whether it is the first or the second effect that dominates is an empirical matter.

While accounting for intrahousehold inequality appeared to be important for assessing levels of inequality and poverty, Haddad and Kanbur also found that the pattern of inequality and poverty over social groups hardly changed when intrahousehold inequality was neglected.

12.5 The distribution of happiness

What does the distribution of income tell us about the distribution of happiness? The economic concept closest to happiness is utility, so economists may like to study the distribution of utility. However, utility functions only represent a person's, or a household's, preferences with respect to consumption, leisure and so on. As such it is an ordinal function: any monotonic increasing transformation of a utility function will again represent the same preferences. No interpersonal comparisons are possible with such a utility concept and it cannot be used to determine the distribution of welfare. In the period of pioneering economists such as Adam Smith (1776) and Jeremy Bentham (1823), welfare comparisons were thought to be possible because utility or welfare was a property connected with a good. Bentham defined utility as 'The property in any object whereby it tends to produce benefit, advantage, pleasure, good or happiness'. The more of these goods you got, the better off you were. Within these restrictions of materialism, private and social welfare were studied. Social welfare could be improved in two ways: by producing more of the goods that provide utility, and by a redistribution of those goods over the population. It was assumed that welfare comparison between people was possible, so utility was a 'cardinal' concept. Combined with Gossen's (1854) ideas about decreasing marginal utility, this led to the conviction that social welfare could be improved by a redistribution of utility goods.

By the end of the nineteenth century, however, many economists already had their doubts about the assumption that utility could be measured, and that the addition of the utility levels of different people would provide the total utility of the group. This led to what could be called the 'ordinalist revolution'. Pareto (1909) argued that utility was not a property of a good, but a subjective experience of an individual, which in general could not be measured objectively. As a result of this supposition, the interest of economists moved away from welfare of individuals towards concepts such as scarcity and price formation in markets. Pareto showed that consumer behavior could equally well be explained by means of an ordering of preferences of consumers. Consistency of their preferences was almost all he needed to explain optimal choices, as we showed in Chapter 2. The markets are supposed to be perfect and the exchange system works in such a way that, when all consumers have made their optimal choice, no utility gain of any consumer is possible without the loss of utility of at least one of the other consumers. This is called a Pareto optimal distribution (see also Chapter 3). Because of this development, the cardinal utility concept fell out of fashion. Still, the need for a measurable concept of well-being did not disappear.

Van Praag (1968) picked up the cardinal utility concept again, although in a different way. In Chapter 7 we mentioned the income evaluation question, which is used by van Praag to derive subjective cardinal utility functions. The basis for these functions are the opinions of households about the income levels that correspond with a 'very bad', 'bad', 'insufficient', 'sufficient', 'good' and 'excellent' income. In his vision, the meaning of words such as 'very bad', 'bad', 'insufficient', and so on with respect to an income position can be related to utility levels, say $1/12$, $3/12$, ..., $11/12$, on a $[0, 1]$ scale. Log normal distribution functions are fitted to these points to find the individual welfare functions of income. If the words do indeed have the same meaning for different households we would be able to compare their utility levels, corresponding to their own incomes. The translation from verbal evaluations to numbers is characterized by the 'equal interval assumption': the difference in utility level between 'very bad' and 'bad' is equal to the difference between two other successive evaluations, for example, 'sufficient' and 'good'. All are equal to $2/12$ on the $[0, 1]$ scale. In van Praag *et al.* (1988 and van Praag, 1991) it was shown, by asking people to translate words directly into numerical evaluations, that the equal interval assumption holds very well. The distribution of the utility levels that households attach to their own income could be interpreted as a distribution of contentment with incomes.

The quality of life concept is closely related to 'happiness'. Veenhoven (1984) defines happiness as 'the degree to which an individual judges the overall quality of his life-as-a-whole favorable'. This judgment integrates all appreciation criteria used explicitly and implicitly by a person who draws up the balance sheet. It covers past, present and anticipated experiences, but not all experiences are given equal weight. The happiness concept was made operational by Cantril (1965) in a cross-national happiness study he performed in 1960. The question that he asked people to answer was:

Here is a picture of a ladder. Suppose that we say the top of the ladder represents the best possible life for you and the bottom represents the worst possible life for you. Where on the ladder do you feel you personally stand at the present time?

Veenhoven studied the relationship between happiness and one's living conditions: for example, the economic and political conditions of a country; one's place in society; work; and intimate ties. He also looked at the effect of individual characteristics, such as personal resources like physical health and specific abilities, and personal traits. On average the people in poorer countries indicate themselves to be less happy than those in the rich countries, which is illustrated by Figure 12.4. Economic progress seems to have

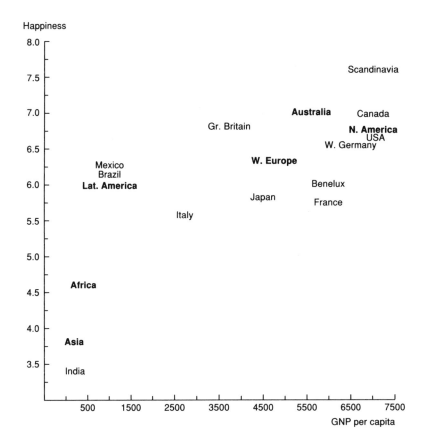

Source: Veenhoven (1984).

Figure 12.4   Average happiness and GNP per capita in different parts of the world, 1975

more effect on happiness for the poor countries than for the rich. This corresponds with the notion of diminishing marginal utility on the micro level.

Happiness is also correlated with household composition. Veenhoven's (1983) results indicate that, in general, people living alone are less happy than people living with a partner. Several explanations have been proposed for this phenomenon. Single people were on average less healthy and had more psychological problems. These may be causes of their unhappiness, but they may also be causes of their being single. Veenhoven also stipulates that nowadays care, affection, warmth, protection and social contacts can almost only be found within marriage, which means that single people get more lonely and have more problems finding care, affection and so on in society.

12.6 Summary

In previous chapters we analyzed various aspects of households' decisions that should lead them to maximum utility in both the short and the long run. In this chapter we saw that their attempts to optimize do not result in a similar income or utility level for everybody. Income distribution is characterized by location and inequality measures, which makes comparison of distribution easier. Poverty is closely related to inequality. Although there is no unique and universally accepted poverty definition, it is recognized that some groups in society are more vulnerable than others, whichever definition is used. Social studies often concentrate on an individual's well-being or happiness rather than on income alone. Some methods are proposed to link economic theory to the happiness concept and to see whether economic variables affect an individual's happiness.

Principles of Duration Models

This appendix presents a brief outline of models of duration. For a comprehensive treatment, the reader is referred to Lancaster (1990).

The key concept of duration models is the *hazard function*, $\theta(t)$, of the transition from one state (being unmarried, for example) to another (for example, being married); $\theta(t)dt$ is the probability that the transition will take place in the (short) time interval of length dt following t, *conditional on still being in the initial state at time t*. The hazard should be clearly distinguished from the unconditional probability of making the transition between t and $t + dt$. As an example, consider the population of men who were born on 1 January 1970. The unconditional probability gives the probability that someone from this population will marry (for the first time) in, say, 1998, whereas the hazard gives us the probability that someone from this population *who is still unmarried on 1 January 1998* will marry in 1998.

A related concept is the *survivor function*, $\bar{G}(t)$, defined as the probability that the transition does not take place before time t. Suppose, in our example, that t is measured in years and that $t = 0$ corresponds to age 18. Then $\bar{G}(10)$ is the probability that a man who was born on 1 January 1970 will not marry before 1 January 1998. The functions $G(t) := 1 - \bar{G}(t)$ and $g(t) := dG(t)/dt$ are the corresponding distribution and density function, respectively, of the duration until transition.

The definition of the hazard implies that the relationship with the distribution function and the density function is as follows

$\theta(t)dt =$
$Pr(\text{transition between } t \text{ and } t + dt \mid \text{no transition before } t) =$

$$\frac{Pr(\text{transition between } t \text{ and } t + dt)}{Pr(\text{no transition before } t)} = \tag{A.1}$$

$$\frac{g(t)dt}{1 - G(t)}.$$

Equation (A.1) is a differential equation which can be solved by integrating both sides from 0 to t:

$$\int_0^t \theta(s)ds = \int_0^t \frac{g(s)}{1 - G(s)} \, ds \tag{A.2}$$

$$= -\ln\{1 - G(s)\} \big|_0^t$$

$$= -\ln\{1 - G(t)\},$$

where we have used the initial condition $G(0) = 0$. Rewriting Equation (A.2), we obtain:

$$G(t) = 1 - \exp\left\{-\int_0^t \theta(s)ds\right\}. \tag{A.3}$$

Differentiating Equation (A.3) with respect to t to obtain the density function yields:

$$g(t) = \theta(t)\exp\left\{-\int_0^t \theta(s)ds\right\}. \tag{A.4}$$

Note that if one function of the triplet $\theta(t)$, $g(t)$ and $G(t)$ is known, the other two functions can be derived using Equation (A.1), (A.3) and (A.4).

The simplest model arises if the hazard rate is constant over time, that is, $\theta(t) = \theta$. In this case the corresponding duration follows an exponential distribution, that is $g(t) = \theta e^{-\theta t}$, $G(t) = 1 - e^{-\theta t}$, $\bar{G} = e^{-\theta t}$ and $E(t) = 1/\theta$.

If, in our example, $\theta(t) = \theta = 0.1$, the expected age of marriage of someone from our population is $18 + 1/\theta = 28$ years (recall that $t = 0$ corresponds to age 18), whereas the probability of getting married before the age of 30, for example, is $G(12) = 1-\exp(-0.1*12) = 0.699$. The probability that someone who is still unmarried on 1 January of year t will marry in year t is:

$$\frac{G(t + 1) - G(t)}{1 - G(t)} = \frac{\exp(-0.1*t) - \exp(-0.1*(t + 1))}{\exp(-0.1*t)} = \tag{A.5}$$

$$= 1 - \exp(-0.1) = 0.095.$$

Note that it is independent of t, which is a reflection of the constancy of the hazard rate.

In econometric research, the hazard function for individual i is usually made dependent not only on time, but also on a vector of (time-invariant) explanatory variables x_i. A popular specification in empirical work is the proportional hazard (PH) model. The PH specification, which assumes that the ratio of the hazard of two individuals is constant over time, is written as:

$$\theta(t, x_i) = \exp(x_i' \beta) \cdot \psi(t). \tag{A.6}$$

The function $\psi(t)$ is known as the 'baseline hazard'. A specification for the baseline hazard that has been used frequently in applied work is $\psi(t) = \alpha t^{\alpha-1}$, with $\alpha > 0$. In this case, the density function $g(t)$ of the duration is a Weibull distribution. The hazard increases or decreases monotonically, depending on whether $\alpha > 1$ or $\alpha < 1$. For $\alpha = 1$, the hazard is time-independent, which brings us back to the exponential model.

Cox (1972) has proposed an estimation procedure, the 'partial likelihood method', which allows consistent estimation of the parameter vector β, without specifying the 'baseline hazard' $\psi(t)$. The PH model is sometimes extended by adding a random disturbance term v_i, representing the effect of omitted variables:

$$\theta(t, x_i, v_i) = \exp(x_i'\beta) \cdot \psi(t) \cdot v_i. \tag{A.7}$$

Equation (A.7) is known as the mixed proportional hazard (MPH) model. In empirical work, v_i has often been assumed to follow a Gamma distribution with mean 1, a choice which has computational advantages. An approach that is computationally more difficult but preferable from a conceptual point of view is to estimate the distribution of v by means of non-parametric methods, as proposed by Heckman and Singer (1984).

The Expected Present Value of Discounted Flows

In a dynamic environment, households or individuals are assumed to discount future costs and benefits. Discounting reflects the notion that one dollar that will be received (paid) after some time is presently valued less than one dollar received (paid) now. In continuous time models, we discount a benefit or cost incurred at time t according to the function $g(t) = e^{-\delta t}$ with $\delta > 0$. Note that $g(0) = 1$ and that $g(t)$ is monotonically decreasing, with $0 < g(t) < 1$, for $t > 0$. Thus, the farther away in the future, the stronger the discounting. The discount factor applied to benefits or costs incurred after one unit of time is $e^{-\delta} \approx 1 - \delta \approx 1/(1 + \delta)$; δ therefore represents the discount rate per time period. (See Section 9.3 for comments on this way of discounting.)

If the household receives a benefit (income, utility or 'minus costs'), B, *at one point in time*, say t, then the present value of the benefit equals $B.e^{-\delta t}$. If the household receives *a continuous benefit flow* (or stream), $b(s)$, during the time period $(0, t)$, the present value of the discounted flow is given as:

$$V(t) = \int_0^t b(s) \cdot e^{-\delta s} ds. \tag{B.1}$$

In many circumstances, t is uncertain and is therefore treated as a random variable. The *expected present value* of the discounted benefit flow is then given by:

$$E_t[V(t)] = \int_0^\infty V(t)f(t)dt, \tag{B.2}$$

where $f(t)$ is the probability density function of t. Integration by parts allows us to write this in the alternative form:

$$E_t V(t) = \int_0^\infty b(t)\bar{F}(t)e^{-\delta t}dt, \tag{B.3}$$

with $\bar{F}(t)$ being the probability that the benefit stream will last at least until t.

In the special case where the benefit stream is constant, that is, $b(t) = b$, the present value of a flow until t is:

$$V(t) = b.\int_0^t e^{-\delta s}ds = \frac{b}{\delta}(1 - e^{-\delta t}), \tag{B.4}$$

which approaches b/δ if t tends to infinity. If t follows an exponential distribution with parameter $\lambda > 0$, the expected present value equals:

$$E_t[V(t)] = \frac{b}{\delta} (1 - Ee^{-\delta t}) = \frac{b}{\delta} \left(1 - \frac{\lambda}{\lambda + \delta}\right) \qquad (B.5)$$

$$= \frac{b}{\lambda + \delta},$$

where we have used:

$$Ee^{-\delta t} = \int_0^\infty \lambda e^{-(\lambda+\delta)t} \, dt = \frac{\lambda}{\lambda + \delta}. \qquad (B.6)$$

Comparing the right-hand side of Equation (B.5) with the expression for the present value of a flow having an infinite duration with certainty, b/δ, we see that the uncertainty acts like an increase in the discount rate.

Since $V(.)$ is a concave function, it follows from Jensen's inequality that the present value evaluated at the expected duration of the flow is larger than the expected present value. The bias can be expressed as:

$$\text{Bias} = \frac{V\{E(t)\} - E\{V(t)\}}{E\{V(t)\}} = (1 + \lambda/\delta)(1 - e^{-\frac{\delta}{\lambda}}) - 1. \qquad (B.7)$$

If $\delta = 0.10$ and $E(t) = 10$, for example, the bias is 26 per cent.

Bibliography

Abel-Smith, B. and P. Townsend (1965) 'The Poor and the Poorest', *Occasional Papers and Social Administration*, no. 17 (London: Bell and Sons).

Ahn, N. (1994) 'Effects of the One-Child Family Policy on Second and Third Births in Hebei, Shaanxi and Shanghai', *Journal of Population Economics*, vol. 7, pp. 63–78.

Alderman, H. and P. Gertler (1989) 'Family Resources and Gender Differences in Human Capital' (mimeo) Rand Corporation.

Alessie, R. and A. Kapteyn (1991) 'Habit Formation, Interdependent Preferences and Demographic Effects in the Almost Ideal Demand System', *The Economic Journal*, vol. 101, pp. 404–19.

Alessie, R., A. Kapteyn and B. Melenberg (1989) 'The Effects of Liquidity Constraints on Consumption: Estimation from Household Panel Data', *European Economic Review*, vol. 33, pp. 547–55.

Antill, J. K. and S. Cotton (1988) 'Factors Affecting the Division of Labor in the Households', *Sex Roles*, vol. 18, pp. 531–53.

Antonides, G. (1991) *Psychology in Economics and Business* (Dordrecht: Kluwer).

Antonides, G. and W. F. van Raaij (1990) 'Income and the Advantages and Disadvantages of Work' (in Dutch) (The Hague: Ministry of Employment and Social Affairs).

Atkinson, T. (1970) 'On the Measurement of Inequality', *Journal of Economic Theory*, vol. 2, pp. 244–63.

Baanders, A. N. (1991) 'Leaving the Parental Home; Changes Since the Fifties' (in Dutch), *Huishoudstudies*, vol. 1, pp. 14–21.

Baudrillard, J. (1970) *La Société de Consommation* (Paris: Gallimard).

Becker, G. S. (1962) 'Investment in Human Beings', *Journal of Political Economy*, vol. 70, pp. 9–49.

Becker, G. S. (1965) 'A Theory of the Allocation of Time', *Economic Journal*, vol. 75, pp. 493–517.

Becker, G. S. (1975) *Human Capital, A Theoretical and Empirical Analysis, with Special Reference to Education* (New York: Columbia University Press).

Becker, G. S. (1981) *A Treatise on the Family* (Cambridge, Mass.: Harvard University Press).

Becker G. S. and K. M. Murphy (1988) 'A Theory of Rational Addiction', *Journal of Political Economy*, vol. 96, pp. 675–700.

Becker G. S., M. Grossman and K. M. Murphy (1994) 'An Empirical Analysis of Cigarette Addiction', *American Economic Review*, pp. 396–418.

Behrman, J. R. (1990) 'Intrahousehold Allocation of Nutrients and Gender Effects: A Survey of Structural and Reduced Form Estimates', in S. Osmani (ed.), *Nutrition and Poverty* (Oxford University Press).

Bentham J. (1823) 'An Introduction to the Principles of Morals and Legislation', in A. N. Page, *Utility Theory, A Book of Readings* (New York: John Wiley).

Berg, G. J. van den (1990) 'Nonstationarity in Job Search Theory', *Review of Economic Studies*, vol. 57, pp. 255–77.

Berg, G. J. van den (1994) 'The Effects of Changes of the Job Offer Arrival Rate on the Duration of Unemployment', *Journal of Labor Economics*, vol. 12, pp. 478–98.

Biddle, J. E. and D. S. Hamermesh (1990) 'Sleep and the Allocation of Time', *Journal of Political Economy*, vol. 98, pp. 922–43.

Bjorn P. and Q. Vuong (1984) 'Simultaneous Models for Dummy Endogenous Variables: A Game Theoretic Formulation with an Application to Household Labor Force Participation', working paper, California Institute of Technology.

Bjorn P. and Q. Vuong (1985) 'Econometric Modeling of a Stackelberg Game with an Application to Household Labor Force Participation', working paper, California Institute of Technology.

Blackburn, M. L., D. E. Bloom and D. Neumark (1993) 'Fertility, Wages and Human Capital', *Journal of Population Economics*, vol. 6, pp. 1–30.

Blood, R. O. and D. M. Wolfe (1960) *Husbands and Wives: The Dynamics of Married Living* (Illinois: Free Press of Glencoe).

Blundell, R. and A. Lewbel (1991) 'The Information Content of Equivalent Scales', *Journal of Econometrics*, vol. 50, pp. 49–68.

Blundell, R. and I. Walker (1982) 'Modeling the Joint Determination of Household Labour Supplies and Commodity Demands', *Economic Journal*, pp. 351–64.

Booth, C. (1892) *Life and Labour of the People in London* (London).

Brechling, V. and S. Smith (1992) *The Pattern of Energy Efficiency Measures Amongst Domestic Households in the UK* (London: Institute for Fiscal Studies).

Bresnahan, T. F. and P. C. Reiss (1991) 'Empirical Models of Discrete Games', *Journal of Econometrics* vol. 48, pp. 57–81.

Brookshire, D. S. and T. D. Crocker (1981) 'The Advantages of Contingent Valuation Methods for Benefit–Cost Analysis', *Public Choice*, vol. 36, pp. 235–52.

Bruyn-Hundt, M. (1985) *Housekeeping = Unpaid Work* (in Dutch) (Deventer: Van Loghum Slaterus).

Browning, M. (1991) A Simple Non-additive Preference Structure for Models of Household Behavior Over Time', *Journal of Political Economy*, vol. 99, pp. 607–37.

Browning, M. (1992) 'Children and Household Economic Behaviour', *Journal of Economic Literature*, vol. 30, pp. 1434–75.

Browning, M. and A. M. Lusardi (1996) 'Household Saving: Micro Theories and Micro Facts', *Journal of Economic Literature*, to appear.

Browning, M., A. Deaton and M. Irish (1985) 'A Profitable Approach to Labor Supply and Commodity Demand over the Life-cycle', *Econometrica*, vol. 53, pp. 503–43.

Buhmann, B., L. Rainwater, G. Schmaus and T. M. Smeeding (1988) 'Equivalence Scales, Well-Being, Inequality and Poverty: Sensitivity Estimates Across Ten Countries Using the Luxembourg Income Study (LIS) Database', *Review of Income and Wealth*, vol. 34, pp. 115–42.

Burns, S. (1977) *The Household Economy* (Boston, Mass.: Beacon Press).

Buttner, T. and W. Lutz (1990) 'Estimating Fertility Responses to Policy Measures in the German Democratic Republic', *Population and Development Review*, vol. 16, pp. 539–55.

Cain, G. G. (1976) 'The Challenge of Segmented Labor Market Theories to Orthodox Theory: A Survey', *Journal of Economic Literature*, vol. 14, pp. 1215–57.

Cantril, H. (1965) *The Patterns of Human Concern* (New Brunswick: Rutgers University Press).

Central Bureau of Statistics (1992) Housing Needs Survey (in Dutch), The Hague.

Central Bureau of Statistics (1972–95) Statistical Handbook (in Dutch), The Hague.
Chaloupka, F. (1991) 'Rational Addictive Behavior and Cigarette Smoking', *Journal of Political Economy*, vol. 99, pp. 722–42.
Chiappori, P. A. (1988) 'Rational Household Labor Supply', *Econometrica*, vol. 56, pp. 63–89.
Chiappori, P. A. (1992) 'Collective Labor Supply and Welfare', *Journal of Political Economy*, vol. 100, pp. 437–67.
Coleman, M. T. and J. Pencavel (1993a) 'Changes in Work Hours of Male Employees Since 1940', *Industrial and Labor Relations Review*, vol. 46, pp. 262–83.
Coleman, M. T. and J. Pencavel (1993b), 'Trends in Market Work Behavior of Women Since 1940', *Industrial and Labor Market Work Review*, vol. 46, pp. 638–53.
Collins, W. (1868) *The Moonstone* (Signet Classic).
Cooney, T. M. and D. P. Hogan (1991) 'Marriage in an Institutionalized Life Course: First Marriage Among American Men in the Twentieth Century', *Journal of Marriage and the Family*, vol. 53, pp. 178–90.
Cooper, G. and A. Katz (1977) *The Cash Equivalent of In Kind Income*, Report to the Department of Health, Education and Welfare (Stanford, Conn.: Cooper and Company).
Coulter, F. A. E., F. A. Cowell and S. P. Jenkins (1994) 'Family Fortunes in the 1970s and 1980s', in R. Blundell, I. Preston and I. Walker (eds), *The Measurement of Household Welfare* (Cambridge University Press).
Cox, D. (1972) 'Regression models and life tables', *Journal of the Royal Statistical Society*, series B, vol. 34, pp. 187–220 (with discussion).
Cramer, J. S. (1969) *Empirical Econometrics* (Amsterdam: North-Holland).
Cutler, D. M. and L. F. Katz (1992) 'Rising Inequality? Changes in the Distribution of Income and Consumption in the 1980's', *American Economic Review (Papers and Proceedings)*, vol. 80, pp. 546–51.
Dalton (1920) 'The Measurement of the Inequality of Incomes', *Economic Journal*, vol. 30.
Deaton, A. (1989) 'Looking for Boy–Girl Discrimination in Household Expenditure Data', *World Bank Economic Review*, vol. 3, pp. 1–15.
Deaton, A. and J. Muellbauer (1980) *Economics and Consumer Behaviour* (Cambridge University Press).
Deaton, A. and J. Muellbauer (1981) 'Functional Forms for Labor Supply and Commodity Demands With and Without Quantity Restrictions', *Econometrica*, vol. 49, pp. 1521–32.
Deaton, A. (1992) *Understanding Consumption* (Oxford: Clarendon Press).
Deaton, A. S. (1981) 'Theoretical and Empirical Approaches to Consumer Demand under Rationing', in A. S. Deaton (ed.), *Essays in the Theory and Measurement of Consumer Behaviour*, in Honour of Sir Richard Stone (Cambridge University Press).
Dobbelsteen, S. (1996) *Intra-household Allocation of Resources: a Microeconometric Analysis*, Ph.D. thesis, Wageningen Agricultural University.
Duesenberry, J.S. (1949) *Income, Saving and the Theory of Consumer Behavior* (Cambridge, Mass.: Harvard University Press).
DuRivage, V. L. (ed.) (1992) *New Policies for the Part-Time and Contingent Workforce*, Economic Policy Institute series (Armonk, NY: M. E. Sharpe).
Eck, R. van and B. Kazemier (1988) 'Features of the Hidden Economy in The Netherlands', *Review of Income and Wealth*, vol. 34, pp. 251–73.
Eden, F. M. (1797) *The State of the Poor* (London).
Elster, J. (1983) *Sour Grapes: Studies in the Subversion of Rationality* (Cambridge University Press).
Elster, J. (1986) *Ulysses and the Sirens, Studies in Rationality and Irrationality* (Cambridge University Press).

Engel, E. (1883) 'Der Werth des Menschen, Teil 1: Der Kostenwerth des Menschen', *Volkswirtschaftliche Zeitfragen*, vol. 37–38, pp. 1–74.

Engel, E. (1895) *Die Lebenskosten Belgischer Arbeiterfamilien Früher und Jetzt* (Dresden).

Engel, J. F., R. D. Blackwell and P. W. Miniard (1986) *Consumer Behavior* (New York: CBS College Publishing, The Dryden Press).

Engels, F. (1892) *The Condition of the Working Class in England* (London: Granada).

European Trade Union Institute (1988–9) *Collective Bargaining in Western Europe in 1988 and Prospects for 1989*.

Eurostat (1988) *Europe in Figures* (Luxembourg: Office for Official Publications of the European Communities).

Eurostat (1992) *Demographic Statistics* (Luxembourg: Office for Official Publications of the European Communities).

Evenson, R., B. Popkin and E. Quizon (1980) 'Nutrition, Work and Demographic Behaviour in Rural Philippine Households' in H. Binswanger *et al.* (eds), *Rural Household Studies in Asia* (Singapore University Press).

Festinger, L. (1957) *A Theory of Cognitive Dissonance* (Evanston, Illinois: Row, Peterson).

Fields, G. S. (1975) 'Rural-Urban Migration, Urban Unemployment, and Job Search Activity in LDCs', *Journal of Development Economics*, vol. 2, pp. 165–87.

Fields, G. S. (1989) 'On the Job Search in a Labor Market Model: Ex Ante Choices and Ex Post Outcomes', *Journal of Development Economics*, vol. 30, pp. 159–78.

Firestone, J. and B. A. Shelton (1994) 'A Comparison of Women's and Men's Leisure Time: Subtle Effects of the Double Day', *Leisure Sciences*, vol. 16, pp. 45–60.

Fitzgerald, J. and J. Wicks (1990) 'Measuring the Value of Household Output: A Comparison of Direct and Indirect Approaches', *Review of Income and Wealth*, vol. 36, pp. 129–41.

Fogel, R. W. (1990) *The Conquest of High Mortality and Hunger in Europe and America* (Cambridge, Mass.: NBER Working Paper no. 16).

Fuchs, V. (1982) 'Time Preference and Health: An Exploratory Study', in V. Fuchs (ed.), *Economic Aspects of Health* (Chicago University Press).

Galbraith, J. K. (1962) *The Affluent Society* (Harmondsworth, Middlesex: Pelican).

Gärtner, W. (1974) 'A Dynamic Model of Interdependent Consumer Behavior', *Zeitschrift fur National Ökonomie*, vol. 34, pp. 327–44.

Gately, D. (1980) 'Individual Discount Rates and the Purchase and Utilization of Energy-Using Durables: Comment', *Bell Journal of Economics*, vol. 11, pp. 373–4.

Goldscheider, K. and F. Goldscheider (1993) *Leaving Home Before Marriage* (University of Wisconsin Press).

Goode, W. J. (1963) *World Revolution and Family Patterns* (New York: The Free Press).

Gossen, H. H. (1854) *Entwicklung Der Gesetze Des Menslichen Verkehrs* (Amsterdam: Liberac).

Graham, J. W. and C. A. Green (1984) 'Estimating the Parameters of a Household Production Function with Joint Products', *Review of Economics and Statistics*, vol. 66, pp. 277–82.

Grift, Y. K., J. J. Siegers and G. N. C. Suy (1989) *Time Use in The Netherlands*, Report no. 65 (in Dutch) (Den Haag: SWOKA).

Gronau, R. (1980) 'Home Production – A Forgotten Industry', *Review of Economics and Statistics*, vol. 62, pp. 408–16.

Groot, W. and H. Pott-Buter (1992) 'The Timing of Maternity in The Netherlands', *Journal of Population Economics*, vol. 5, pp. 155–72.

Haddad, L. and R. Kanbur (1990) 'How Serious Is the Neglect of Intra-Household Inequality?', *Economic Journal*, vol. 100, pp. 866–81.

Hagenaars, A. J. M. and S. R. Wunderink-Van Veen (1990) *Soo gewonne, Soo Verteert (The Economics of the Household Sector)* (in Dutch) (Leiden: Stenfert Kroese).

Hagenaars A. J. M. and K. de Vos (1988) 'The Definition and Measurement of Poverty', *The Journal of Human Resources*, vol. 23, pp. 211–21.

Hall, R. E. (1978) 'Stochastic Implications of the Life-Cycle Permanent Income Hypothesis: Theory and Evidence', *Journal of Political Economy*, vol. 86, pp. 971–87.

Harrington, M. (1962) *The Other America* (New York: Macmillan).

Harris, J. R. and M. P. Todaro (1970) 'Migration, Unemployment and Development: A Two Sector Analysis', *American Economic Review*, vol. 60, pp. 126–42.

Hausman, J. (1979a) 'Individual Discount Rates and the Purchase and Utilization of Energy-Using Durables', *Bell Journal of Economics*, vol. 10, pp. 33–54.

Hausman, J. (1979b) 'The Econometrics of Labor Supply on Convex Budget Sets', *Economics Letters*, vol. 3, pp. 171–4.

Hausman, J. (1981) 'Labor Supply', in H. Aaron and J. Peckman (eds), *How Taxes Affect Economic Behavior* (Washington DC: The Brookings Institute).

Hausman, J. (1985) 'The Econometrics of Nonlinear Budget Sets', *Econometrica*, vol. 53, pp. 1255–82.

Hausman, J. and P. Ruud (1984) 'Family Labor Supply and Taxes', *American Economic Review*, vol. 74, no. 2, pp. 242–8.

Heckman, J. J. (1979) 'Sample Selection Bias as a Specification Error', *Econometrica*, vol. 47, pp. 153–61.

Heckman, J. J. and B. Singer (1984) 'A Method for Minimizing the Impact of Distributional in Econometric Models for Duration Data', *Econometrica*, vol. 52, pp. 271–320.

Heckman, J. J. and J. R. Walker (1990) 'The Third Birth in Sweden', *Journal of Population Economics*, vol. 3, pp. 235–75.

Heckman, J. J., V. J. Hotz and J. Walker (1985) 'New Evidence on the Timing and Spacing of Births', *American Economic Review* (Papers and Proceedings), vol. 75, pp. 179–84.

Hiedemann, B. (1993) 'Retirement Decisions in Dual Career Households: Development and Estimation of a Stackelberg Model', working paper, Duke University, Center for the Study of Aging and Human Development.

Hill, M. S. (1985) 'Patterns of Time Use', in F. T. Juster and F. P. Stafford (eds), *Time, Goods and Well-being* (Ann-Arbor, Mich.: University of Michigan Press).

Hodgkinson, V. and M. Weitzman (1984) *Dimensions of the Independent Sector: A Statistical Profile* (Washington DC: Independent Sector).

Homan, M. E. (1988) *The Allocation of Time and Money in One-Earner and Two-Earner Families; An Economis Analysis* (Ph.D. thesis, University of Rotterdam).

Howe, H. (1975) 'Development of the Extended Linear Expenditure System from Simple Saving Assumption', *European Economic Review*, vol. 6, pp. 305–10.

Hsiao, C. (1989) *Analysis of Panel Data* (Cambridge University Press).

Hurd, M. D. (1990) 'Research on the Elderly: Economic Status, Retirement, and Consumption and Saving', *Journal of Economic Literature*, vol. 28, pp. 565–637.

Intomart (1985, 1990) *Analysis of Time Use* (in Dutch) (Hilversum: Intomart).

Juster, F. T. and F. P. Stafford (1985) *Time, Goods and Well-being* (Ann Arbor, Mich.: University of Michigan Press).

Juster, F. T. and F. P. Stafford (1991) 'The Allocation of Time: Empirical Findings, Behavioral Models, and Problems of Measurement', *Journal of Economic Literature*, vol. 29, pp. 471–522.

Juster, F. T., M. Hill, F. Stafford and J. Parsons (1983) *Time Use Longitudinal Panel Study, 1975–1981: User's Guide*, vol. 47 (Ann Arbor, Mich.: Inter-University Consortium for Political and Social Research).

Kagel, J. H., R. C. Battalio, and L. Green (1995) *Economic Choice Theory; An Experimental Analysis of Animal Behaviour* (Cambridge University Press).

Kapteyn, A. and P. Kooreman (1992) 'Household Labor Supply: What Kind of Data Can Tell Us How Many Decision Makers There Are?', *European Economic Review* (Papers and Proceedings), vol. 36, pp. 365–71.

Kapteyn, A., P. Kooreman and A. van Soest (1990) 'Quantity Rationing and Concavity in a Flexible Household Labor Supply Model', *Review of Economics and Statistics*, vol. 57, pp. 55–62.

Kapteyn, A., P. Kooreman and R. J. M. Willemse (1988) 'Some Methodological Issues in the Implementation of Subjective Poverty Definitions', *Journal of Human Resources*, vol. 23, pp. 222–42.

Kerkhofs, M. (1991) 'On the Identification and Estimation of Household Production Models', Research Memorandum FEW-42, Tilburg: Department of Economics.

Kerkhofs, M. (1994) 'A Quadratic Model of Household Production Decisions', Discussion Paper TI 94-45 (Rotterdam: Tinbergen Institute).

Kirchler, E. (1988) 'Household Economic Decision Making' in W. F. Van Raaij, G. M. van Veldhoven and K. E. Wärneryd (eds), *Handbook of Economic Psychology* (Dordrecht: Kluwer).

Kodde, D. A. (1985) *Microeconomic Analysis of Demand for Education*, Ph.D. thesis, Erasmus University, Rotterdam.

Kooreman, P. (1986) *Essays on Microeconomic Analysis of Household Behavior*, Ph.D. thesis, Tilburg University.

Kooreman, P. (1994) 'Estimation of Some Econometric Models of Discrete Games', *Journal of Applied Econometrics*, vol. 9, pp. 255–68.

Kooreman, P. (1995) 'Individual Discounting and the Purchase of Durables with Random Lifetimes', *Economics Letters*, vol. 48, pp. 29–32.

Kooreman, P. and A. Kapteyn (1985) 'The System Approach to Household Labor Supply in The Netherlands', *De Economist*, vol. 133, pp. 21–42.

Kooreman, P. and A. Kapteyn (1986) 'Estimation of Rationed and Unrationed Household Labor Supply Functions Using Flexible Functional Forms', *Economic Journal*, vol. 96, pp. 398–412.

Kooreman, P. and A. Kapteyn (1987) 'A Disaggregated Analysis of the Allocation of Time Within the Household', *Journal of Political Economy*, vol. 95, pp. 223–49.

Kooreman, P. and A. Kapteyn (1990) 'On the Empirical Implementation of Some Game Theoretic Models of Household Labor Supply', *Journal of Human Resources*, vol. 25, pp. 584–98.

Kuznets, S. (1941) *National Income and Its Composition, 1919–1938*, vol. 1 (New York: National Bureau of Economic Research).

Lancaster, T. (1979) 'Econometric Methods for the Duration of Unemployment', *Econometrica*, vol. 47, pp. 939–56.

Lancaster, T. (1990) *The Econometric Analysis of Transition Data* (Cambridge University Press).

Lancaster, T. and A. Chesher (1983) 'An Econometric Analysis of Reservation Wages', *Econometrica*, vol. 51, pp. 1661–76.

Lancaster, T. and S. Nickell (1980) 'The Analysis of Re-employment Probabilities for the Unemployed', *Journal of the Royal Statistical Society A*, vol. 143, pp. 141–65.

Lawrance, E. C. (1991) 'Poverty and the Rate of Time Preference: Evidence from Panel Data', *Journal of Political Economy*, vol. 99, pp. 55–77.

Lazear, E. P. and R. T. Michael (1988) *Allocation of Income within the Household* (Chicago University Press).

Lee, L. F. and M. M. Pitt (1986) 'Microeconometric Demand Systems with Binding Nonnegativity Constraints: The Dual Approach', *Econometrica*, vol. 54, pp. 1237–42.

Leung, S. F. (1988) 'On Tests for Sex Preferences', *Journal of Population Economics*, vol. 1, pp. 95–114.

Levy, P. S. and S. Lemeshow (1991) *Sampling of Populations* (New York: John Wiley).

Lewis, W. A. (1954) 'Economic Development with Unlimited Supplies of Labor', *Manchester School of Economics and Social Studies*, pp. 131–91.
Lillard, L. A. (1993) 'Simultaneous Equations for Hazards; Marriage Duration and Fertility Timing', *Journal of Econometrics*, vol. 56, pp. 189–217.
Linder, S. B. (1970) *The Harried Leisure Class* (New York: Columbia University Press).
Lippe, T. van der (1993) *The Division of Labour Between Men and Women* (in Dutch), Ph.D. thesis, Utrecht University.
Loewenstein, G. and R. H. Thaler (1989) 'Anomalies; Intertemporal Choice', *Journal of Economic Perspectives*, vol. 3, pp. 181–93.
Lubell, H. (1990) *The Informal Sector in the 1980s and 1990s* (Paris: OECD, Development Center).
Maddala, G. S. (1983) *Limited-dependent and Qualitative Variables in Econometrics* (Cambridge University Press).
Maddala, G. S. (1985) *Limited-dependent and Qualitative Variables in Econometrics* (Cambridge University Press).
Magnac, Th. (1991) 'Segmented or Competitive Labor Markets', *Econometrica*, pp. 165–87.
Manser, M. and M. Brown (1980) 'Marriage and Household Decision-Making', *International Economic Review*, vol. 21, pp. 31–44.
Mayhew, H. (1851) *London Labour and the London Poor* (London: Woodfall & Son).
McElroy, M. (1985) 'The Joint Determination of Household Membership and Market Work: The Case of Young Men', *Journal of Labor Economics*, vol. 3, pp. 293–316.
McElroy, M. B. (1990) 'The Empirical Content of Nash-Bargained Household Behavior', *Journal of Human Resources*, vol. 25, pp. 559–83.
McElroy, M. and M. J. Horney (1981) 'Nash-Bargained Household Decisions: Toward a Generalization of the Theory of Demand', *International Economic Review*, vol. 22, pp. 333–47.
Menchik, P. L. and B. A. Weisbrod (1987) 'Volunteer Labor Supply', *Journal of Public Economics*, vol. 32, pp. 159–183.
Michalopoulos, C., P. K. Robins and I. Garfinkel (1992) 'A Structural Model of Labour Supply and Child Care Demand', *Journal of Human Resources*, vol. 28, pp. 166–203.
Mincer, J. (1958) 'Investment in Human Capital and Personal Income Distribution', *Journal of Political Economy*, pp. 281–302.
Mincer, J. (1974) *Schooling, Experience and Earnings* (New York: National Bureau of Economic Research).
Mincer, J. and H. Ofek (1982) 'Interrupted Work Careers: Depreciation and Restoration of Human Capital', *Journal of Human Resources*, vol. 17, pp. 3–24.
Moffitt, R. (1989) 'Estimating the Value of an In-Kind Transfer: The Case of Food Stamps', *Econometrica*, vol. 57, pp. 385–409.
Moffitt, R. (1992) 'Incentive Effects of the U.S. Welfare System: A Review', *Journal of Economic Literature*, vol. 30, pp. 1–61.
Montgomery, M. and J. Trussell (1986) 'Models of Marital Status and Childbearing', in O. Ashenfelter and R. Layard (eds), *Handbook of Labor Economics* (Amsterdam: North-Holland) pp. 205–71.
Mood, A. M., F. A. Graybill and D. C. Boes (1974) *Introduction to the Theory of Statistics* (3rd edn) (New York: McGraw-Hill).
Narendranathan, W. and S. Nickell (1985) 'Modelling the Process of Job Search', *Journal of Econometrics*, vol. 28, pp. 29–49.
Neary, J. P. and K. W. S. Roberts (1980) 'The Theory of Household Behaviour under Rationing', *European Economic Review*, vol. 13, pp. 25–42.
Nerlove, M., A. Razin and E. Sadka (1987) *Household and Economy, Welfare Economics of Endogenous Fertility* (London: Academic Press).

Niesing, W. (1993) *The Labor Market Position of Ethnic Minorities in The Nether-lands*, Ph.D. thesis, Erasmus University.

OECD (1992) *Education at a Glance* (Paris: OECD Indicators).

OECD (1995) *Historical Statistics, 1960–93* (Paris:).

O'Higgins, M., G. Schmaus and G. Stephenson (1990) 'Income Distribution and Redistribution', in T. M. Smeeding, M. O'Higgins and L. Rainwater (eds), *Poverty, Inequality and Income Distribution in Comparative Perspective* (New York: Harvester Wheatsheaf).

O'Neill, J. (1985) 'The Trend in the Male–Female Wage Gap in the United States', *Journal of Labor Economics*, vol. 3, pp. S91–S116.

Ott, N. (1991a) 'Analysis of the Hazard Rate of Divorce' (in German), in R. Hujer, H. Schneider and W. Zapf (eds), *Herausforderungen an den Wolfahrtsstaat im Strukturellen Wandel* (Frankfurt).

Ott, N. (1991b) 'Fertility and Division of Work in the Family: A Game Theoretic Model of Household Decisions', working paper, University of Frankfurt.

Pahl, J. (1990) 'Household Spending, Personal Spending and the Control of Money in Marriage', *Sociology*, vol. 24, pp. 119–38.

Pareto, V. (1909) *Manuel d' Economie Politique* (Paris: Gicard & Brière).

Piore, M. (1979) *Unemployment and Inflation: Institutional and Structuralist Views* (White Plains, NY: M. E. Sharpe).

Pitt, M., M. Rosenzweig and M. Nazmul Hassan (1990) 'Productivity, Health and Inequality in the Intrahousehold Distribution of Food in Low-Income Countries', *American Economic Review*, vol. 80, pp. 1139–56.

Pollak, R. A. (1976) 'Interdependent Preferences', *American Economic Review*, vol. 66, pp. 309–20.

Pollak, R. A. and T. J. Wales (1978) 'Estimation of Complete Demand Systems from Household Budget Data: The Linear and Quadratic Expenditure Systems', *American Economic Review*, vol. 68, pp. 348–59.

Pollak, R. A. and T. J. Wales (1979) 'Welfare Comparison and Equivalence Scales', *American Economic Review*, vol. 69, pp. 216–21.

Pollak, R. A. and T. J. Wales (1981) 'Demographic Variables in Demand Analysis', *Econometrica*, vol. 49, pp. 1533–51.

Poppel, F. van (1992) *Marriage in The Netherlands; An Historical–Demographic Study of the 19th and Early 20th Centuries* (in Dutch), Ph.D. thesis, Wageningen Agricultural University.

Pott-Buter, H. A. (1993) *Facts and Fairy Tales about Female Labor, Family and Fertility* (Amsterdam University Press).

Praag, B. M. S. van (1968) *Individual Welfare Functions and Consumer Behavior* (Amsterdam: North-Holland).

Praag, B. M. S. van (1985) 'Linking Economics with Psychology; An Economist's View', *Journal of Economic Psychology*, vol. 6, pp. 289–311.

Praag, B. M. S. van (1991) 'Ordinal and Cardinal Utility', *Journal of Econometrics*, vol. 50, pp. 69–89.

Praag, B. M. S. van, A. J. M. Hagenaars and W. van Eck (1983) 'The Influence of Classification and Observation Errors on the Measurement of Income Inequality', *Econometrica*, vol. 51, pp. 1093–108.

Pradhan, M. P. (1994) *Labour Supply in Urban Areas of Bolivia*, Ph.D. thesis, Tilburg University.

Pradhan, M. P. and A. H. O. van Soest (1995) 'Formal and Informal Sector Employment in Urban Areas of Bolivia', *Labour Economics*, vol. 1, pp. 275–97.

Pudney, S, (1991) *Modelling Individual Choice, The Econometrics of Corners, Kinks and Holes* (Cambridge: Basil Blackwell).

Quah, E. (1987) 'Valuing Family Household Production: A Contingent Evaluation Approach', *Applied Economics*, vol. 19, pp. 875–90.

Rader, T. (1963) 'The Existence of a Utility Function to Represent Preferences',

Review of Economic Studies, vol. 30, pp. 229–32.

Reid, M. G. (1934) *Economics of Household Production* (New York: John Wiley).

Ritzema, H. J. and M. E. Homan (1991) 'Debts and Assets in The Netherlands' (in Dutch), (The Hague: SWOKA Institute for Consumer Research).

Rosen, S. (1977) 'Human Capital: Relations between Education and Earnings', in M. Intriligator (ed.), *Frontiers of Quantitative Economics*, vol. 3b (Amsterdam: North-Holland).

Rosenzweig, M. and T. P. Schultz (1982) 'Market Opportunities, Genetic Endowments and Intrafamily Resource Distribution: Child Survival in Rural India', *American Economic Review*.

Rosenzweig, M. R. and T. P. Schultz (1983) 'Estimating a Household Production Function: Heterogeneity, the Demand for Health Inputs, and Their Effects on Birth Weight', *Journal of Political Economy*, vol. 91, pp. 723–46.

Rothbarth, E. (1943) 'Note on the Method of Determining Equivalent Income for Families of Different Composition', in C. Madge (ed.), *War-time Pattern of Saving and Spending* (Cambridge University Press).

Rowntree, B. S. (1901) *Poverty: A Study of Town Life* (London: Macmillan).

Rust, J. and C. Phelan (1993) 'How Social Security and Medicare Affect Retirement Behavior in a World of Incomplete Markets', monograph, University of Wisconsin.

Saunders, P., H. Stott, and G. Hobbes (1991) 'Income Inequality in Australia and New Zealand: International Comparisons and Recent Trends', *Review of Income and Wealth*, vol. 37, pp. 63–79.

Scanzoni, J. and G. L. Fox (1980) 'Sex Roles, Family and Society: The Seventies and Beyond', *Journal of Marriage and the Family*, vol. 42, pp. 743–56.

Schor, J. B. (1991) *The Overworked American* (New York: Basic Books).

Schultz, T. P. (1993) 'Investment in Schooling and Health of Women and Men, Quantities and Returns', *Journal of Human Resources*, vol. 28, pp. 695–734.

Schultz, T. W. (1960) 'Capital Formation by Education', *Journal of Political Economy*, vol. 68, pp. 571–83.

Scitovsky, T. (1976) *The Joyless Economy* (London: Oxford University Press).

Slesnick, D. T. (1994) 'Consumption, Needs, and Inequality', *International Economic Review*, vol. 35, pp. 677–703.

Smith, A. (1759) *The Theory of Moral Sentiments* (London: Henry J. Bohn).

Smith, A. (1776) *An Inquiry into the Nature and Causes of the Wealth of Nations* (reprinted 1981) Liberty Class.

Soest, A. van, P. Kooreman and A. Kapteyn (1993) 'Coherency and Regularity of Demand Systems with Equality and Inequality Constraints', *Journal of Econometrics*, vol. 57, pp. 161–88.

Stigler, G. J. (1960) 'The Economics of Information', *Journal of Political Economy*, pp. 213–25.

Strauss J., P. J. Gertler, O. Rahman and K. Fox (1993) 'Gender and Life-Cycle Differentials in the Patterns and Determinants of Adult Health', *Journal of Human Resources*, vol. 28, pp. 791–837.

Subramanian, S. and A. Deaton (1990) 'Gender Effects in Indian Consumption Patterns', Discussion Paper no. 147 (Princeton University: Research Program in Development Studies).

Sussman, M. B. and S. K. Steinmetz (1987) *Handbook of Marriage and the Family* (New York: Plenum Press).

Takayama, A. (1985) *Mathematical Economics* (Cambridge University Press).

Thaler, R. H. (1981) 'Some Empirical Evidence on Dynamic Inconsistency', *Economics Letters*, vol. 8, pp. 201–7.

Theil, H., C. F. Chung and J. L. Seale (1989) *Advances in Econometrics, International Evidence on Consumption Patterns* (Greenwich, Conn.: JAI Press).

Thomas, D. (1990) 'Like Father, Like Son: Gender Differences in Household Resource Allocation', working paper, Yale University.

Tilly, C. (1992) 'Short Hours, Short Shrift: The Causes and Consequences of Part-Time Employment', in V. L. duRivage (ed.), *New Policies for the Part-Time and Contingent Workforce*, (Armonk, New York: M. E. Sharpe).

Tilly, L. A. and J. W. Scott (1987) *Women, Work and Family* (London: Methuen).

Townsend, P. (1983) *Poverty in the United Kingdom* (Harmondsworth: Penguin).

Tummers, M. P. (1994) 'The Effect of Systematic Misperception of Income on the Subjective Poverty Line', in R. Blundell, I. Preston and I. Walker (eds), *The Measurement of Household Welfare* (Cambridge University Press).

Varian, H. (1992) *Microeconomic Analysis* (3rd edn) (New York: Norton).

Veenhoven, R. (1983) 'The Growing Impact of Marriage', *Social Indicators Research*, vol 12, pp. 49–63.

Veenhoven, R. (1984) *Conditions of Happiness*, Ph.D. thesis, Erasmus University.

Vuong, Q. H. (1989) 'Likelihood Ratio Tests for Model Selection and Non-nested Hypotheses', *Econometrica*, vol. 57, pp. 307–33.

Wasserman, J., W. G. Manning, J. P. Newhouse and J. D. Winkler (1991) 'The Effects of Excise Taxes and Regulations on Cigarette Smoking', *Journal of Health Economics*, vol. 10, pp. 43–64.

Weiss, Y. and R. Gronau (1981) 'Expected Interruptions in Labour Force Participation and Sex-Related Differences in Earnings Growth', *Review of Economic Studies*, vol. 48, pp. 607–19.

Whittington, L. A., J. Alm and E. H. Peters (1990) 'Fertility and the Personal Exemption: Implicit Pronatalist Policy in the United States', *American Economic Review*, vol. 80, pp. 545–56.

Willis, R. J. (1986) 'Wage Determinants: A Survey and Reinterpretation of Human Capital Earnings Functions', in O. C. Ashenfelter and R. Layard (eds), *Handbook of Labor Economics*, vol. 1, pp. 525–599.

Winston, G. C., (1982), *The Timing of Economic Activities* (Cambridge University Press).

Wolfe, D. A. (1987) *Child Abuse, Implications for Child Development and Psychopathology* (Newbury Park: Sage).

Wolff, E. (1994) 'Trends in Household Wealth in the United States, 1962–83 and 1983–89', *Review of Income and Wealth*, vol. 40, pp. 143–74.

Woodside, A. G. and W. H. Motes (1979) 'Husband and Wife Perceptions of Marital Roles in Consumer Decision Processes for Six Products', in Beckwith *et al.* (eds), *Educators Conference Proceedings*, Series 44 (Chicago, Ill.: American Marketing Association) pp. 214–19.

Wunderink, S. R. (1988) 'Applications of a Budget Allocation Model', Ph.D. thesis, Erasmus University.

Zeldes, S. (1989) 'Consumption and Liquidity Constraints: An Empirical Analysis', *Journal of Political Economy*, vol. 97, pp. 305–46.

Zhang, J., J. Quan, and P. Van Meerbergen (1994) 'The Effect of Tax-Transfer Policies on Fertility in Canada, 1921–88', *Journal of Human Resources*, vol. 29, pp. 181–201.

Subject Index

Author Index

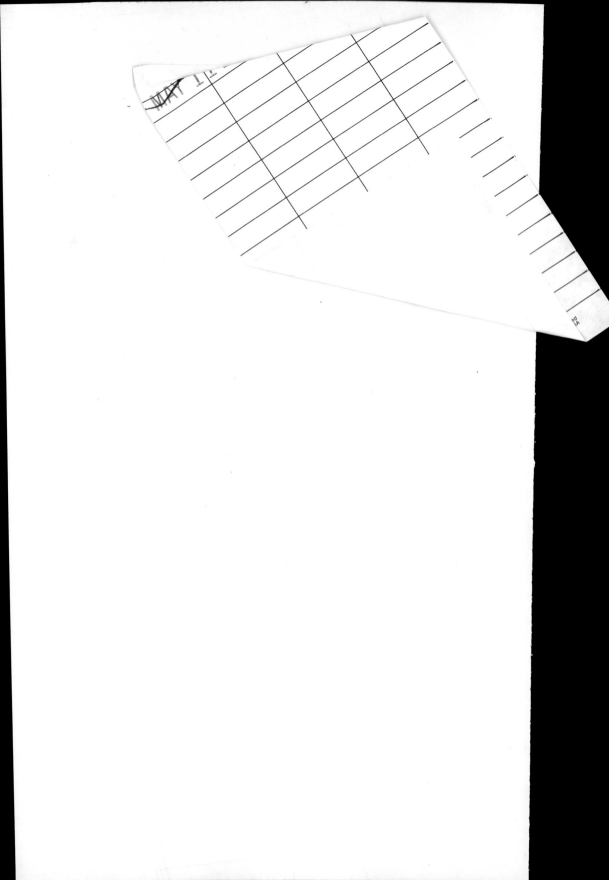